WHAT MATTERS MOST

Sweet Auzy!
So glad we met!

P.S.D.

Intimate
Interviews
with
Notable
Nashvillians

by Paul Samuel Dolman

WHAT MATTERS MOST

To Tricia,
For continually showing me What Matters Most.

SUCCESS

To laugh often and much; to win the respect of intelligent people and the affection of children; to earn the appreciation of honest critics and endure the betrayal of false friends; to appreciate beauty, to find the best in others; to leave the world a bit better, whether by a healthy child, a garden patch or a redeemed social condition; to know even one life has breathed easier because you have lived. This is to have succeeded.

-Ralph Waldo Emerson

Acknowledgements

I would like to thank several people who not only made this book possible but a true labor of love for me:

My wife, Tricia Marie, for your patience and support through the entire project. Your kindness and unconditional love continues to be an inspiration to me.

My brother, Chris, for being my best friend over the past thirty-three years. I respect you in so many ways and feel blessed that we have shared so many magical moments.

The amazing Bonnie Johnson, who helped me put the pieces back together.

My Father & Mother, for all the sacrifices, support, time, talks, hugs, and kisses.

Sherry Stephens, who believed in me before I did.

Brothers and Sisters: Steve, Annette, Phil, Jana, Joey C, Chris Faulconer, Donna, Mr. T, Stephanie. You give me more than mere words can express. What a blessing to have you in my life.

The Sunday morning meditation group and all my friends in the practice around the world.

Soul sister Angela Bevins, my unofficial official advisor/sister. For telling me I'm "<u>NOT</u>" crazy.

Mark Kaufman, my editor, for telling me I "<u>AM</u>" crazy. Mark, your work made this a joy.

Susie Garland Rice, for generously sharing her artistic talents and friendship over the years.

Charlie & Michelle, for taking such wonderful pictures.

Donna Paz, for her professional and personal support throughout the project.

All the gracious folks who helped me set up the interviews with the subjects. They quietly work so hard for little of the glory. Thanks for patiently putting up with ALL my calls.

Dr. Bob Hoehn and Margaret Smith, for their support and guidance.

Ellen Lehman, for helping me help others through The Nashville Community Foundation.

The people IN the book. For being so open and honest. For caring enough to get involved by donating your time and wisdom. For everything you do in this world to make it a little better. I feel you are my new friends.

God, whose infinite generosity makes everything possible.

TABLE OF CONTENTS

INTRODUCTION

My life and this book are about the same thing: building bridges between people for the greater good. In writing *What Matters Most*, my goal was to take the wonderfully diverse, collective wisdom of Nashville and raise it up to a place of unification. And in the process show that, despite our superficial differences, despite how we may define success, or what name we might call God, deep down in our core we are all basically the same. Dr. T.B. Boyd said it quite well, "We may have come over on different ships, but we are all in the same boat."

In our culture, success is mostly defined in terms of money and status. The goal of this book is to broaden the paradigm of success. It is about the qualities people possess — how they see and react to life — and how that contributes to their success.

The book reflects intimate interviews I conducted with 40 noteworthy Nashvillians. Each person answered my questions, sharing wisdom in his or her own words.

These people are examples of what can happen when we get in touch with our hearts, follow our hearts, and truly live life. There is potential within each of us to do the same and make a difference in the world.

This book is also about tolerance and acceptance. I ask that you read it with an open heart. I hope you can see through the theoretical divergence to a common ground where ideas intersect — like making a contribution to your fellow man and selflessly serving the greater whole.

Throughout the interviews, I found myself repeatedly inspired by the participants. While I did not always agree with their opinions, I greatly respected their convictions and their choice to share them so openly and honestly. I encourage you to focus on the transcendent qualities of the human spirit, rather than how these people might be different from you.

A second goal for the project was to create a scholarship fund that would help underprivileged children go on to higher learning. This dream was realized when I met Carl Carlson and learned of his heroic efforts in leading the YMCA's Y-CAP program. Through the Nashville Community Foundation and the help of its Director, Ellen Lehman, I established the What Matters Most Endowment. This fund will benefit deserving youngsters of Y-CAP and other children around the community in their pursuit of secondary education. With the goal of changing lives through education, fifty percent of my writer's royalties will go directly into the endowment. This book is only the beginning. It will also be used as a kickoff for other fundraising efforts on behalf of the What Matters Most Endowment. Carl Carlson and the Y-Cap program have begun a process that can transform an element of society that most have abandoned as hopeless. By reaching out to homeless children, juvenile delinquents and their families, children's lives are being transformed. Yet Y-CAP only goes as far as the completion of high school. The What Matters Most Endowment will take these children through college and complete the transformation of the delinquent, abandoned child to a well-educated adult capable of making a positive contribution to the community.

This book is a way of saying, "look how different we are ... but how much alike." Through the Endowment, I am saying, "let's join together and make a difference. Y-CAP has laid the foundation, let's take it the extra mile and really make a difference that will affect the entire community for generations to come." Children are our future, so let's invest in their education.

By rallying together, the community has the phenomenal possibility of transforming itself from within. Nashville now has the opportunity to make it possible for any child with the desire to attain a higher education to do so.

For me, success is really about the dignity of the human spirit and one's ability to reach out to others and make a positive difference in the world. No act of love, kindness or compassion is *ever* too small. I want to thank you for choosing my book, and invite you to join me and my guests on a wonderful journey of discovery as we talk about and share *What Matters Most.*

Paul Samuel Dolman
Nashville, TN
January, 1997

Bill Moyers

Journalist, Author, and Educator

"Never get too old or grow too sophisticated to stop being a student. I don't know of any way to cope with the perils of life, the hazards of existence, and the demands of society, than to learn something new every day."

PSD: *Was your interview with Joseph Campbell and the Power Of Myth series a personal turning point?*

BM: I don't see it as a turning point because I find a certain consistency to my curiosity over the years, of which the Campbell series was certainly one manifestation. It was probably the most popular series I ever did in terms of the response. I didn't anticipate its success. The series aired with almost no promotion and no publicity to a very small rating by commercial standards and modest by public television standards. But word of mouth spread, almost contagiously. People were calling up public television stations and pleading with them to repeat the series. It just grew into a phenomenon in it's own right that I never anticipated, didn't intend, and didn't know how to evaluate.

PSD: *You started out in traditional media, yet your journalistic path has taken on a very spiritual element over the years. Was there a catalyst earlier on in your life or career that shifted your paradigm? Or were you always curious, with this road just a natural extension of your quest?*

BM: Well, I am a journalist first and foremost. I started studying journalism at the age of sixteen, and have had some detours along the way. I went into government politics for seven years. I studied theology and ethics for four-and-a-half years. So I was aware of the importance of religion in people's lives, unlike journalists who have not had any theological training.

I knew that, for millions of Americans, faith matters. Faith is a subjective reality that drives, animates, and influences their behavior. It was natural for me, when I had the chance, to try to cover that beat as a journalist. Because I knew it was important, and I had already covered everything else: government, politics, economics, sports, sometimes even the weather. So I don't think there was any one thing or catalyst. It is not that I am on any kind of

mission, I just recognize the role that religion plays in millions of people's lives, and any time I cover it, the response confirms that intuition. I do a lot of conventional journalism: documentaries on public education, documentaries on politics and government in Washington, the environment. But nothing I do has the impact like the programs I do that deal with religion in one way or another.

PSD: *How do you define success for you personally?*

BM: I never have thought about that. (He pauses.) It is being able to have an idea for something original and see it emerge as a television series six months or two years later. It is the knowledge that, as a public educator, I have one of the largest classrooms in the country. Television is a university without walls. Life is a continuing course of adult education and I have a great classroom, into which I invite some of the most interesting people, stories, and ideas of our time.

So success for me is knowing that I have had an idea that I can share with a larger audience whose own world is then enlarged by that experience.

PSD: *Does that bring you great pleasure in life?*

BM: Yes, though my greatest pleasure is spending time with my family —my wife, children, and my grand-kids. But it gives me the greatest professional satisfaction.

PSD: *Do you ever think about how you would like to be remembered?*

BM: I really don't. I haven't ever been asked that question! For one thing, I don't think people in television are remembered very long. It is an ephemeral, passing, fleeting, transient medium. The best a journalist can do is serve his time and move on. So I don't really think of being remembered, except by my family. I want them to remember me for the fun we had together and the intimacy we shared.

PSD: *If your grandchildren asked for a little guidance as they were about to go out in the world on life's path, what would you tell them? To coin your friend Joseph Campbell's phrase, how to "follow your bliss?"*

BM: Never get too old or grow too sophisticated to stop being a student. I don't know of any way to cope with the perils of life, the hazards of existence, and the demands of society, than to learn something new every day. If people consider themselves life-long students, no matter what they do, they are never going to get bored. They may have periods of doubt, they may be out of a job, they may be sick or have infirmity, or lose friends and family. But as long as you think of every day as an invitation to learn, you will never find a day that fails you.

PSD: *What do you do to stay grounded and get in touch with your inner self?*

BM: I do just what I advise other people to do. I am always listening, reading, and enjoying the company of people who know more than I do. I don't come away from a lunch with strangers or with friends where I haven't learned or shared something. So keep good company — people who can teach you something.

PSD: *After all these years, what keeps you going?*

BM: People like you who think it matters.

T.B. Boyd

President and CEO, The National Baptist Publishing Board

"You can work hard, but it is not always what clicks and jingles in your pocket that matters, but what clicks in your heart. While it is good to know all the dance steps, don't forget where the steps to the schoolhouse and church are."

PSD: *Are you a philosophical person?*
TBB: My general philosophy on life is that you must first learn about yourself. Realize your potential and stretch your limitations. If you never forget where you have come from, you can appreciate where you are while you dream about where you are going. This is the daily catalyst to what I do here at the publishing board. This institution has been in my family now for one hundred years and I am very proud of it.

PSD: *Who does the Publishing Board serve?*
TBB: Our clientele is about three and a half million people, three thousand bookstores, and we are on just about every continent.

PSD: *The Publishing Board — this whole institution — seems to be founded on the paradigm of giving. The focus seems to be completely outward. Does this come from your father, his father, and his father?*
TBB: Absolutely. I am the fourth generation.

PSD: *This way of life was handed down through the generations.*
TBB: As a child, I was taught by the example of how my daddy loved this work. Most of all, it is work that helps to influence the lives of other people in a very positive manner, which I feel is the main purpose of this institution — to have a positive influence and promote the values of family, giving spiritual inspiration to people all over the world.

PSD: *Did you have any choice in your vocation? Were you pressured at all?*
TBB: Oh yes, I had a choice. I was taught as a child to do this particular work. I wasn't indoctrinated because you have to like this kind of work. No one can talk you into liking it. One thing my Daddy never did was try to influence me or make me do this work. He said, "If you don't see it, then it is not for you." I really had a lot of respect for him. I am extremely blessed and fortunate to have

had enough sense to see the potential in this family business.

PSD: *Did you feel called to do this work?*
TBB: No, I wasn't called, but it is all I ever wanted to do. I remember coming down here when I was six years old getting in the way and stacking books. So I never had a second thought because I always wanted to do it. I just loved to do it, it gets in your blood. I never considered not doing it.

PSD: *Your forefathers were up against serious inertia in terms of segregation and prejudice. What do you think allowed them and this institution to survive?*
TBB: They had backbone and tenacious will, the absolute dedication to get it done no matter how long it took. If you stop to think about it, the last thing anyone would have wanted to sell a black man after the civil war would have been a printing press, even more so than a gun. It was a dangerous instrument to sell a former slave. A cannon might do a little damage, but a printing press? When you think that this press has since printed hundreds of millions of books and the influence they have had, it is mind-boggling.

PSD: *Your forefathers were courageous, too.*
TBB: Yes, very courageous. Remember, though, that they didn't do it by themselves. They had lots of help from some very good white friends along with their own people.

PSD: *There are always good people who go against the grain in the name of truth. They don't care what the norm is, even if their lives are at stake.*
TBB: There always are. My great-grandfather had instances at auctions when a very good white friend would buy the equipment for him because he was not allowed to purchase what he needed. He would watch from the window and give signals.

PSD: *Where did his financing come from?*
TBB: His wife had the money. She had saved three thousand dollars. So he was able to get the equipment and his business caught on very quickly. It was a natural. He didn't change the scriptures, but gave opportunities for his own people to reflect their views.

PSD: *These men had an uncanny sense of survival.*
TBB: You had to be on your toes, because there was adversity all of the time. For these people, every day was an emergency so they always had to come up with new things. Like when there was a run on the banks in the 1920s. When the lines formed for withdrawals, my great-grandfather took all the money out of the vault and placed it in the windows. People thought this bank must be really solid, so by the end of the day, the line for deposits was longer than the line for withdrawals. They actually ended up turning a profit that day.

PSD: *Coming from this tradition you must feel an enormous responsibility. You are measured against myth.*
TBB: That's right. And the only way to outmeasure myth is to go off the seams and start your own path. This is a very important point you have made. It is hard to earn respect, especially in your own home town where everybody remembers you growing up. They used to call me "Young Boyd." I use the word respect not in terms of people being polite, but in terms of what you have accomplished and being able to run the show.

PSD: *What do you do to separate yourself from the weight of the past?*
TBB: I am always looking forward. Hopefully the Lord will grant me a few years to do the things I want to do. I have a major building project I want done. Part of my drive comes from knowing that I have something that I am measured by. At the same time, I must remain cognizant of the fact that I didn't create this institution. I am just a part of it.

PSD: *How do you start your day?*
TBB: The first thing I do when I get up in the morning is thank the Lord for the gift of another day. I am thankful that my name has remained on his agenda for another day. I get up with the attitude that you should live every day as if it were your last, and be as appreciative of it as if it were your first.

PSD: *How do you measure yourself when you go to bed at night? It is obvious to me there is more involved than just numbers.*
TBB: Well, sales are still important. But the way I measure myself at night is to take some time and count my blessings, both personally and professionally.

PSD: *What is your greatest fear in life?*
TBB: To live a full life, then pass off the face of the earth with nobody even knowing you were here. And even worse, nobody even caring you were here. I have always wanted to do something to leave behind for someone else — to have a positive influence on people. It is fascinating to me that I can influence a person's life who I may never meet or ever see.

PSD: *You are not only a CEO but also a father.*
TBB: My children range in age from 5 to 25 years old. I may be CEO and Chairman, but that doesn't mean one thing when I come home in the evening and walk through that front door. I have a five year old who demands that I get on my knees and play horse. Every day!

PSD: *Quite humbling.*
TBB: Very humbling. And he will not take no for an answer, no matter how tired you are. He is one of my blessings. I take family very seriously. For me, it is a driving force to provide for them.

PSD: *What advice would you give to someone who came to you asking, "How can I be a good parent?"*

TBB: I would say a good parent is someone who gives parenting 100%. Now that can vary, but it is giving all you can. Some people are physically able to do more, some are emotionally able to give more, some spiritually. The greatest investment you will ever make is in your children, in both the short and long term. As long as you give 100% you know you are being the best parent you can be.

PSD: *You can't be perfect, though.*

TBB: You're right. You can't be perfect. Just spend as much time as possible and do the best you can. A child's training starts at birth, not when he or she is eighteen. I think it is imperative for us to give our kids a good essence of what life should be about. We should teach our girls that it is good to be a mother, but you should be a woman first. We should teach our boys that it's not how many babies you can make, but what you make for your babies. We have to bestow these kinds of things upon our children. It pays for itself.

PSD: *There seems to be a lack of role models and responsibility.*

TBB: We like to send our kids out the door and expect our school teachers to teach home training and values. This is not their role. It is the obligation of parents, who cannot delegate this to anyone. It is imperative that we teach the child in the home so they will know how to act outside of the home.

PSD: *You mentioned teaching a child what is important in life. What is important for you?*

TBB: To know that whatever I do, I do to the very best of my ability. It is important for me to know that, and only I can know what that means. Just think what you can do if you really put yourself out. Think of what you can accomplish.

PSD: *You seem very grounded. Does this come from your spiritual foundation?*

TBB: Yes, that and experience. After you run into enough stone walls you start to realize the path to take is not the one that leads to the same wall again. It takes awhile, but you will discover a path that will be both beneficial to you and those around you. That is what I am trying to do in my life.

PSD: *How do you stay on that path and avoid the stone walls? How does one stay passionate without being ego-driven?*

TBB: I guess every situation calls for it's own solution. Overall, the drive to do what you know is right keeps you going even if it is an unpopular choice. Sometimes that feeling may run you straight into that stone wall, but you still have to face it.

PSD: *As was the case with your forefathers.*

TBB: That's right. Sometimes stone walls come down. Many of them did. You have to follow your convictions, no matter where they lead.

PSD: *If it was a young man or your son sitting here and asking, "How do I find myself? How can I succeed?" What would you say?*

TBB: First of all, I would tell him he has to get an education. That is imperative in order to succeed in today's world. It is also imperative that we prepare spiritually so that we can deal with the problems we are going to encounter in life. And you will encounter problems, no matter who you are. Preparation is so important. And do what you believe is right.

I often tell the African-American men I counsel it is good to wear the symbol of the African continent around their neck. It is good to show pride in one's history and where one comes from. But it is also important to be able to point to it on the map.

You can work hard, but it is not always what

clicks and jingles in your pocket that matters, but what clicks in your heart. There is a big difference between the two. While it is good to know all the dance steps, don't forget where the steps to the schoolhouse and church are. This all goes back to the parent who teaches that anything worth having, you really have to work for.

PSD: *Do you counsel a lot of young African-American males?*
TBB: I talk to young people around the country and around the world. One of the most outstanding programs is the 100 Black Men. I served in this program as its local founding president. We all take a day out of the month and substitute teach in local schools.

PSD: *Tell me about this program.*
TBB: It started in the 1960s in New York. It has been very successful. There are now about 67 chapters nationally. It is primarily a mentor program for young men, but here we try to start the process before they become teenagers. There was a study done that showed young black males to have developed a basic resentment of female authority by the time they get to the fourth grade. In the secondary school system, that means you are automatically programmed for failure because 90% of the teachers are women.

PSD: *This may be idealistic and a long way off, but do you think we will some day be able to come together where we can be proud of our African heritage — or wherever our ancestors may be from — yet transcend our differences to be a nation of people where race or creed does not matter?*
TBB: I think it is important for African-Americans to know and be proud of where we came from because we were brought over here against our will. Our complete history was wiped out. I think it is very hard to understand that from an outside position. I

can trace my family as far back as the 1820s. Before then, it is completely untraceable. Kids were sold off and families split up. It was a terrible injustice to a people. Plus our homeland was always viewed as a bad place to be from.

PSD: *Can we hang on to our cultures and still be a brotherhood?*
TBB: I think it is important that we learn to live together, even though we have some cultural differences. You have to be able to learn to live in this society. We may have come over on different ships, but we are all in the same boat.

PSD: *There are more things we have in common than there are differences, no matter who we are.*
TBB: Absolutely! I feel you can be proud of where you came from and where you are going and still get along with your brother. I consider myself an American who has African roots. I was born here and I want to stay here. This is the finest country on the face of the earth. I love this country. My ancestors fought and died for this country.

PSD: *How do you define success?*
TBB: Success can only be defined by one's own personal measure. For me, success is being a good husband, a good daddy, and a good employer — one who has respect for the hundreds of people and their families whom I support.

PSD: *What else?*
TBB: Not so much as all the assets that can be acquired or all the fame and glory, but going to bed at night knowing that I have put in a good day's work to secure the well-being of both my family and the people I employ. To make sure they continue to have a place of employment, and that place is a comfortable place to work. Then I can go to sleep at night and feel successful.

PSD: *Does success come from the inside out?*
TBB: Yes, because I believe to have the feeling of success you have to feel good about yourself. If I'm not feeling good about myself there is no way I could say that I am successful. This comes from knowing one's self. Integrity is very important because you can't do bad things to other people and still feel good about yourself.

PSD: *Your view is humanistic.*
TBB: And I don't think it is idealistic, I think it is realistic. It's the way you should live — the way that I try to live.

PSD: *Do you take quiet time to find this inner center?*
TBB: Not nearly enough ... but you do have to take the time. I like to go jogging at Radnor Lake. That place has a spiritual awakening to it.

PSD: *Are you ever satisfied with what you have achieved?*
TBB: I feel like I have never done enough — that there is always something else to be done. You could probably live a thousand years and still have more goals that need to be accomplished.

PSD: *Do you ever think about how you would like to be remembered?*
TBB: I guess I would like to be remembered as a man who appreciated all that life had to give, and who gave life all he had to give. In other words, a man who put forth the best he possibly could, hopefully to make a difference in someone's life that would be beneficial. There's an old song that would sum it up, "If I could just help somebody, my living would not be in vain."

Mike Reid

Songwriter and Composer

"One of the things that drives me so hard is that this is not a rehearsal — this is the show, this is life. I may be tired, and my back may be hurting, but these are conditions I fully accept. Life is not meant to be enjoyed, it is meant to be experienced."

PSD: *You strike me as a focused person.*

MR: If I look back on the way I do things, I guess I am. I don't think it is an actual conscious decision where I say 'I have to focus now.' What I tend to do is take on things that are beyond me, that are beyond what my mind tells me I can do. Frost said, "One must begin on insufficient knowledge." It was exciting to hear that come from a great writer. I think a sense of inadequacy is generally always there for me because you are always beginning on insufficient knowledge.

Elliot spoke of every start being a little failure. I'm not sure it is a little failure, but it is always a new beginning into places you haven't been before. So I always have the sense that the equipment is not going to be up to the task.

Another thing that factors into it is how my father raised my brothers and me. He used to say, "If you tell somebody you are going to do something, damn it, you do it." We live in a time where that is not really the case. But once you are raised that way, you never stray very far from it. By telling somebody, 'Yes, I will write this, I accept this commission to write this opera,' your mind is saying, 'You are an idiot.' But you proceed on insufficient knowledge, except the suspicions about doing it reside in the body.

PSD: *Not in the mind.*

MR: Not for me. I walk around in this stuff and sense I have a notion of what the music should be. That is what you have to do. You need to focus, so you begin to understand your intent. Once you understand your intent, then it is a matter of rolling up your sleeves and moving the words and music around until you're really getting close to your intent.

PSD: *Are you saying to begin with the end in mind?*

MR: No, I don't think it is necessarily so pat that you can begin with the end in mind. I swear to you that is a challenge, that is a hard thing for anyone who wants to write. 'What am I intending here?' Writers of all kinds should write every day. They should think about walking around in this stuff even for ten minutes. It is using that part of your decision-making process, which is what I think writing is ultimately about.

PSD: *Are you talking about the subconscious and the mysterious?*

MR: You can't ever, ever consider writing without considering that. Because what I am trying to do — and what other writers are trying to do — is get into it. There is this neat little box called the ordered mind, the conscious mind, the mind that says 'These are the decisions I make about who I am.' Well, baby, all this royal stuff underneath is too much a part of who you are to discount it.

PSD: *An escape from the pragmatic mind to the unknown?*

MR: I am 48 years old and I see it in my eight-year-old, who comes forth with stories, involuntarily. It is like breathing for her. My biggest job with her is to protect her imagination, to nurture this part of her. She is bringing it out of this place in the mind we're talking about.

Poets can get into this place. What is a little bothersome about education and socialization is that it is set up to protect you. Erroneously we say, 'We don't want these ions of original energy that the child brings into the world. We want the child to get through life as painlessly as possible, and one of the best ways to do that is to act like everyone else.'

Fortunately, there are people who say, "I can't *be* like everyone else. I can't." They go off and write Beethoven's Fifth Symphony. Or they become Steven Spielbergs or turn into Arthur Millers and Paul Simons. They just can't behave like everyone else.

There are also people who behave like everyone else far too long, then by the grace of something, realize it is not too late to discover the lost self. That is me. Then there are people who never address the ebbs and flows and pushes and pulls of their own impulses. They just continue to be like everyone else.

PSD: *Inner success — the love of the process — is sacred. Like writing this book.*

MR: The book is 'ashes from the volcano.' The volcano is personal and powerful to experience, but the thrilling thing is to see the ashes and expect something to happen. This human act of following what you expect to be the right course is a powerful act. When your suspicions prove to be correct, that is your reward. And it is a profound reward. It helps further us along in the singular problem that all human beings have had, the search for who in hell they are. "Who am I?"

PSD: *I sense in you some real change going on, some questioning on a very deep level.*

MR: All this is imperfect stuff, but we can dig around and see what we can find. I mentioned the phrase, 'The recovery or the reclaiming of a lost self.' I grew up in Western Pennsylvania in a traditional working family. What you did if you were a kid like me was to be an athlete. I think there are some deep psychological things that go on with this. In some people, there are little alternative selves that you have to be kind to because they really are survival mechanisms. Jung talks about individuation, the point in life where you take the mask off and say, 'I am really going forth with me.'

I remember the first time I fell in love with a girl when I was seventeen. It was throughout the course of a summer. Of course, she was very cool about the whole thing. Then I went out on a Friday night in the first football game of my senior year and ran for 225 yards and scored five touchdowns, thus becoming 'big news.' A star was born. Before the game, I

had asked if she was going to the dance afterwards, and she was saying, "Maybe I'll see you there or something." Then I have this big game, Dad gives me the car, and there is that girl mooning me with her eyes saying, "Can I go to the dance with you? I only want to be with you."

Looking back without too much analysis, a little war begins there. The Football Mike says, "All right, everybody, listen up. I'm in charge from here on out. This feels way too good to let Mike The Writer call the shots. No one is going to screw this up." Mike The Football Player was in charge, and football paid my way through college.

PSD: *You won the Outland Trophy for being the best lineman in the nation.*

MR: I was the Outland Trophy winner.

PSD: *Did you work as hard in athletics as you have in writing?*

MR: I was always working out to be in shape, but I have worked far harder as a writer. Writers work much harder than athletes. The most difficult thing in life is the choices one makes and being responsible for them. Athletes don't have to do that, they just have to get in shape and drive themselves. There is no choice to that. It is just an animal reacting to a stimulus.

That is the tough thing about writing. The opera that I wrote was an hour and twenty minutes of choices.

PSD: *Are you satisfied with what you have accomplished?*

MR: Hell, no! I remember a couple of years ago when somebody said, "Make a record. Here is some money, go in there and be yourself." It sounds inviting until you get in there and find out you haven't a clue as to who the hell you are. You need to travel through some neighborhoods where you don't belong to figure out and identify your self.

But you take a look at your stuff, your commercial success, the success you have had in the public sector. A hit songwriter is hoping to get the public's attention. I took a look at this stuff and I said, 'All right, there is something missing. What is missing here from this work?' And I identified what was missing. ME! ME!

One of the testicular density checks in life is being able to listen and pay attention to what your life is asking you to do.

PSD: *Popular songwriting seems a lot like the jingle business.*
MR: Hit songwriting is generally about a journey outward, away from the self, into the external world. When you have had success doing that, the tough thing is when life comes along and says, "What I ask of you now is to go inward." This means you may write more truly. You may write something that you find an amazing peace about, that you never had before. But you write at the expense of the audience. You may lose a lot of people.

PSD: *More tough choices.*
MR: As a maker of music, do you want to be a slave to the five million people who buy your records on their terms, or have an audience of 350 people that you are really connecting with?

PSD: *Do the answers for you have to come through music, or can they also come through your children? Is it all funneled through the prism of your work?*
MR: I have to work very carefully on that. My children came into the world bearing huge gifts for me and my wife. We just listen to them and pay attention to them.

PSD: *What is your biggest challenge right now?*
MR: In an age of unbelievable technology where we are literally overrun with information and noise, one of the great challenges for

me is to not stop caring. About everything. To figure out a way to continue to be engaged. To not take that baby out of gear.

PSD: *But is it really life that we see on CNN every hour?*
MR: You know what the big information picture does? The most harmful thing it does is to destroy local culture. Local cultures used to exert a centripetal force. But we have all become part of feeding the big picture centripetal, so centrifugally it spins out to us the same books, the same CNN bull___, the same Sylvester Stallone movies, the same, the same, the same. Television does that, too. Something you never see people do on TV is watch TV.

They are doing what we used to do, which is relating to one another. Shows like *Cheers*, where you have a little community of people telling each other their stories. In telling each other our stories, we knew one another. In knowing one another, we trusted one another. And when we trusted one another, we helped one another. We don't do that anymore.

PSD: *How do you define success?*
MR: I have no definition for it. I don't feel successful, I don't feel unsuccessful. The only thing that I have done that causes me to think that I am a success is that I am in control of my life. My life is not being pulled in any direction by someone else. I am in control and I am the architect of my life.

PSD: *Do you love to create?*
MR: When someone says, "I write because I have to," I always think that is such a horse ____ answer. That may be because I don't feel that way, and I insist that other people feel like me. That is always what arguments are about. You know the number one problem that my wife and I have? She just refuses to be like me. (He laughs.) I don't know why.

PSD: *When you can obviously see what is right.*

23

MR: Exactly. (He laughs.) Why wouldn't she want to be like me? She probably wonders why *I* want to be like me. We have been together for 22 years.

PSD: *I'd call that a form of success.*
MR: My friends who are divorced say that the overwhelming feeling they are left with is that they have failed. I don't understand that. How can you measure success or failure in interpersonal relationships?

PSD: *Do you think the natural course of action is laziness or entropy?*
MR: I always watch those nature shows, and really envy the Silverback gorilla whose only mission in the course of the day is to eat. I have never thought about it, but laziness is natural for me.

PSD: *Was the 'real' Mike Reid a poet and a writer, born into an athletically gifted body, who ended up on the gridiron as a sports hero through the natural inertia of cultural acceptance?*
MR: I have only just felt that I could stand up and say that. And I said it to somebody out of frustration in an interview. Whether you like it or not, athletics was never a purpose. It was what I did on the way to discovering my purpose.

So the answer is yes. It is not an easy thing, at least for me, to stand up and say over the arc of my life, 'I am this writer of music.' It may be bad or it may be good. The quality of what you do is not the issue. Sometimes at night when I am really fatigued and most vulnerable, I begin to wonder if I don't really belong coaching a junior high school football team somewhere.

PSD: *Is doubt what drives you so hard?*
MR: Maybe so. One of the things that drives me so hard is that this is not a rehearsal — this is the show, this is life. I may be tired, and my back may be hurting, but these are conditions I fully accept. Life is not meant to be enjoyed, it is meant to be experienced. I look back over the 48 years of my life and say, 'It has been a good one.' But it has been a good one because I have put some effort into it. Something in me finds the natural impulse towards laziness to be completely unacceptable, particularly at my age when you discover that the most beautiful and valuable thing you have is time. What are you going to do with it? You can't choose the time in which you live, you can only choose what to do with that time while you live.

PSD: *What would you tell your son if he was 18 years old today and looking for some direction?*
MR: I would say, 'Pack up a few things in a bag. Take off and find out what it is that engages you, what resonates within you.' That is the whole key to the rest of your life — finding out what is sufficiently meaningful so that you can spend the rest of your life with it.

PSD: *The beauty is that things can change. You are a perfect example of that.*
MR: I am and I am not. I don't put music into categories. I have often felt that if you really fell passionately in love with writing, you would write your way into obscurity. When you go down to places that you haven't been, the audience that knew an easier side of you is not going to want to go there.

PSD: *But if you have enough money, who cares?*
MR: That's the practical part to this. I have enough money right now. If I won the lottery, I wouldn't change anything in my life. I would give Mac Pirkle enough money to buy his own 400-seat theater. I do worry about my kids having too much.

PSD: *That is a real challenge. How do you keep the well-fed hungry?*
MR: What a great question! Have you ever said that before?

24

PSD: *No, it is a wonderful part of the whole process of personal exploration manifested through the book.*

MR: "How do you keep the well-fed hungry" is a really great question. It feels like there are some rather vacuous forms of entertainment that are generating huge sums of money. The reason they are generating these sums is that people pay to see them. I think it is curious why we as a culture seem to need these empty, vacuous forms of entertainment. I haven't figured out why this is. America has never been excited about the inward journey. But we are finding out now that the alternative is not working. There is a pervasive sense of dissatisfaction across the country.

PSD: *Are you a spiritual person?*

MR: Belief-wise, what makes sense to me is my belief in God through the divinity of nature. One of the disadvantages as a human is to look out there and see that the tree is crooked and think, 'That tree should be straight.' I look up at the stars and go, 'Ah!' You encounter art in the same way. You encounter Brahms in the same way. You think what a wonder this is.

PSD: *Do you have a spiritual center?*

MR: I have almost come to a place where I think if we can know our spiritual center, then that is not it. God, art, and love are things we cannot know. We insist on knowing them, and I think that insistence gets us in trouble. We can't know these things. Jerry Falwell might say that I will burn in hell for saying that I cannot know God. But I believe that the most you can do is experience these things and then wonder about them.

I have pain like everyone else, but middle-age has brought me to the place where I find it less and less necessary to make the pain go away. The difficulties of life are what life is. We continually make moral judgments about things, where nature does not. Nature just *is*.

Identify the questions that mean something and embrace the question. The best we can do is to live the question. If we live long enough, and if we live the question truly enough, we might live our way into an answer or two. The necessity to know things that are unknowable only creates sadness, frustration, and unnecessary heartache. Life is difficult. We must accept that.

PSD: *Do you believe the inner part of you to be connected to something transcendent?*

MR: The inner part of me is absolutely connected to something bigger. I don't believe that I am going to come up before God, and he is going to go down a list of bad things I have done, and say, "I'm sorry, you can't get in." The assumption that you were born bad — original sin — is a bad way to begin this whole thing we call life.

PSD: *Have you ever loved anything as much as your children?*

MR: No. This whole notion of love beyond condition with a stranger I view very suspiciously. But I think you love your kids without condition.

PSD: *How would you like to be remembered?*

MR: I don't care about that. In terms of my kids? Someone who was fair and listened to them. If I could somehow get them to know one thing, it would be that they made my life better. That their gifts to me were substantial. That they enriched my life more than they will ever know.

Thomas Frist, MD

Founder, Hospital Corporation of America

"I love people more than anything. The reason I practiced medicine is because I love people. I wouldn't give all the money in the world for the good things I did practicing medicine."

PSD: *By all rights, you are a success on a lot of levels, so how would you define success?*

TF: Being a good family man, working hard, and doing something for the good of people.

PSD: *How did you come upon the idea to found a hospital chain?*

TF: I was practicing medicine awfully hard, night and day, from eight in the morning to eleven in the evening. My only break would be to go home and see my children for an hour, maybe just to throw a baseball with them. I was also teaching medicine at Vanderbilt. Vanderbilt Hospital was always full, so was Saint Thomas — you couldn't get in there — and so was Baptist. So I said to four or five other doctors, 'Let's develop a small hospital for old folks because these other places always have a waiting period just to get in.'

We developed Parkview, which was a fifty bed hospital and a hundred bed nursing home. We designed it this way so if it wasn't successful as a hospital we could turn it into a nursing home. It was so successful we turned the nursing home part into a hospital.

One day, my son Tommy called me while he was in the Air Force as a surgeon in training. He said, "Daddy when I come back let's start a chain of hospitals." I said, 'Son, are you crazy? You need to practice medicine.' He then called his mother and said, "I am going to do it anyway, even if Daddy doesn't help me." So the next day I called him back and told him I would help. We didn't have any money, so we got an investor, Jack Massey, who had a lot of money because he had recently sold his ownership of Kentucky Fried Chicken. Jack furnished the money for us to start HCA, Hospital Corporation of America, a name my wife came up with.

PSD: *What is it about medicine that you loved enough to devote your life to?*

TF: My father died when I was eight years old. He was the station master in my hometown, Meridian, Mississippi. One day he saw a lady holding a baby standing on the train track. She appeared to be hypnotized as the train was coming down the track. So he rushed out and pushed her off the rail. He saved the two of them, but he was killed.

We had no money at all, so my mother took in boarders to help pay the rent on our old three-story house. We had some interesting boarders, one of whom was a doctor. I went to work for him and he became my best friend. He was such a great doctor, I decided I had to be a doctor, too, because I loved what he was doing and I loved people.

PSD: *You love people.*

TF: I love people more than anything. The reason I practiced medicine is because I love people. I wouldn't give all the money in the world for the good things I did practicing medicine. Helping patients was one of the greatest things in my life. I loved them and they loved me. I was always very close to my patients.

PSD: *Why do you love people so much?*

TF: I guess because my father died when I was so young and I missed him so much. Also because my mother, who was so great, loved people. If you love people, they will love you. I just cared so much about every patient I saw.

PSD: *Was anyone of great influence?*

TF: My brother was by far the greatest man I have ever known. By far. He was four years older than me. He was a father, a friend, and the best brother in the world to me. He died from colon cancer when he was only 50 years old but he helped me in so many ways. He was a minister and a great human being. I still miss him.

PSD: *Why is family so very important to you?*

TF: Family means more to me than anything in the world. In our family, no one has ever smoked a cigarette or anything. These are good kids. I have a good wife, especially as a doctor's wife, with me working every night. She was a great mother. She never complained at all. She gave all of her time to me and the children. You know, our son Billy came last and was a surprise. She was 40 at the time and I was 41. He was a big surprise.

PSD: *That big surprise is a United States Senator now.*

TF: Billy was the best thing that happened in my life. He is a wonderful boy.

PSD: *How did you try to be as a father?*

TF: I never spanked a child, I never cursed. I never did anything but talk to them and compliment them.

PSD: *What advice would you give to a young man or woman to help them be successful — not only in terms of monetary reward but all-encompassing success?*

TF: If you are successful, money will come naturally. But I wouldn't give my children money because I think they should earn it on their own. Money never meant much to me. I have given most of it away. I still drive a Chevrolet that is six years old. I never spend any money on myself. In fact, they say I'm pretty tight. But I was brought up to be careful. The two worst things in the world are having no money and having too much money. Am I talking too much?

PSD: *Heavens, no. This is all about you! What advice would you give on how to be happy?*

TF: That's an easy one. The most important thing by far is to marry the right girl. And I have been very lucky in this way. She has been a wonderful mother and wife.

PSD: *And in terms of a career or a calling?*

How does someone who doesn't know what they want to do find that magical thing like you found?

TF: That is a very good question, but a very difficult question. If that doctor had not lived in my house when I was a boy, I probably would not have gone into medicine. My brother was a minister and I thought about doing that, but knew I couldn't give a sermon every Sunday. I wasn't smart enough. I am really street-smart but not very book-smart.

PSD: *For all you have accomplished, you don't seem to have a big ego. You come across as very humble.*

TF: I have always had a very big inferiority complex, and in fact, I still have it. I can't walk in the doctors' lounge without feeling inferior.

PSD: *Why do you think this is so?*

TF: I don't know, but it is terrible. I never thought that I was smart. I have felt inferior for a long time. In one way, I think it is good because when a person is cocky, it is one of the worst things in the world.

PSD: *Do you think this inferiority complex may have been one of the things that drove you so hard?*

TF: Yes, I think so. I have worked really hard in my life.

PSD: *It must be very challenging to grow old, especially with your mind being as sharp as it is.*

TF: I will tell you briefly about my illnesses. I was always healthy growing up, but twenty-five years ago I had a heart attack and almost died. I had to then have a heart replacement and had a second transplant eight years ago. I have had cancer of the colon and the prostate, but both were caught early so I am OK. I had a stroke during my first open heart surgery that paralyzed my right side. I got the movement back but I have trouble with my speech. I am also blind, deaf, and dumb! (He laughs.)

PSD: *What keeps you going through all that physical adversity?*
TF: My love of people and the joy I get in watching things grow. Trying to help people keeps me going.

PSD: *Did you have any fear of dying during those hard times?*
TF: Yes, I did. But Billy came down and stayed with me the whole night long. He encouraged me so much that I didn't have as much fear. All my children were there for me. Having had two heart replacements is pretty rare, but I have had great doctors who have saved my life.

PSD: *Do you ever feel like modern medicine is becoming completely technological thus losing the personal touch that you so embodied ?*
TF: I don't think I could be a doctor now for anything because of all the changes, which are enormous. But the things happening in medicine are also remarkable. I used to see people die from typhoid fever and other infectious diseases. Life will be lived a lot longer now.

PSD: *What will be the most important thing you leave behind?*
TF: My children.

PSD: *What is your greatest challenge right now?*
TF: Just to be alive and to stay alive. I want to see HCA become a great company and continue to improve.

PSD: *When you wake up every morning, do you feel that it's a great gift?*
TF: Oh, yes. I am 85 and should have been dead a long time ago with all the ailments I had. So I don't dread death at all. I just hope my death passes quickly and doesn't linger. I

have had such a perfect, perfect, life. Nobody had a more joyful life or a better family. My life has been unbelievable. Losing my father and brother were the about the only real bad things in my life.

PSD: *Why is it so important for you to give back to the community?*
TF: When you give back, you get back. When you give to people, not only with money, you get so much back. Medicine is a wonderful life to lead if you love people. And you have to really love people.

PSD: *How would you like to be remembered?*
TF: I told my preacher, 'Don't say too much. When someone dies, the preachers go on for thirty minutes or an hour. Don't do that. Just say he was a good man, a good father, a good doctor. That's all.'

PSD: *And he loved people?*
TF: And he loved people.

Rosetta Davis

Graduate Student and Social Activist

"**Being able to make a difference, whether in one individual's life, with a whole family, or the neighborhood. If I can hear that inner voice say, 'A job well done,' then that, for me, is success.**"

PSD: *What makes you get involved in community service?*

RD: There is something within that drives me. Believe me, I have tried to think the other way since I started an MBA program, to think 'for profit', but there is something from within that drives me towards community service, towards non-profits, and towards the underdog. Driven towards the ones who don't have. I said to myself, 'Now Rosetta, you really need to learn to make money. You can make a more dramatic impact if you have more money.'

PSD: *Is business a new road?*

RD: I have always had this business thing. I even started the Young Entrepreneurs Program at Edgehill and seem to be destined that way. There is just something that is part of my makeup. While some people are in that 'gain, gain, gain, get, get, get' mode, I seem to be in the 'give, give, give' mode. But I don't really know why.

PSD: *So it is an internal thing?*

RD: One time, I told a group of kids over at Hillsboro High School that it was part of the 'Master Plan'. I tried to deviate from The Plan, when I was an antique buyer for T.G.I. Fridays. I also had a plan to start a home video rental store, long before Blockbuster Video. But God had a way of redirecting me, because in August of 1985, I was asked to become the director of the Edgehill Center. At the time, I was planning to resign my position at Edgehill in order to make more money.

PSD: *Talk a little about Edgehill.*

RD: It was the South Street Community Center when I got started there back in 1981. In 1990 we changed the name to Edgehill to be more clearly identified with the community. We were getting a lot of good publicity with the name South Street, while there was a lot of negative publicity for the community of Edgehill. The Edgehill rapist, the Edgehill gangs, the Edgehill crime rate, and so on. So, by changing the name of the community center to Edgehill, there was a balance where kids could also read something good about their community.

PSD: *What were the Edgehill Center's programs?*

RD: We had a child care program and youth programs through 18 years of age. We also had a number of early intervention programs for kids: alcohol, drugs, teen pregnancy — which all basically started with self-esteem. While working there I learned that just because we were black, we didn't have any formula for dealing with black children. So as African-Americans, we had to learn about ourselves. One of the things that fostered that was my sister encouraging me to attend the National Black Development Conference. They had some real interesting programs being presented that we later incorporated.

It was at that conference that I became convinced that we should be identified as African-Americans, because as a group we had been given so many names like Negro, Black, African, Colored, American, and now African-American, so we were kind of confused. I think you need to know who you are to know where you are going. Our kids were missing out on that sense of who they were and not learning about the greatness of a people. If you look in books, you're not there. If you look at television, it's "There I am, I am a basketball player." Or "I shoot people." But if kids learn that they come from civilization, and a great civilization at that, this could be very important.

PSD: *Many of the great African civilizations were destroyed by white colonization, a record of which is strangely absent in our so-called history books.*

RD: There was an article in *Discovery* magazine that said Africa was the cradle of civilization. That 'Eve' was even African. So if you believe in creation, then we are all connected. You are my brother and I am your sister.

PSD: *Even if you believe in evolution, you would have to think that we are all connected.*
RD: That's right. Our similarities are greater than our differences.

PSD: *What was it like to grow up in the projects of Nashville?*
RD: Wonderful! I grew up in the John Henry Hale projects on Joe Johnston Avenue. It was great. When I was born, we lived on Donaldson Street in a shotgun house — you could look in the front door and see right out the back. We had no indoor plumbing and coal heat. To move into the projects where we had running water and heat was a big step up. There were six of us. Now this was a good example of the old African proverb, 'It takes a whole village to raise a child.' Because the community helped raise you, the neighbors would help discipline you. The families there took care of each other.

PSD: *Did your parents have a profound influence on you?*
RD: Oh, yes. My mother was very religious, but we didn't appreciate it at the time. My father worked a lot. He had three jobs and I can even remember him having the mumps as an adult and walking miles to go to work at the Shell station. I think seeing the work ethic in my father had a great impact on me. We were poor but we didn't know it. Other kids pointed that out. We had food and we had clothes. Sometimes the clothes were hand-me-downs from the place where my mother did day work. But we were happy.

PSD: *Where did your self-esteem come from?*
RD: Well, I didn't always have it. I was really quiet and shy as a kid. I think it evolved from having a number of people like church members and teachers helping me. I can remember my siblings telling me I was smart but I didn't feel as capable or as adequate as some of my classmates. There was a wonderful math teacher in junior high school who really helped me. He worked with me after school until I started to think 'I can do this.' I really got into my homework and felt good when I got praise from my teachers. Then I remember how things changed when I made the honor roll. The Fort family took a real interest in me. Chloe Fort was a good friend. They took me everywhere.

PSD: *For a little girl from the projects, what was your first experience with integration?*
RD: I guess the real awakening came when we were looking for a house. I didn't know there was any difference until then. We were in East Nashville and there was this little white girl we were playing with. Her mother called her over and when she came back she said, "My mama told me I can't play with niggers." So we wanted to know what a nigger was. We had never heard that word before.

PSD: *That had to be hard for a kid.*
RD: It was. We were taught in church to love everybody. We had some white friends and they were just people. It wasn't until that experience that we realized we were different, or that people would perceive us as being different. And when they wouldn't play with us, that hurt.

PSD: *You work a lot with kids. Are you concerned about the lack of male role models?*
RD: Oh yes, that is what we worked with at Edgehill. I was fortunate to have some great people like James Threalkill and Andrew Bradley, who were two excellent male role models. I have had parents tell me it made a big difference to them that we were willing to come into their homes and show support.

PSD: *How would you define success?*

RD: That is a hard question. Sometimes I feel successful when I get a phone-call from a kid who reminds me where I have made an impact in her life. Or, having served on the Affordable Housing Board, seeing a family going into a home where the kids have a yard to play in. I can really relate to that. My idea of success doesn't comply with the normal definition, so to speak. If I think what I have done is in compliance with God, that is success. Being able to make a difference, whether in one individual's life, with a whole family, or the neighborhood. If I can hear that inner voice say, "A job well done," then that, for me, is success.

PSD: *What advice would you give a young person on how to get in touch with what matters most?*
RD: I'm not sure, but one of the things that I am thankful for is the fact that I was exposed to God. I feel for people who don't have that connection. I feel that bond with Jesus and I am so happy that I can talk with Him and have a relationship. So Jesus is with me all the time. I don't have to go to a church to find Him, or to talk to Him and ask for guidance. It is within me. I am working on hearing and listening to that inner voice. I guess my advice would be to get in touch with your spiritual being or self. You can do this in the morning or late at night. It depends on the individual. For me, sometimes it is hearing the birds, or just seeing the stars. Know that it is all within you. Everything that we need is in us, it is there.

PSD: *You are still in the process of discovering who you are.*
RD: I am, and it is constantly changing. People ask why I am in an MBA program at this stage in my life. I am constantly evolving. I have this insatiable appetite for learning and knowledge. We will always be learning, because you can never really master everything. Not only learning concepts, but learning who we are.

PSD: *Do you have a sense of why you are here?*
RD: Not really, but I ask constantly for direction to help me pursue and fulfill my purpose.

PSD: *What do you think your purpose is?*
RD: I don't know exactly, but I know my purpose has to do with mankind. I love people. I get really excited to work with people or do things with people. To be able to connect with someone.

PSD: *You have a sister who is struggling with a drug problem. What lessons has that taught you?*
RD: I have learned how to let go. I have learned what tough love really means, and that is hard. I have learned that Rosetta doesn't control anything, I am not God. I can't force her to enter a treatment center or to get help. I have learned not to enable her. It is really, really, hard. I know a lot of people who have a family member with drug problems and it is so frustrating. I wonder 'Why her?' or 'How?' We talked about self-esteem and she says that hers is very low. As kids we did everything together growing up, because she is only one year younger than me. It is a mystery to me but it is all about choices.

PSD: *What is your biggest challenge?*
RD: Taking care of and raising my eleven-year-old niece. Doing the right thing with her. School can also be a big challenge. My father died in March, so that was a challenge, although I feel he is still with me. But I do miss being able to talk to him. He gave great advice. He was the most brilliant man I have ever known, even though he only had a third grade education. I really respected him. I miss him.

PSD: *How would you like to remembered?*
RD: She really tried, she made a difference. She didn't just sit back and watch things, she

tried to help and she was fair. She tried to really make a difference.

PSD: *Are you optimistic in terms of our kids and the future?*
RD: Oh yes, I have seen some real changes in attitudes and beliefs. They are more spiritually in touch with themselves and others. They are concerned about the environment. I know there is another segment that is way out there. I do hope there are enough who are grounded and who will be able to carry on.

PSD: *What are your own plans?*
RD: I don't really know, but I think I will be guided and know when it is right and what to do. God brings people into my life just at the right moment. I am working on recognizing those things that I need to do to take care of myself.

PSD: *What do kids today really need?*
RD: They need love. I used to have teenagers come by my office all the time just for hugs. The kids — especially the little ones — just want a sense of belonging and respect. They want to feel valued and they want to contribute. The greatest self-esteem booster for our kids was for them to do something for their community. To be needed and included. I trusted our kids, so we didn't have the problem of theft because the kids took ownership. I said 'This stuff is yours and if somebody steals it, you won't have it.' They couldn't believe I would let them have the code for the alarm, but we had no theft. They protected the place.

PSD: *You just love to give, don't you?*
RD: Yes, and to change someone's mindset. I sometimes question why I can't just have a normal life with less stress, but I think this is my calling and my destiny. The children are our future and I have to do my little part for the brotherhood of man.

Carl Carlson

Director, YMCA Y-CAP Youth Programs

"There are many children in need around the world that I can't do anything about, but I can impact my little bit of society right here."

PSD: *What is the Y-CAP Program?*
CC: We work with kids who have been dealt a bad hand from the word 'go'. What do I mean by bad hand? Well, 90% of these kids are coming from homes with no father. The father had abdicated his responsibilities and run off. Compound that with suffering from poverty or neglect, and the basic necessities like food, clothing and medical concerns. I would say at least 50% to 60% of our kids suffer from some kind of physical or sexual abuse. Sometimes they have been abandoned. I could go on and on with individual stories that would probably move you. True stories, unbelievable stories. But this is what we do at Y-CAP. We do a lot of things to try to help these kids.

PSD: *What does Y-CAP stand for?*
CC: The YMCA Community Action Project. I founded it with Ed Hunley, the juvenile court chaplain, 11 years ago. We have five programs. The community-based program works with boys 9 to 14 who are referred to us through the courts. We pick these kids up from school and do all kinds of things to help get them back on track. Thirty-five percent of kids today drop out of school before they graduate. So we have a heavy emphasis on academics here.

PSD: *How did you end up in this position?*
CC: In essence, I used to *be* one of these kids. That is the bottom line. My father died when I was 3 and our mother just abandoned us. She ran off. I have a brother and a sister. We were raised in orphanages until an aunt took me, which wasn't a good situation. When I was 11, I was put into a state reformatory for running away and spent a year there. A year later, I went back into the reformatory for stealing and spent another year. When I got out, I stole a car, then went to a Federal reformatory where I spent two and a half years. I got out when I was 18, got a job in a steel mill, until I was drafted and sent to

Vietnam. I went to Vietnam and served my country honorably, but I discovered drugs over there. It was like a drug store. I got out of the military and made some really bad decisions.

PSD: *What happened?*
CC: We were in the middle of a recession and I had taken training in brick-laying while in the military so I would have a trade when I got out. But I went to construction site after site and couldn't get a job because there was no work. I was driving over a bridge one day in my truck. I was so frustrated, I got out and threw all my nice brick-laying tools in the river. Then I went out and got a job working in a bar. One night, a guy came up to me and asked if I wanted to make ten grand. At the time, I was half-crazy messing around with dope, drinking, and chasing women. This guy was a middle-man who wanted me to burn down a building for some businessman. I did it, and that lead to some other things. The long and short of it is that I got busted here in Tennessee and ended up getting a 15 year prison sentence for armed robbery and did some hard calendar years in the prison.

One day, my brother Philip came out to visit me in the prison. It was the only time he had ever come, and he started talking about God and Jesus. You have to understand that if you talk to preachers, 80% of their daddies were preachers, and preachers are paid good money to talk about God. But there was my brother, born and raised like I was — dirt poor — talking about God. I saw something in him. I saw a Light, if you will. He was telling me how the Lord Jesus Christ had made a difference in his life. I will never forget it to the day I die, and I will be 50 years old this year. I turned around and said, 'Philip, do you see these walls? There are 2000 men inside and there ain't no God in here. There are men dying, there's drugs, homosexuality, pain, and despair. God is not in here, son.'

37

But what Phil did was plant a seed. Later, when I was locked up in the hole for trying to escape a couple of times, after the guards had jammed me up pretty good, I remember crying out to God. And He came into my life in a mighty way. He changed the way I thought at the time. I thought money was the most important thing, along with drugs, women, and power — basically a gangster lifestyle. I still had a million miles to go, but God planted a desire in me.

PSD: *Was it a gradual thing, or like "BOOM"!?*

CC: At first it was like that. BAM!!! What I said later was that the hand of God touched me because it put such a zeal in me. Unless you have had this kind of experience, you won't know what I am talking about. It put a zeal in me, yet at the same time, He gave me such a sense of peace. And what was probably most important, a sense of assurance that He really loved me. I had never felt that in my life, especially having been abandoned. It changed my life.

PSD: *What did you do when you were released?*

CC: When I got out of prison, I walked into the detention center, on my own, and said that I wanted to work with these kids. That was 16 years ago. Though each case is unique, it is always basically about abandonment and rage.

So for sixteen years I have been working with these kids. My message is this: 'I know where you are coming from because I have been there. It doesn't have to be this way, or it can be this way if you want it to be this way. If you are determined to end up in prison or dead that is fine, but it doesn't have to be this way. It can be different, you can have a decent life. You can get married and have children one day. You can break the cycle like I broke the cycle.'

PSD: *Do you have a family?*

CC: My wife and I are blessed with four fine sons. She is a very Godly woman. She is the best thing that ever happened to me, she really is.

PSD: *There is a miraculous element to this story.*

CC: There is no question. None. God is the author. When you talk about Y-CAP, I really believe with all my heart and soul that we have done some great things. We have kids who have come to us broken and who are now strong, young adults who are going to be contributors to society. All because of Y-CAP, and Y-CAP is because of God. It is as simple as that and the bottom line to the story.

PSD: *How do you define success on a personal level?*

CC: Being the best husband and the best father that I could possibly be. That is one of my most consistent prayers. For God to help me be a better husband and a better father to my children. Also, to help provide them with the opportunity to be compassionate men who contribute to society. Where one day they truly understand that success is not just academically or athletically oriented, but also comes from helping your fellow man — helping people less fortunate than yourself. I get my older sons involved in the ministry. Every Christmas they come with me to the inner city and meet people. They buy gifts from their own money and we have in our home what we call a Jesus box. All year we put money in it, everyone in the whole family, and at the end of the year we go out and buy nice gifts, not junk, but quality gifts for some child in the inner city. I want them to understand how blessed they are, because they are indeed blessed. There are many children in need around the world that I can't do anything about, but I can impact my little bit of society right here.

PSD: *And in doing that you do impact the world.*

CC: Absolutely. So for me, success is raising my children to be all that they can be and at the same time providing the leadership, fire, and passion for the Y-CAP Program to continue its mission. We are getting ready to open an incredible new facility with a 1.5 million dollar grant we received locally. We have had a dream to build a facility for several years and we are going to build it. There is no telling how many children we are going to be able to reach with that.

I'm talking about excellence, not numbers. I'm not into numbers. I believe in quality over quantity. You can't just turn these kids around like that, it takes time, a lot of time. So for me, that is success — making a difference and providing an opportunity for these kids to be all that they can be.

PSD: *What advice would you give to kids or parents in finding the kind of success you have talked about, their 'inner resonance?'*

CC: Kids today are facing more than they have ever faced before and I think in order to succeed, or even survive, they have got to have a foundation. This foundation, I believe, has got to come from God. Their parents need to guide them and talk about the Lord at home. What we tell our kids here is that they have got to stay in school and get an education. They have to hang around with people who are like-minded, because too many times, who you hang around with can drag you down. They have to have that spiritual grounding. To believe in hard work and a work ethic, even though that is not popular these days. There must be balance.

PSD: *How do you find balance between your family and such a demanding profession?*

CC: It is tough, an incredible challenge. What I try to do is synthesize things. That is why it is my most consistent prayer, because it is so difficult to maintain. I am getting better at giving myself a little bit of time.

PSD: *Do you get discouraged by all of the suffering you witness?*

CC: Oh yes, because it is literally out of control. Violent juvenile crime in Nashville has increased 400% in the last 25 years. Look at illegitimate births in the last 30 years. In 1960, 5% of white babies and 22% of black babies were born out of wedlock. Fast forward to 1991, when 24% of white babies and 65% of black babies were born out of wedlock — and in the inner cities, the rate is 90%. Strictly from a monetary standpoint, America can't handle it. That's not to mention the pain, despair, and all the other variables. This country has serious problems. But if enough of us get involved, if enough of us try to fight it, if enough of us stay in there and fight, we can win this thing.

PSD: *It must affect you.*

CC: Do I get discouraged? Yes, it is overwhelming sometimes. We just had a kid that we buried from a crack cocaine overdose. Another kid's father ran off after their mother died last week. I have a 12-year-old girl who is pregnant. I just went to visit a kid in prison I have been working with for 7 years and he broke down on my shoulder. He deserves to be there because he did wrong, but it is still hard for me because I always think of the ones who slip up and how we could have better helped them.

PSD: *Is our country in denial about these problems?*

CC: I don't know any more. I think the big, inner cities may be too far gone but we can still win this here in Nashville. The key is to get serious about it and get our minds off money and power.

PSD: *Are you basically trying to save one child at a time?*

CC: That is what Y-CAP is all about. We

have been turned down so many times for grants because we are not working with enough kids. But you can't do this kind of work on a grand scale. It has to be focused. Quality over quantity.

PSD: *This sounds like a very hands-on, super-intense program with a lot of focus.*
CC: Well said. We don't fix anything over night. We also match up every kid with our own big brothers.

PSD: *These kids don't have any role models.*
CC: Exactly. We also provide counseling. I have a Master's in Counseling but what I'm talking about is much more down to earth in it's style. We get into the issues of rage. We try to work with the parents so they may become more effective.

PSD: *Do you recycle some of these kids where they come back into the program as counselors?*
CC: Some of them do, yes. And everything I said about the boys is the same for the girls. We have a group home in East Nashville.

Remember, we don't charge a nickel to any of the families. They could never afford it any-way, but when I got into this, I said I would never charge for it. Consequently we have to raise all our own money.

PSD: *I hear a lot of commitment from you towards these kids.*
CC: We are in this for the long haul. There are no quick fixes. We hold these kids responsible for all their actions. Just because they were abused, they have no right to do wrong. The bottom line? The foundation is God Almighty and Jesus Christ.

PSD: *This all shows what one person can do with a dream.*
CC: Yes. When I started, it was just me and my wife. Now we have seventeen people on staff.

PSD: *How would you like to be remembered?*
CC: For three things. I did the best I knew how to honor God. I did the best I knew how to raise my children and be a good husband. And I did the best I knew how to give kids who were born into a very difficult situation a chance at a decent life. That is it.

PSD: *One person really can make a difference.*
CC: I believe that, but God gets the honor here and I mean that. I think God does a lot of our work here in spite of me.

Bonnie Johnson, RN

Holistic Healer

"What I would say is that the God force or Great Spirit is greater than our skepticism. It is not limited by us. The idea that we have to have faith in order for spirit to work in this world is ludicrous to me. It is egotistical."

PSD: *How did you get involved with holistic healing?*

BJ: Going way back in my life, you'd see that what I have always been doing, in one way or another, is caring for people — even as a small child. I have always been a caregiver for children. I loved kids. So what I got interested in was finding some way in which I would be interacting with and caring for children. That's what led me to nursing, where I experienced the fullness in caring for children. At the same time, I was aware that there was so much that we weren't doing for people.

PSD: *The nursing profession has gone through a lot of changes.*

BJ: I am an old nurse, you see. I graduated from nursing school back in 1965, and have seen nursing go through all kinds of changes. A lot of those changes took us further and further away from contact with people and more and more into giving pills and operating machines. When I trained, I learned how to give a back rub to somebody in the morning, afternoon, and evening. That was just what you did. There are not many nurses who get trained to do that now, or who would even think about it. Not only were we working more and more with machines, but the patients were treated like machines, too. So I became very dissatisfied with that kind of treatment.

PSD: *There must have been a sense of alienation.*

BJ: I soon became aware that my view of people — my way of interacting — was not the same as other nurses. I thought, 'Am I the only one who wants to know patients on an individual basis, who believes that patients are in charge of their own healing?' The attitude that I saw a lot of was that the nurse, the doctor, and the health care facility knew what was best. To me, this wasn't right. I felt like I was in a desert, knowing that there was water

out there somewhere. So I started searching for some way to bring more of what I knew instinctively and intuitively into the work I do with people.

PSD: *You made a break with traditional nursing practice?*

BJ: It led to me going on what I call a spiritual journey twelve years ago. And it was an intentional spiritual journey. I decided to set aside a year without being actively involved in any social situations — I was just going to take care of my family. What a laugh! As if you only needed to take a year to do a spiritual journey. It actually took me a whole year just to find some books I could read and people to converse with about what I was looking for. I wasn't even sure what I was looking for! Some time into the second year, a very good friend I had gone to college with recommended a book to me, *Therapeutic Touch*. When I read it, I said 'This is it! This is what I want to do!'

PSD: *So a light went on?*

BJ: Yes. From that moment on, there was never any doubt that this was my life's work. I just studied that book from the inside out. I talked to anybody and everybody who would listen to me about the phenomena of therapeutic touch. The process itself is very simple, so I read the book and did what it said to do. Then if someone said, "I have a headache," I would say 'Let me try this.' Of course, I had no real idea of what I was doing. I remember, at the time, I was working as a pediatric nurse at Vanderbilt. A good friend took me aside one day and said, "I am really worried about you and this stuff. I'm afraid the devil has got you!" And I thought, 'What is she talking about?' None of my experiences with this practice had been harmful in any way, so how could she say this? It was just a sincere question coming from a good friend.

PSD: *A lot of people are afraid of metaphysi-*

cal and holistic approaches, believing they might be satanic or evil. Is that out of fear and ignorance?

BJ: There are a lot of people that have been taught there is only one way to live, and if you deviate from that one way, you will be in great harm. A force will take you over. They believe that is true.

PSD: *How many years have you been doing holistic healing?*

BJ: Probably 9 or 10 years. I am still studying.

PSD: *How would you best explain the process of therapeutic touch to someone who was unfamiliar with the experience?*

BJ: It is very hard to put into words, but very easy to show. Most people have actually experienced it as children or even as adults when they were sick. Often times when people have fevers, one of the things others will do in caring for them is use their hands to brush the hair back from the forehead. This brushing motion is often therapeutic touch, because all the elements are there: a person who is in need, and a person who cares. The caring person brings her love, care, focus, and compassion — which is a basic element of therapeutic touch — to the one who is in need. All of this, along with the brushing, helps to restore order to the person and bring harmony. It is mystical and magical, and is unexplainable in terms of how something so simple could do so much.

PSD: *Is the practice you have described similar to the laying on of hands in the biblical tradition?*

BJ: Yes. One of the major differences is that both the healer and the person who is ill 'must believe' in order for the laying on of hands to work. This is not the case with therapeutic touch. One can actually be skeptical and still provide for the person's needs. Many therapeutic practitioners do have faith and

strong belief, but it is not mandatory for the process to work.

What I would say is that the God force or Great Spirit is greater than our skepticism. It is not limited by us. The idea that we have to have faith in order for spirit to work in this world is ludicrous to me. It is egotistical.

PSD: *How would you define success on a personal level?*

BJ: Success is being fully who I am and really being true to that. Kind of staying in line with who I am and honoring it.

PSD: *To thine own self be true. That can be very difficult.*

BJ: I basically live a peaceful life. I was brought up in the tradition of a Protestant work ethic, and productively worked many years in that lifestyle. So I sometimes get caught up in the fact that there are a whole bunch of people out there that are very, very physically and/or emotionally ill. Since I have technical nursing skills, why am I not out there bandaging people, running machines, and throwing medicine at them on top of everything else I do? It's hard when I get challenged by that. So I tell myself, 'You have already done that for thirty years. They only ask for twenty in the army.' (laughs)

PSD: *It's not as if you are laying out back on the hammock.*

BJ: Right. But what comes up is the fact that right now what I do is so easy for me, because this is my life's work.

PSD: *We are sometimes culturally brainwashed to believe that it has to be difficult.*

BJ: Yes. In the work I do, self-care is essential. So a lot of my day is self-care, in one form or another.

PSD: *Can you talk about some of the things you do to help maintain self?*

BJ: The kind of self-care that I do is to

spend a lot of time with myself so I know who I am. One of the ways I lose track of who I am is to be really, really busy. So I am a strong guardian of my time, because I've had years of experience of being busy, busy, busy.

PSD: *Unstructured time?*
BJ: Yes. Just time where I am not with anybody else and I'm not doing anything else. I will spend time going for a walk, but usually do a walking meditation as part of it. Or I do Tai Chi, which is energy-moving. Creative movement is the new word for it. I read an article stressing exercise, suggesting that it sounds better to say, "I'm going to do my creative movement now." I also do a sitting-still meditation.

There's another recent practice called 'ceaseless praying'. I had gone for a walk, and while walking, was praying for procrastinators. The reason is that I had been in a conversation with my husband, and he said, "Well, pray for me, will you?" because he's a procrastinator. So I'm walking and praying for procrastinators. As I was just about to turn into my driveway, this little red Toyota caught my attention. A woman rolled down her window and said, "I'm looking for Bonnie Johnson. Do you know where she is around here?" And I said, 'Yes, I'm Bonnie Johnson.' She was just checking out where I was because somebody had given her my name. We got to talking and she said, "You know, I have this real problem with procrastination."

PSD: *Synchronicity! So the key, for you, is to guard your time. That's where you have a weakness.*
BJ: Yes. The part that's so hard for me is that I love being with people and doing things — something fun.

PSD: *How would you suggest that people find themselves, then be true to what they find?*

BJ: A lot of times, young people do not have enough consciousness or awareness. So the journey to discovering who they are comes through stumbling. You get into all kinds of experiences without realizing that they're helping you know who you are. The most helpful way is through self-observation. How do you do that? How do you learn to observe anything? If you don't know how to observe yourself, start by observing other people, the environment. Watch what the cat is doing. Learn the skill, then go inward to observe your self.

PSD: *What's your biggest challenge right now?*
BJ: Let me think. Do I have a challenge? It doesn't seem like the right word for me. I keep exploring the best ways for me to be present with the gifts I have, so I'm open to where that will be.

PSD: *Is life about service?*
BJ: Yes. That is why I am here. I have had many invitations to leave, but I turned them down. I'm here for the duration, to see it through. To be here with people, with this universe, in a way that can assist and help. So I stay here to do that.

PSD: *The challenge is to bring the core of who we are to wherever we go.*
BJ: Yes. My son is in prison, so I visit the prison once a week. I spend three to six hours there. It is not an easy place to be. But I can choose to be present wherever I end up being.

PSD: *Family usually presents us with challenges and learning.*
BJ: Yes. My biggest challenge comes from seeing somebody in need, knowing I have the skills to be of assistance, yet they cannot receive. To watch someone in pain and suffering is so hard for me at times. I have to remember that the offer of healing is suffi-

cient. When people can receive it, they will. My work is to keep on offering the healing and being there for them.

PSD: *Do you ever get discouraged or feel overrun by the vast amount of suffering there is in this world of ours?*
BJ: I get really angry about it and tend to rail at God. If we are supposed to be learning from all of this pain and suffering, then it's a screwed-up system. So I get angry. This usually happens when I have lost who I am. I'm out there pounding against a rock going nowhere. I have a really hard time with the suffering we inflict on each other. I question the whole idea that we or our souls have chosen to come here.

PSD: *Who do you admire?*
BJ: The people who I admire most are the ones who are willing to put themselves and their wounds out there. By doing so, they are helping others and themselves heal.

PSD: *What would you like your friends to say about you when that beautiful moment of passing finally comes?*
BJ: I want people to wear bright colors, to dance and sing, to eat hot fudge sundaes, to enjoy that day. What I would like someone to say is "She was there when I needed her, and I could count on her. She was present."

Henry Foster, MD

Senior Advisor to President Clinton on Teen Pregnancy Issues

"What I appreciate more than anything is life. Life is a very precious gift which should be used in a constructive and positive way. I really believe that when all the scripts are written, you won't be measured by what you got in life, but by what you gave."

PSD: *You have had quite an interesting time of it lately, especially with the President.*

HF: Yes, really interesting. Let me tell you a story. When I had been nominated for Surgeon General, I was sitting in one of the rooms of the White House reading a book. And you know how sometimes you can be so engrossed in a book? Well, I didn't notice that someone was standing over me. It was the President. He said, "If you don't mind, what are you reading?" I said, '*Sleep Walking Through History* by Haynes Johnson.' When we got up to the Oval Office, I saw that he had a lot of books that we both had read. He gave me this marvelous book called *The Gettysburg Address* by Gary Wills.

This is truly a marvelous little book. First of all, the Gettysburg Address was preceded by a speech that lasted three hours. The Gettysburg Address itself is only 272 words long and is the more profound speech. The point I wanted to make, though, is that after that speech, this country was referred to as 'The' United States. Prior, it had always been 'These' United States. It changed us from a fragment to a oneness.

PSD: *Lincoln was a magical human being. Is he one of your heroes?*

HF: Oh yes, absolutely. You know why he is one of my heroes? Because he reminds me in many ways of my own approach to problem-solving. I recognized very early in life that having the right answer or knowing the right thing is only part of the puzzle. The real challenge is how you implement the answer, how you make it work. It is great to have the right idea for world peace, but if you can't make it happen, what good is it? I have learned this through the years, but it is very difficult for some people because they see it as a compromise. You have to be able to balance idealism with pragmatism to reach a goal. Lincoln did so adroitly, balancing the factions around the issue of slavery. He kept walking the line to keep the country together.

PSD: *Were you influenced to be this type of problem-solver and thinker, or was it more of an innate thing?*

HF: Sometimes you are a certain way and you really don't know why or how it happened. I think a part of it is in my DNA, my intrinsic make-up. But another part of it is in my own family's make-up. I grew up in the segregated south, in Pine Bluff, Arkansas, and I watched how my people negotiated the system. I think the most important thing, if you are looking for the great anchor, was that my folks had the greatest faith in the essence of the American way. My father used to tell us that freedom and justice were locked in the American Constitution. The key, he said, was education.

PSD: *There must have been some thick, hard walls for you to penetrate.*

HF: I think something else happened which I have a knack for. I find commonalities as opposed to differences. I don't care who the people are or what groups they belong to, but people basically have a lot more in common than they do differences. I have always been an optimistic, open person. I have faith.

You get prepared by doing things. I went to the University of Arkansas and was the only African-American in a class of deep southerners. I was also the youngest person in the class, so I negotiated those four years, just like I had watched so many others do.

PSD: *What led you into medicine?*

HF: A few things come to mind. First, my father graduated from Morehouse College in 1928. That is the same college I graduated from in 1954. The family story was that my father was a pre-med student at Howard University in Washington, but didn't have the money to continue. This was during the height of the depression. So he took a job in Arkansas as a science teacher at a local high school to help support his family, because my mother was pregnant with my older sister. In a vicarious sort of way, going into medicine was fulfilling one of my father's desires.

Second, one of my father's best friends in life was Dr. Clyde A. Lawlah. We had an avuncular relationship. He was a black man who finished the University of Chicago Medical School in 1932. I used to follow him around and carry his bag.

There is a third, more pragmatic factor. Opportunities were extremely rare for African-Americans in that genre. I knew this was a good way to help people. I liked medicine and had a pretty good aptitude for it.

PSD: *Is it not what you do in the end but the process that matters?*
HF: Indeed. I think, too, that somehow, I have never reached a point where I feel I have done enough. I am always looking for something else to do and I think that makes a difference. Some people are never completely satisfied with what they accomplish.

PSD: *You get juiced on the process.*
HF: Absolutely. And I enjoy challenges. When things fail, I pick up the pieces and try another approach. What I appreciate more than anything is life. Life is a very precious gift which should be used in a constructive and positive way. I really believe that when all the scripts are written, you won't be measured by what you got in life, but by what you gave. I really believe that!

PSD: *I have found this to be the case with many of the people I have been interviewing.*
HF: There is another aspect to giving. There are two kinds of broad definitions of wealth. One is occidental, the other is oriental. Basically, the occidental definition of wealth is the acquisition and accumulation of possessions. But the oriental definition is having few needs. If you have few needs, I think it's true that you are wealthy. Because if you

have all the money in the world but are unhappy and unfulfilled, then you are really quite poor.

PSD: *If you are Taoist in nature, just sitting by a stream in bliss, then you are quite rich.*
HF: Absolutely. That is what it is all about. I have always been pleased with the things I have given. I am writing a book, by the way, which I think you would enjoy reading. I may call it *Promises To Keep*. The book is written around three themes: my early life, my healthcare years, and the nomination process. I want to write a second book about how to intervene in the lives of inner city kids in a positive way.

PSD: *You don't strike me as bitter about what happened during the nomination process.*
HF: The main reason I didn't get bitter was because I was pretty observant. A few hours after I was nominated, there were all kinds of people coming out to take stands opposing me. These people knew nothing about me. In fact, I could have walked into their offices and they would have had no idea who I was. So I realized very quickly that it was not about me, Henry Foster. That is why I came through personally unscathed. The hearings were my forum to address these accusers and reassure those who supported me. I wanted to also show my kids — because I have a future with them — that when a battle comes, you have to put up the best fight you can.

PSD: *I was very pleased to see Senator Frist support you.*
HF: I was, too. He backed me based on my qualifications. One thing that was most disappointing was that I looked upon a Senate Committee as seeking truth. But the people who were on that committee who opposed me were not interested in truth. Had they known the truth and knew nobody else knew about it, they would have suppressed it. I guess I was a little naive.

PSD: *That is scary, isn't it?*

HF: Yes, and that is what was so disappointing. They were not interested in the truth. We even had a sworn affidavit from the State of Alabama and from the patient that I was nowhere near the meeting in question. I was operating on a woman. The committee wanted to ignore the facts and still try to place me at this meeting.

PSD: *That's sad. If they were just grilling you to make sure you were worthy of the position, you could have respected that.*

HF: Of course. But once they had the truth and still chose to ignore it, that was disappointing. That is how politics has gotten. The real downside is that it is getting harder and harder to find people willing to subject themselves to that kind of scrutiny.

PSD: *This was a good test of your positive philosophy. Not to trivialize it in any way, but for you, this was just a minor setback.*

HF: You're right, especially from a personal standpoint. In January, 1996, President Clinton appointed me his Senior Advisor on teen pregnancy reduction issues. So I am doing a lot of things. Life goes on. I have two wonderful, independent adult children who are out there being good citizens, so life goes on.

PSD: *What is Bill Clinton like as a person?*

HF: Great. I really love him. He is such a neat person. I mean look at his background. His father was killed in a car accident when his mother was two months pregnant with him, so he never even knew his father. His mother worked in fill-in jobs and she was, as a woman, paid less. He is obviously very bright. You don't lead your law class at Georgetown University and become a Rhodes Scholar by being an idiot.

PSD: *Are you a political person?*

HF: Actually, most people assume that I am a Democrat but I am actually independent. I

supported Lamar Alexander for two terms. He was a good governor.

PSD: *What was your philosophy in terms of raising your children?*

HF: To let them know that, no matter what they thought, the best friends they would ever have in this world would be their mother and father. Second, I never pretended to have all the answers. I tried to make them aware of my foibles. Third, I had to make them aware of how the system worked. I had to be the one who was responsible for making the mistakes. I guess a lot of it is luck. I have seen friends of ours, who are good people, have kids that seemed absolutely possessed. We never even got a call for one of our kids throwing a spitball. Remember, kids pay a lot more attention to what you do than to what you say.

PSD: *Based on your varied experiences, what advice would you give a young person?*

HF: Realize how important it is to give of your talents. This is what I heard growing up from my family — "When you pass away from this place and your slate is written, you want it to be said that you did something to leave this world a better place than you found it." This is a fundamental philosophy. Everybody who has difficulty basically seeks relief. I am here to try to provide relief where and when I can to those who need it. And I try to seek relief when I need it.

PSD: *So seek to give first rather than to receive?*

HF: Think about it. When you really enjoy giving, as opposed to getting, you control your own fate and happiness. If I can be happy by providing for you then I am in control. But if I have to wait to get something from you, then I am at your mercy. This is true. When I was dealing with those poor, rural women in Alabama, nothing made me feel better than to put a smile on one of those faces. Nothing! Or a thank-you for being kind. To give these people a little respect just by referring to them as Miss Williams instead of Lucy.

PSD: *You love people. Is that another innate quality?*

HF: Yes, and it, too, is part of my upbringing. I grew up in an enclave so I was protected from a lot of the harshness of segregated American society. It never crossed my mind that anybody was better than somebody else just because of their birthright. I didn't think it worked like that. I figured God gave people different talents, and I was fortunate that God gave me a particular talent.

PSD: *What's your take on race relations?*

HF: Some things are better and some things are worse. It depends what you focus on. I like to look at what is getting better. Sure, there is a bigger gap between certain classes because of what happened in the Reagan years. But what is happening to children in this country is unconscionable in terms of the amount of poverty. Six million children under 5 years of age live in poverty — here in the greatest of any industrialized nation in the world. Those things are all bad.

PSD: *Why do we allow that?*

HF: Because we are insensitive and uncaring. There are two reasons why it happens.

PSD: *The cult of materialism?*

HF: Greed and avarice is a major part of it. It is unconscionable that this nation, the wealthiest nation in the history of mankind, does not provide universal healthcare access to pregnant women and babies — the most vulnerable amongst us. It's not like the country is trying to tackle the problem of what to do with some 35 million people that are unemployed at any given time. That would be a monstrous task. Do you know how easy it would be to provide care for mothers and babies? It would be virtually nothing. There are only 4 million births in this country each year, and of that number, only 22% have inadequate access. We are talking about 880,000 people. We can provide superlative care for that whole cadre of women for the cost of two stealth bombers. The cost of one of those planes is 750 million dollars, and that does not include research and development.

PSD: *The real tragedy is that we don't even need any of those planes.*

HF: I know. We already have over 20 of them. And to think that we could take about two-and-a-half of those bombers and provide all of that care. This is the biggest investment we can make in this country, assuring the quality of human reproduction.

PSD: *Yet there is so much indifference.*

HF: Indifference! I read that during World War II, pregnant women were given double rations in England. Not only did that not occur in this country, I doubt if anyone even thought about it. Our society has tended to punish women and pregnancy for the reasons of dollars and business.

PSD: *Why don't we provide the services you advocate?*

HF: I don't know. The bigger problem in this country right now is that we are getting government by default. Only 39% of Americans voted in 1992, and in 1994, only 37% — barely one in three. That boggles my mind. When I think about how this country was founded, your ancestors had come to escape serfdom and persecution, where you couldn't rise above your father's position at all. They came over here and built the greatest kind of democracy, have the franchise, then fail to exercise it. To me, it is the weirdest thing how people fail to vote in this country. I think 80% of the people vote in Israel.

PSD: *So the enemy is apathy?*

HF: Yes, that's right.

PSD: *What can we do?*
HF: There are a lot of things we have to do. We have to increase sensitivity. We have to put people in office who are more sensitive. We have to realize the value of investment. The author of *Megatrends*, John Naisbett, devoted a whole chapter showing the advantages of the long term over the short term. He also talked about how this country got so far behind by not planning ahead and investing in the future. Basically, when you take care of mothers and babies, what you are doing is investing in the quality and future of the country. But the country only looks at the cost of what it would take to care for these women. Maybe it costs two billion dollars. That is still only two of those airplanes.

PSD: *Ours is, sadly, a very profit-oriented culture.*
HF: Right. I remember during the Nixon administration a phrase coming up that I just loved. It talked about the Republicans back then as 'people who know the price of everything and the value of nothing.'

PSD: *But the babies you are talking about are the future of this country.*
HF: Which reminds me of another point, that the greatness of this country has always come through it's diversity. We need to make sure to maximize this diversity. Chuck Yeager, who grew up very poor, said he could have never done the things he had accomplished if he hadn't had access to such an excellent education. What happens when we see an elitist type of government forming is that we start squandering our most precious resource — brainpower. And it is something you cannot buy.

PSD: *This needs to be addressed on a national level.*
HF: What this country really needs is a domestic Marshall Plan. The best schools, the best day care, should be in the inner cities, or in Appalachia, where the needs are greatest. That is where the teacher/pupil ratio should be the highest — not the way it is now.

PSD: *Do you see that happening?*
HF: Well, that goes back to my previous thoughts about voting. It depends on what kind of people we choose to lead us. If we sit around and don't vote, what chance do we have? Churchill said, "Democracy is absolutely the worst form of government that has ever been created. Except for all the others."

PSD: *Funny.*
HF: But he is so right. You see the magic when the people who created this democracy were sitting around the Acropolis thousands of years ago. They did so at a time when you really had to sit around and think. There were no IRS forms to fill out, no TV. The magic is lost when you stay at home. We need to do a better job of teaching civics and responsibility. We did this with the civil rights movement in the '60s. I think schools should be turned out on election day and all the kids should be allowed to go the polls with their parents.

PSD: *How much responsibility does the media have because of the tremendous amount of influence it possesses?*
HF: There is certainly no codified responsibility, though there is a moral, human one to help these kids understand that their actions may lead to their deaths, like with AIDS. Where the paradox occurs is when those of us in this so-called free, open society want to teach our children about human sexuality and how to protect themselves, the conservative element rises up and says, "No, education is dangerous. It will make kids become more sexually active." How foolish can you be? All you have to do is turn on the TV and you'll see all kinds of behavior there. How can teaching them about the danger of HIV or AIDS hurt these kids?

What validates what I am saying is that in every industrialized nation where the pregnancy rates are 10% to 50% as high as ours, everyone has complete family life education in grades one through twelve. Teachers are not harassed or brow-beaten. We have to change all this.

PSD: *How would you like to be remembered?*
HF: As someone who tried to make the world a better place. Someone who was creative and had ideas, who had hope, and who had faith. Someone who operated on four major principles. I tried to engage every task using intelligence, energy and enthusiasm, integrity, and persistence. That is how I try to approach problems.

PSD: *Are you a spiritual man?*
HF: Yes, I am very spiritual. I am proudly spiritual. We are all spiritual beings. We all have spirits. There is definitely a soul.

Phil Bredesen

Mayor of Nashville

"I think something that everyone has to go through is to finally recognize that the answers really are inside and that you ought to listen. You need to learn to listen to that voice."

PSD: *What makes you want to be here with all the scrutiny, working hard, when you could be taking it easy somewhere?*

PB: I have a lot of people ask, "Why don't you just retire?" And I would say that the same impulses that get you to the point where you are able to retire are exactly the same ones that won't ever let you do it. I came of political age back in the Kennedy era, he was President while I was in college. I always thought that one of the things that I would like to do at some time was to be part of government in some fashion. Kennedy made it one of his legacies that serving in government was an honorable thing that good people ought to strive to do. If I had been in college during the Nixon era, I might have felt entirely different about it. This was just something I wanted to do and the opportunity presented itself when I was in my 40s. So that is what I did.

PSD: *So you already had an eye ahead on political life when you were younger?*

PB: I guess I always thought that I would like to be involved in government in some way. But, to be honest with you, I got out of college and was busy earning a living, building up, getting some security and doing that kind of stuff. It wasn't until twenty years later when the disease reoccurred — the political desire — that I went out and did it.

PSD: *You strike me as basically a shy and private person. Has it been a stretch for you on a personal level to be out in front with a very public persona?*

PB: No. I am not as shy now as I used to be. I don't think you can be Mayor for 4 or 5 years and stay at the same old level. But I basically am shy, and think of myself as a shy person. When I first thought about running for office, I thought the really hard thing was going to be having a grasp of all the issues that somebody would think about. That turned out to be no problem at all, because in any election, there are only about ten things anybody cares about anyway. The hardest thing for me was just wading into a crowd, shaking hands, and making friends. That is what proved to be difficult.

PSD: *And having a public persona wherever you go ...*

PB: Someone will always want to talk about something.

PSD: *Do you have a personal definition of success?*

PB: I think it is several things. One piece of success for me has always been security, which I would define as not being beholden to someone else. I think the impulse that causes me to be an entrepreneur is not wanting to work for someone else. I think another piece of success for me goes beyond that by having some appreciation for the wider world that humans have created. I think you ought to be good at health care or good at being a Mayor, but that doesn't mean you shouldn't understand what is going on in the world of physics. Or what is going on in the world of art and literature. So a piece of success for me is to structure your life so that you are not one-dimensional. That way, you have an appreciation for all the different things that human beings have achieved.

PSD: *Like Leonardo DaVinci's Vitruvian Man, a renaissance approach so to speak?*

PB: I don't think you can be a renaissance man anymore. The world is too big. But I do think you can have some appreciation for all the different areas in which human beings have accomplished great things. I think this is an important piece of success.

PSD: *How about the human side of success in terms of being a husband and a father?*

PB: Well, family has always been extremely important to me. I am somebody who grew up in a household without a father. So being there for my son transcends everything else. Short of being successful in family life, I would not consider myself a success.

PSD: *You grew up without a father figure. Who had the major influence on your early life?*
PB: My mother and grandmother. They were the big influences in the household where I grew up.

PSD: *What type of life philosophy did they try to expound?*
PB: Oh, I guess my grandmother was very much 'family first'. She had eleven children, ten of whom lived in this town of 1,100 people where I grew up. So in that sense it was a very close-knit family. Both she and my mother had the characteristic of spending no time complaining about whatever the world dealt them. They just took it, figured out how to get around it, and moved on to the next thing. I think one the of things that has helped me a lot over the years is this notion. I basically believe that everything is in my control — that all of my failures are my fault. It's the sense of 'you really are the master of your own destiny', nobody else is, and there really are no excuses. This is something I have deeply, deeply ingrained.

PSD: *Do you read a lot?*
PB: Yes, I read a lot, depending on the timing of things. While the 'NFL Yes' vote was going on, I didn't read too much fiction. (He laughs.) But I enjoy reading different kinds of books from different sources. I would say a fairly wide-ranging, eclectic group of topics. I certainly don't have a bent for self-examination. I don't read a lot of self-improvement books or those kinds of things.

PSD: *One word that comes to my mind with you is integrity. Even with the NFL vote and all its controversy, no one attacked your integrity.*
PB: It is hard to talk about integrity

because there isn't a politician in the world who doesn't like to talk about what great integrity he or she has. I just figure that is something you don't talk about. You just let people observe your actions, then decide what they want about your character and integrity. What integrity means to me is more about its root, integral — that the way you are presenting yourself to the world is consistent with the way you are working inside. That is very important to me.

PSD: *What is your style of leadership?*
PB: Let me say this. One of the criticisms made of me is, "He is arrogant and he doesn't listen to people." I think where that comes from is what I really believe leadership to be about — listening to some people, then deciding on a course of action and pursuing it. Now, I don't believe in grassroots anything — that you ought to conduct your business by listening to the way the wind is blowing or to a thousand different people before you decide. What I think you should do is learn as much as you can through as many different channels as you can, then decide on some course of action and try to sell the rest of the world on that course of action.

PSD: *That is the opposite of what we have now in government, where the latest CNN poll dictates what the course of action will be this week.*
PB: Yes. I believe the fundamental problem of government is there are too few people who undertake some course of action that does not have 50.1% approval rating in the polls on the day you start.

PSD: *I don't get that sense from you.*
PB: No, not at all. We started the arena down here, when about 17% of the people approved of it and wanted it built. It is now a popular project.

PSD: *You cannot govern effectively with an*

eye towards approval and the polls.

PB: No, you can't. If you want to get re-elected, that's the way to do it. But if you want to accomplish something, you have to go off from that.

PSD: *With all the things going on in your external universe, how do you nurture your private universe?*

PB: I would say, first of all, I don't do that literally in the morning, but certainly my schedule in the office here is built around keeping mornings free to work on big projects. Anything worth doing takes two or three hours of concentrated time at a shot. So I try to do that. I try to have the afternoons, and sometimes the evenings, for interviews and such. I like to keep the mornings, when I feel I'm at my best, for the larger projects. Afternoons are more for the mechanics of doing the job. I think this has worked out very well for me.

PSD: *And personally?*

PB: I try hard not to spend lots of evenings or weekends away from home. So I guess the recharging time for me is literally sitting down for dinner and having a chance to talk. To kind of unwind from the day and talk to people about what went on during the day. I guess that is sort of the centering time.

PSD: *Are you a person that writes down goals or are your goals more internally tracked?*

PB: I think achieving goals is a kind of mixture, and I don't think I can put words around it. On one hand, you have longer-term goals and on the other hand, being able to take advantage of targets of opportunity. It is a funny mixture. People that just run after the target of opportunity and don't keep their heads up as to where they are going don't ever get there. The same is true of people who spend all their time looking at long-term goals. I really believe that the way you make big things happen is to make lots of small

things happen. Try to have the big picture in mind, but don't lose focus on the fact that in order to get from here to there, you need to take step one, step two, and step three.

PSD: *It is a balancing act.*

PB: Exactly.

PSD: *In terms of the enormity of your job, is balance hard for you?*

PB: No. I came into office with the requirement that this was not going to be a damaging thing to my family life. People expect of someone in public office that if they invite them to something on a Saturday night they will show up. I just took the attitude of being hard-nosed about it. Obviously, I do some things in the evenings and occasionally on Saturday nights, but if you want me to give a speech, you have a lot better chance of getting me there if you have it at 5:30 or over lunch. I found people being mad at me for about a year over this, but they all settled in and decided that this was reasonable. I work hard, but if somebody is going to have a dinner meeting and they want a speaker, maybe they can accommodate it at 6:00 before dinner, rather than at 8:00. And that lets me go home and have some family time.

PSD: *Have you always been a very disciplined person?*

PB: No. I'm not a disciplined person.

PSD: *You're not?*

PB: No. I'm not a disciplined person at all. I struggle constantly with that.

PSD: *Then what do you think are the factors that have attributed to your success or achievements?*

PB: First of all, I wouldn't get too carried away with my success or achievement. I'm happy, but I'm the Mayor of a small city. Lots of people have done a lot better. I don't think there is any magic to it. I was just lucky enough to be born or brought up with some personality and character. I certainly believe to a fault in deferred gratification. I mean I am now 52 years old, and decided I better get on with some of the things I enjoy. I think that has helped. I am a reasonably hard worker in the sense of getting up early and working hard. But I don't consider myself disciplined. I have to struggle with keeping priorities straight, making sure I work on the important things, not the urgent things.

PSD: *What advice would you give to your son if he was 17 and said, "Dad, you have done what you wanted to in life in a few different areas. How do I find my passion?" Or as Joseph Campbell might say, 'follow my bliss?'*

PB: I guess I would say a couple of things. One, it is inside of you. It is not something that anyone can tell you about. When you spend your time going to school, then going to college, and then working for people in a job, it is easy to fall into the hold of other people being the drivers of your destiny. I think something that everyone has to go through is to finally recognize that the answers really are inside and that you ought to listen. You need to learn to listen to that voice. The other thing I would say is to be open to experience. It is a wonderful, big world out there, beyond the scope of what anyone could imagine in fiction. I think the ones who are successful and happy are the ones who really are open to new experiences.

I am on a career that is totally different than running a healthcare company, which was totally different than studying physics and computer programming. I figure I have a couple more in me, but I don't know yet what they will be. But there's a sense of being open to new experience, seeing what life has in store, and reacting to it well. I think this is an important characteristic of success and a good life.

So I would say to him, look inside for the

ultimate guidance on these things and be original, don't be imitative. Just be open to experience.

PSD: *Do you ever stop in awe of the miraculous wonder of it all?*
PB: Oh, there is nobody who enjoys living more than I do. I promise you that. Maybe my son. No, you can't name something I don't enjoy.

PSD: *You love life and in a sense there is a spiritualism in that.*
PB: I just find it so remarkable that we have this great universe around us and I have this spark of consciousness that lets me understand a little bit of it. I just eat it up.

PSD: *You are on a learning journey?*
PB: Yes.

PSD: *What brings you the most pleasure and satisfaction in your life?*
PB: Well, setting aside family, which is an easy thing to say, we talked about some of the things that are important. The notion of being effective when you go through the world and it somehow knows you were there in a good way. And the notion of being able to think about things, marshal your resources to get things done, and have some effect on the world. That is real important to me and that is probably the most rewarding thing about this job. It can be very frustrating in a lot of ways, but for getting around the city and thinking it is better off because of something you did. I particularly enjoy seeing the arena go up or watching people walking up and down Second Avenue — those kind of things that you have worked on.

I didn't speak of it earlier, but that notion of being effective is an important piece of what drives me. I don't mean that in the narrow kind of business sense of the word. I mean effective in the sense that you are not passive, that you do things that change the world around you. That you are sort of master of your fate and the fate of a few things around you while you are at it. I think this is real important.

PSD: *What I hear between the lines is service to others. Even though your gratification and validation are inwardly derived, your focus and energy are flowing outward in an attempt to make a positive difference. Is that what Phil Bredesen is about as a person?*

PB: I think that is a fair way of putting it. In trying to think of a synonym for effective that adds to this notion ... it is the notion that you want to act on the world, not have the world act on you. I guess depending on your personality, you could be Mother Teresa or Adolf Hitler in the way you act on the world. But the basic impulse to be active rather than reactive is a basic characteristic of a lot of people who are successful.

PSD: *What I hear is that you are not only proactive, but proactive with a sense of service. Being elected Mayor was proactive. But by trying to improve the community rather than enhancing one's personal means is proactive with a sense of service.*

PB: I hope that is the case. But I think it's the notion of being active, if you are trying to talk to people about the psychology. I think that is a larger concept. I choose to be active in the Mayor's office and in the community for what I hope to be the right reasons — for service and to make things happen. But that activity is the same impulse that causes you to go start a company. The thing that scares me the most is to just be a passive observer. I have talked about the joy I think people ought to get just living, just being around, being able to see and experience things, and so on. And I think a piece of that is me saying, 'Oh, by the way, I don't want to just passively experience things.' I really want to engage this outer world. At the moment, I happen to be engaging with it, in one sense,

as Mayor — doing things I hope are the right things. That gives me pleasure because I like to do things for the good of the community and I feel good about trying to help people and making things happen. But if my personality were different and I was trying to get ahead in politics, that same sense would still be there. It would just take a slightly different coloration depending on what your motivations are in making it happen.

PSD: *I heard what you said, and this is what I focused on. Your motivations are not in self-interest.*

PB: Well, I hope not. It is important to me that this is not what it is. What I am trying to say is this notion of engaging the world has nothing to do with the morality with which you engage the world.

PSD: *The manifestation is not important. It is the process.*

PB: It is important to me to be active, and I hope that I have the character to be active in a way that helps people and contributes to the good of society. If you are strong, you are strong whether you use it to beat people up or help old ladies up the stairs. You are still strong. It's the same sense of being active in the world, which I feel is an important thing for me to be. But I hope that it takes the manifestation of doing things that are moral and good for the community. Build the foundations that we all stand on. But I don't think there are two different notions.

PSD: *This is almost an Eastern way of holistic thinking. Similar to the yin/yang. It is beyond right or wrong, dark or light. It is whole. It is One.*

PB: That is accurate.

PSD: *As of this moment, what is your biggest personal challenge?*

PB: The biggest challenge in this job or a situation like this is remaining centered, though I hate the phrase because it is a little trite. People need this sense of balance where the various things that are important to them are balanced in their lives. I find that is harder to do in something like this. Going through this whole NFL thing, which is not my first set of priorities, sort of gets you way over in one corner on the balancing scale. I think just trying to get balanced again so you can let things settle down to what is really important.

You can imagine your motivations, and this is the physicist in me speaking. It is almost like you have all of these little balls that are connected together by strings in this three dimensional mass of things. If you just sort of leave it alone, it will settle down where everything is in balance with one thing or another. But if you grab one thing and pull it out there, and you let it go, it takes a little while where it oscillates a bit. Then it kind of comes back together. So that sense of balance where you feel you have things together, I find that hard to keep going.

PSD: *Is your family your great grounding rod?*
PB: It is a grounding force in the sense that, yes, that is the moral grounding. But I am not going to tell you that I go home every night and as soon as I sit down to supper, suddenly everything is in balance again.

PSD: *Like the Cleaver family.*
PB: No, it doesn't happen that way. But certainly putting at the top of the list what the family needs and expects from you is part of how you achieve that balance.

PSD: *How would you like to be remembered as a person?*
PB: I guess I would like them to say that he was a good man. He was a good father, he was a good husband. 'Decent' is a word I would use.

Debbie Runions

Educator, Member of President Clinton's HIV Advisory Council

"We in America have placed all of our eggs in the materialism basket, but I have never been materialistic. I have always believed that success has more to do with how much people love you, how much you are able to love other people, whatever it is that you have done to uplift mankind."

PSD: *Tell me why you see yourself as successful.*

DR: Because I have always had a plan, and definable, achievable goals. I come from a family that requires perfection, which is dysfunctional. So what I had to learn as a child was that you set goals you could achieve. That way, you could see yourself as a success. What I said was 'I'm going to graduate from college;' then I did. Or 'I'm going to be a writer — not a famous writer, just a writer;' then I did that, too. If people assigned me something to do, my goal was to get it done and be on time. Because of these goals, I became a successful writer with a reputation as a person who could get things done.

PSD: *What kinds of things did you write?*

DR: Magazine articles. I wrote for *Nashville* magazine for eight years as a freelance writer. I am still a freelance writer. And I have a new book out called *Sabrina's Gifts* — it's a fairy tale about learning to fly by the seat of your heart.

PSD: *You are also a speaker and quite a communicator.*

DR: I learned to be one, because speaking is a terrifying thing to do. I didn't ever want to become a speaker. But after I became HIV positive, I realized that I was going to have to learn how to speak publicly. I hooked up with Jana Stanfield, a professional speaker, who helped me learn.

It wasn't as hard a leap as I thought it would be. It helped that I already knew how to structure a topic. The difference was that you try to be as objective as possible when writing, but in speaking, you try to pull people in, to get them to make an emotional commitment.

PSD: *Talk about your story, because I believe it will inspire people.*

DR: The thing that makes my story different — in fact, my whole life story — is that my karma is immediate. The first and only time I had sex, I became pregnant. Oddly enough, we didn't even know we had had sex at the time. We didn't know we had done anything wrong. But within two weeks I said, 'Harry, I'm not feeling well.'

PSD: *How old were you at the time?*

DR: Seventeen. This was middle Tennessee in the '60s and nobody talked about sex, because they didn't know anything to tell us. When I was 15, I remember reading this article in *True Confessions* magazine at the beauty shop, because Mama wouldn't allow such trash in the house. (She laughs.) It said "They kissed, and she got pregnant." So in my mind, you got pregnant through kissing. I asked this girl on the school bus, who knew more than me because she was 16, if this is how you got pregnant. She said, "No, silly, a boy has a seed and he plants it inside the girl and this is how it is done." I wondered out loud what this seed looked like. She said it was clear and about the size of a pumpkin seed, but no one had ever seen it. So I figured if I just stayed away from clear pumpkin seeds, I would be fine.

When the doctor said I was pregnant, I said 'That's impossible. I'm a virgin!' This is when my life of suffering started. We got married, and I went from a life a privilege to a place of poverty. Then Harry was in an explosion and almost died. A year later, he was in another explosion. It was a series of events I call suffering. I had to learn how to be happy amidst all of the tragedy. You can't let all this junk drag you down. We went to college, had kids, held down jobs, and lived on $250 a month.

PSD: *After the close calls, Harry still died young.*

DR: In 1980, at age 32, he died in a car accident leaving me with two kids. Something else to overcome! Then my father died, my father-in-law died, my mother developed leukemia, and my step-mother, who was one of my favorite people, got Alzheimers. I lost her even before she died, a piece at a time.

All of this prepared me for my diagnosis of HIV. I had already learned that you can't base your happiness on people, on money, or even on love. You have to find a center within yourself where you can find a sense of peace. Because I had already learned how to do this, the HIV coming along was just one more piece to overcome.

PSD: *Life is hard, even without such dramatic tragedies. How did you find that inner peace?*

DR: I'll tell you a story that might explain my foundation, and why it hasn't been as hard for me as it has been for other people. My first memory was at my grandfather's funeral in October of 1953. In those days, they used to lay the body out in the front parlor. He was in the front room of Granny's house, and we used wooden Coca-Cola crates to climb up and view the body, since I was so tiny. I looked at his body and thought 'That looks exactly like Dad Fields,' but then looked into the corner of the living room and there he stood. I looked at him, looked at the body, then looked back at him and thought, 'Isn't that funny.' I got all excited because I knew my Mama was really upset. So I went to her and Granny, and said 'Don't cry. He is right over there in the corner!' They said, "Don't come to us with your Ellen Gordon stories today of all days!" (Ellen Gordon was the madwoman of the community.) At that point, Dad Fields put his finger to his lips. He knew I could see him, but it wasn't time to share just yet. So I have always known that death may have one appearance, but it is not real. Because my little three-year-old eyes could see what was real. The body was fake.

I have always been a very philosophical child, a spiritual child. They tell me I used to have conversations with people I couldn't see, even though I don't remember this, and quoted scripture as soon as I could talk, but I wasn't taken to church until much later. In fact, Dad Fields used to say that I was a better preacher than any he had ever heard.

The other gift I have is the ability to detach and really observe. I also have a firm foundation in fundamental Christianity, which was a major hindrance for a while because it is filled with so much shame and guilt. But it gave me a foundation so that when Harry died, I had a rock under me. Then I found Unity Church, and after that, *A Course In Miracles*. I would say that *A Course In Miracles* has done more to help me find a place of peace than any other thing. That and Co-dependents Anonymous.

PSD: *The result is that you found that inner place that is separate from all the suffering.*

DR: Every single challenge comes with an equal opportunity for either blessing or tragedy. If you love somebody, that is a blessing. If that person dies, then it is a tragedy. But it then opens up another door for new blessings. You just have to wait, and be patient that the blessings will arrive.

PSD: *How did you contract the HIV virus?*

DR: I got it from a man with whom I had a seven month relationship in 1989, someone I loved who was not a good person. I had broken off the relationship and we had been separated for two years when he called me. I spent one night with him, and that was the only time we had ever had unprotected intercourse in all of our relationship. There's that 'immediate karma' again — I contracted HIV that evening.

PSD: *What made you decide to be brave and begin educating people about this disease?*

DR: People see it as brave, but I don't see it that way at all. I have learned that we are only here for one reason and that is to learn how to love. I always ask 'What is the loving thing to do for myself and the world around me?' The loving thing was to speak it, because secrets make you sick. It is the shame about this disease that causes people to die before their bodies die. If someone with a high profile will speak out, then people on the street will get a clue that this is not a disease of street-people injecting drugs, or a disease of sexual preference. It is not a disease of people that are stupid, or people who do not care about themselves or the community. It is a disease that affects people.

PSD: *Your involvement is a generous act, no matter how you look at it.*
DR: I have always been told that I am part of a bigger community and that every man is my brother. Since there is no cure for AIDS, then the only thing I can do to help is to work with prevention. AIDS is almost 100% preventable, so it doesn't have to happen to anybody. Since teens are one of the fastest-growing at-risk groups, this is where I thought I could do some good.

PSD: *How did you get started?*
DR: I called the Center for Disease Control and said 'Surely you have money to do this.' They said the person in Tennessee to talk with is Elizabeth Word. I called her that day and she said "I am writing the grant this weekend, and I will write you in." The grant was funded and that is how I got the job. We sent out letters to all the schools in middle Tennessee and the response was amazing. Teachers are afraid to talk about AIDS because they might lose their jobs.

PSD: *What do you tell kids?*
DR: I tell them my story and how important it is to get your information from somebody who knows — not somebody on the school bus. I also tell them how to protect themselves. I tell them that I am not any different from them, that I come from a rural county like most of them do. I tell them that I

thought I was too smart, but smart doesn't have anything to do with it. The children who come are amazing — they follow me to my car, saying that I am the first adult that has ever told them the straight truth. That I was the first adult to say they had sex before they were married. They are literally dying to communicate with an adult.

PSD: *There's an ironic choice of words.*
DR: HIV has forced me to become an adult. America is filled with adult children, people who refuse to take responsibility for themselves and their children. We have given our children away for other people to raise.

PSD: *And to TV sets and the streets.*
DR: Absolutely. That's why we have gangs. They're all lost children trying to find a family.

PSD: *Like the book Lord Of The Flies?*
DR: Exactly. It is sad, yet it is a place where I feel like I can make a difference.

PSD: *So you are out there telling these kids the truth. Do you get discouraged by the enormity of the suffering and the ignorance? In some ways, you are like a cry in the wilderness.*
DR: I do get discouraged. Sometimes when I go into schools these kids talk through my entire program, so I feel like I am spitting into the wind. But then I get some wonderful letters from those same schools, so I guess somebody was listening. One thing that metaphysics teaches is that we are just the instrument. God does the work, we just have to be there.

PSD: *Have you run into much opposition from the religious right?*
DR: Yes.

PSD: *I would imagine part of the problem is denial and the refusal to talk about the situation.*

DR: Some schools place no restrictions. In others, you cannot even mention the word 'condom.' You have to say 'take preventive measures.' Some counties won't even allow someone who is HIV-positive to come into the schools.

PSD: *Fear and ignorance?*

DR: Just plain fear. My message is actually one of abstinence. However, if you are one of the majority of teenagers who are going to have sex anyway, this is what you need to do to protect yourself.

PSD: *What reaction did you have when you first got the news that you were HIV-positive?*

DR: Initially, I was depressed, which understandably is what happens to most people. Then I went into a period of elation because at last I knew what I had been preparing to do all my life. I knew how to write, I learned how to speak, I learned how to promote. Now I have something to say.

PSD: *What does success mean to you?*

DR: The quote by Ralph Waldo Emerson you have in the front of your book. We in America have placed all of our eggs in the materialism basket, but I have never been materialistic. I have always believed that success has more to do with how much people love you, how much you are able to love other people, whatever it is that you have done to uplift mankind, to raise the consciousness of humanity, and knowing your own integrity and living it consistently. And I have done all that! The nicest thing anybody ever said was when my daughter wrote this letter that won us a trip to England. She said, "People always want to know what love is. I look at my mother and I know."

PSD: *That is beautiful, and that is success.*

DR: Yes, I was successful raising my children. I can't sew or cook, but I have been a good friend. If you can be a friend to yourself and the people around you in the world, then you are a success.

PSD: *You met President Clinton. What was that like?*

DR: What a HOOT! When I went to Washington for the first time, I went up to Al Gore and said 'You probably don't remember me, but I...' and he said, "I know you!" Being on President Clinton's HIV/AIDS Advisory Council is fun. It's the most diverse group of people I have ever met.

PSD: *What was your impression of the President? Does he strike you as a sincere person?*

DR: He is very smart and very spiritual. He is sincere, but he is splintered in many directions. I am impressed by the people he has around him. He is a person who cares. He has a photographic memory and never forgets your name, even if he has only met you once. I feel very comfortable with him as President. The best thing about him is that he is flawed, so he has compassion. And I think that compassion shows. Clinton seems in touch with his feminine side and is able to communicate his feelings.

PSD: *What is your biggest challenge?*

DR: This may sound petty, but the thing that drives me crazy is that my time seems to be passing at light-speed. So I want everybody to be on my time clock. I have chaos going on in my body, so I need to have serenity and resonance around me. Now I have a daughter for a roommate who is not very orderly or on my clock, so this is very challenging. (She laughs.)

PSD: *The small things are challenging you in the moment.*

DR: They make me crazy, because they are the only things that I have any control over. I have no control over the big things.

PSD: *You are being challenged for total surrender.*

DR: I just can't give it up, though I do believe my daughter will force me into total surrender. (She laughs.) I am probably the biggest challenge in her life.

PSD: *So your challenge is really about control.*
DR: And it always has been. 'I've got plans, God. Let me do it!!!!' (She laughs.)

PSD: *How do you feel about life?*
DR: I love life, but I don't fear death. I was speaking with some second-year medical students and told them that I wanted to see them get out of the mode of being mechanics and become healers. And the only way to do this is to see death as a friend and not the enemy. Sometimes death is the healer. I love life. But I love life since HIV, and I think that is why HIV came to me. What HIV has done is given me focus and allowed me to be brave. Because of the changes in my life, my children's lives have gotten stronger and more directed. So I love life now, but I am also ready to move on.

PSD: *How is your health?*
DR: Good today, but it comes and goes. I am on steroids, so that makes you feel like you can play football. I feel OK, but I get tired very easily.

PSD: *Since we have such short lives regardless of HIV, what would you tell someone about how to find peace and serenity in this life?*
DR: It is a short life in some ways and a long life in others — when you are not feeling very happy. I would say, 'Follow your bliss. Find out what your passion is and follow it.' You have to find meaning. A book that changed my life was *Man's Search For Meaning* by Victor Frankl. It doesn't matter what your circumstances are, you have to find a meaning to be alive.

We need to learn that we are all children of God, and God cannot be whole without us. I discovered that our only goal is to learn to love and learn to be loved, and even if we fail at that, God loves us and Grace makes up the difference. You come so far and Grace carries you the rest of the way. If we could give ourselves a break and stop being so urgent in our doing and learn how to be, we could be happy.

PSD: *How would you like to be remembered?*
DR: I can tell you what is on my tombstone.

PSD: *You already have it picked out?*
DR: When Harry died, I bought mine, too. It says, 'Friends.' Harry and I didn't have a passionate love, but we were best friends. I want to be remembered as 'People's best friend.' I hope my daughter and my son will say this about me. I know Harry would. So would the people in my circle. I would like for God to say "She was one of the best friends I had on earth."

Emmett Turner

Chief of Police, Metro Nashville

"I am always optimistic, because if I wasn't, I couldn't come to work. Some days are worse than others, but every time I come in here it is with a positive attitude. If you change one or two lives ... if you change a couple of things ... if you help people in this department ... if you help people in the community ... then I feel good."

PSD: *Were you like most kids who wanted to be a policeman when they grew up?*

ET: Believe it or not, law enforcement was the farthest thing from my mind as a career. I never even thought of it. How I ended up applying for a job at the police department was sort of coincidental. I was employed by Avco working on an aircraft wing assembly line. I had worked there prior to getting drafted and going into the service.

So when I was discharged from the Army, I went back to work at Avco. One of the people I worked with had been trying to get a job with the police department for five years. He kept saying to me, "Why don't you go down and fill out an application for the department." I kept saying I didn't want to be a police officer.

We had gone on strike at Avco. One day, I was walking downtown and coincidentally walked past the Civil Service office on Third Avenue. I don't think I even knew it was there before that day. I stood there on the corner for a minute and thought, 'Oh well, maybe I'll go in there and fill out an application.' That is how my career at the police department started in 1968. I began the academy in January of 1969.

PSD: *That was a bit serendipitous.*

ET: The strange thing about it is the guy who had encouraged me to come down and fill out the application, whose name was U.M. Ware, was one of the people killed when the F-14 Navy jet crashed into those houses recently. When I got to the site of the plane crash and was given the names of the people who were killed, I saw the name U.M. Ware. I thought, 'Is this the same guy? This is impossible. It can't be the same guy.' Later on, I found out that it was him.

PSD: *The odds of that happening are almost incalculable. Is there an element of fate involved here?*

ET: There might be a mysterious element in life that brings people or sends people in certain directions.

PSD: *What was it about police work that you enjoyed?*

ET: It was interesting at first, something that really kept you motivated. At the time, I was trying to do something to better myself and better the living conditions for my family. After I had been working at the police department for about a year, I decided to go back to college and take a full load while still working. I had had two years of college previously.

Going back to school was key. It is very important when you deal with young people to stress the importance of education. One thing that I can tell young people now is that if I had not gone back and finished my degree, I would have not been considered for the position that I am in today.

PSD: *At that point were you casting an eye towards a future with the police force?*

ET: I set myself up on a time-line. If I didn't get promoted in five years, then maybe I would look at some other options. While I didn't get promoted to the rank of sergeant within five years, I was able to move up within the department. I worked in a preventive youth program.

PSD: *Did you ever think you would rise to the level of chief?*

ET: The first ambition of most people who come to the police department is to just get promoted to the rank of sergeant. I had a major here tell me that the hardest rank to make is sergeant. So I had no idea that I would get as far as I did.

PSD: *Do you like the job as Police Chief?*

ET: I enjoy the challenge. It never gets dull around here. It is a new adventure every day you come to work.

PSD: *Do you feel any extra pressure being the first African-American to hold this position? Is a magnifying glass on your every move?*

ET: Whenever you are a Chief of Police in any city, you almost live under the glass. In my particular case it sort of magnifies itself. I do think I am in a situation where you have to think about every single thing you do.

PSD: *That is an unnatural position for a human being.*

ET: You have to be very careful, on every level, about the decisions you make. You have to be very aware of your social life. We all need time away to wind down and relax, but you have to be very careful. It is very difficult for me to go anywhere in this city now where I am not recognized. Sometimes that is a disadvantage.

PSD: *A price you pay for your position is a loss of privacy.*

ET: A total loss of privacy. I walk into places and people come up to me and introduce themselves, in the grocery store or anywhere I go. The other evening I went to a cigar bar that had just opened up, because sometimes I like to occasionally smoke a cigar. Well, the media was there. I tried to encourage the cameraman that I was just here to relax, that I had been invited by the people who own the place to just drop by. I just wanted to have a cigar. He said, "Oh no, we need to get the Chief on TV smoking a cigar!!!" The downside was a couple of days later when I went to get a shot for my allergies and the nurse said, "We caught you, we caught you. We saw you on TV smoking that cigar. You know you are not supposed to be smoking those things!" (He laughs.)

PSD: *Other than smoking a cigar, what do you like to do to relax?*

ET: Sometimes, when I am able to dedicate the time to it, I like to travel. Just to get away on weekends. I sometimes 'play at golf' or just stay home. I deal with people so much that when I get home, especially on the weekends, I sometimes like to have a little quiet time. I usually try to get out of here at lunch time, if I can, and get away for an hour or so.

PSD: *What brings you the most pleasure these days?*

ET: One of the things that really motivates me and keeps me going is looking at and trying to help young people. Let me give you an example ... the drill team at the Baptist Publishing Board's banquet. It was encouraging to look at those kids from ages 7 to 17 and look at the precision in which they performed. You know there had to be an awful lot of hours dedicated to that. They had been taught discipline.

Reverend Benjamin Hooks said that people from 18 to 26 years old make up the largest segment of people in prison today. The victims of the most violent crimes are from 16 to 22. Our jails and prisons are full of young people and the only way to turn it around through education and prevention is to start early with kids.

PSD: *You almost have to start when they are in the cradle.*

ET: You can't wait until they are 16 and 17 years old to try and turn these people around. You have to catch them when they first enter school or earlier. Ideally, if each child who grew up in America had a good family life, and people that they could aspire to be like when they grew up, that would be good. But the reality is we don't totally have that. I think you know that there are a number of single family homes where the female is the bread winner with one or more children. As I grow older, I become a little bit more compassionate for young people and look to provide outlets for them.

PSD: *Children are really the forgotten ones.*

Building more prisons will never solve the problem.

ET: You can't build enough prisons to house all of the people that violate the law. Most law enforcement agencies believe that the majority of people will be law-abiding citizens. Statistically, about 10% of the population commits about 90% of the crime. If we could get the majority really involved with their communities and working with law enforcement agencies, we could reduce that 10%.

PSD: *On something this important, how can we change the paradigm to get the same kind of commitment we saw in bringing the NFL to Nashville?*

ET: To be quite frank with you, I don't have a very good answer to that question. If I did, I would be out on the speaking circuit making lots of money as a motivational speaker. (he laughs) I think there are little things you can do. You have to build confidence and build bridges with the community. It is very important that the community play a role in what they perceive as being important in their neighborhood. That will vary from neighborhood to neighborhood. This department is engaged with a lot of activity related to youth.

PSD: *That is a big key.*

ET: Not only does it help the youngster see a police officer in a different perspective, but it also allows that police officer an opportunity to make a contribution to the community other than his day-to-day job of going out and catching criminals. We have many programs that are outlets for these kids, and we also try to teach self-esteem.

PSD: *Self-esteem is the one thing that is missing.*

ET: In all of the programs we are involved with, we are trying to teach these children how to believe in themselves. Teaching them how to apply for a job. With some of them, we are just trying to teach personal hygiene.

PSD: *Is the problem that these kids don't even have the most basic levels of support? I think a lot of people would take it for granted that they did.*

ET: We take a lot of things for granted. I grew up in a very, very small town. If you did something, everybody knew about it. If you did something away from home, your parents knew about it by the time you got home. The same thing with school. What we are seeing today is that we have gotten away from all that. I know that there are a lot of different philosophies out there about raising children, but we obviously need to go back and look at some of those old, traditional things we did years and years ago.

We live in a very fast and mobile society. You look at some of these children today who see the drug dealer standing on the corner with nice clothes and a nice car. Those kids don't look beyond that. A child that can earn $200 a day doing something illegal will think of himself as rich.

PSD: *Why do you think society has turned so dramatically violent?*

ET: We talked earlier about most kids looking for someone to identify with. They are not finding any positive role models. Instead they are identifying with negative elements of society going on in their immediate environments. Often times, young people are very, very impatient. They want everything very quickly. They don't want to spend the time to go to school, they don't want to work towards accumulating something.

PSD: *Could that be symptomatic of our whole society?*

ET: I think it is.

PSD: *In my opinion, the drug war seems like one of the most futile and expensive programs in America, when you consider that maybe one percent of one percent is interdicted. Won't people always find ways to alter their*

consciousness as they have throughout history?
ET: I will try to give you a good answer, knowing that this problem is so enormous and that we live in a world of supply and demand. This department, like most local law enforcement agencies, does not have the resources to deal with the enormous drug problem we have today. Not even close. It is going to take a combined effort of local, state, and federal agencies and a lot of money and personnel. I firmly believe that, if we can put a man on the moon, we can stop illegal drugs coming into this country.

PSD: *You really believe that physically we can stop it?*
ET: With an enormous effort, but it would take an army.

PSD: *What if we took all the money that is being spent on the back-end, when the person is buying drugs, and focused it in the area you said was important, building self-esteem in youngsters?*
ET: I was going to get to that. When I say supply and demand, I tell people that if you educate young children and teach them the downside of using drugs, if there is no demand there will be no supply.

PSD: *Yet the number one and number two drugs, alcohol and tobacco, are legal.*
ET: Society has pretty much accepted them. Prohibition didn't work, there is a strong effort to put restrictions on cigarettes. I know that it is against the law for children under a certain age to buy tobacco. But is that enforced? No, it is not. You have to look at the resources you have available and ask, 'What are my priorities?' Are you going to go out and arrest a convenience store operator for selling cigarettes to minors? No.

PSD: *Why not use the limited resources we do have toward prevention and education, and also make it possible for anyone, at anytime,*

to walk into a rehabilitation center for free treatment?
ET: Education, prevention and rehabilitation will be the keys to a long-term solution. When you reduce the demand, you will reduce the supply. There aren't any simple answers. There is an enormous amount of money spent every year in this country, by all levels of law enforcement.

PSD: *What would you tell a young person who came to you asking, "What would help me lead a better life?"*
ET: There are three things. Young people have to set their goals high, be persistent and persevere, and work very hard. If they do, there is a good chance that they will be successful.

PSD: *How would you personally define success?*
ET: There are a lot of different definitions and they are all personal. Some people want money, and others will want power. When I pass on, it would be good if someone can say, "He made a difference." I try to live by the philosophy of being fair with people. When I was going through the process of applying for this job, a lot of people came to me asking if they should talk to the Mayor on my behalf. I spent a lot of time at the police department, most of my adult life, in fact. I have worked hard and tried to do the things I thought would help me move up. When I reached the rank of major, I thought I had reached my limit. Then I was appointed assistant chief but I did not think I would be chief.

PSD: *Because of the invisible wall of race?*
ET: Yes. Let me tell you that I am very pleasantly surprised at the support I got from all across this city, from everybody. It regenerates your faith in people. I got so many letters of congratulations from such a cross-section of people in this community.

PSD: *What has it been like for you to deal with prejudice?*

ET: I try to be objective when I see people with a problem in dealing with other people. I guess I have always tried to be very broad-minded. I think that people have a right to worship whomever they want to. They have a right to their sexual preference. They have the right to do certain things as long as that does not infringe upon someone else. When I look at people who may have made certain remarks to me in the 1960s and in the 1970s, I tried to put them in proper perspective and not judge everybody, and really not even be judgmental of that individual. I have tried to live my life that way.

PSD: *That is a beautiful and tolerant attitude.*

ET: All of us have certain prejudices. But if we take a holistic approach, do we discriminate against people? I don't care about people who may not like me, for whatever reason, like my hair is getting thin, or the color of my skin. I remember years ago I was having a conversation with one of my supervisors who said, "I guess I am kind of prejudiced." I responded very quickly and told him I didn't have a problem with that as long as he treated me fairly and he treated me like he treated other people.

PSD: *You are drawing a very nice distinction between prejudice and discrimination.*

ET: For me personally, it wasn't that difficult.

PSD: *Who influenced you in terms of your tolerant philosophy?*

ET: I cannot identify one person in my life. I guess I have taken the good from a lot of different experiences I have had and from a lot of people with whom I have come in contact. That is what I have tried to do with life. You learn by watching and observing, even in this police department.

PSD: *So this is success for you?*

ET: Partially. I think I can lead this police department to a higher level. We have come a long way in the last five years and we need to keep progressing. We certainly don't need to take a step backwards. As long as I can feel some sense of self-satisfaction when I retire, then I will think that I have been successful in my career.

PSD: *Are you spiritual man?*

ET: I started to give you an answer like Dr. Kevorkian. (He laughs.) But in all seriousness, I think that often times spiritual belief comes from within the individual. I believe that people have a certain destiny. Sometimes we are spared or preserved for certain reasons. What those reasons might be, I don't know. I spent a year in Vietnam and was very fortunate to come back home. I thought 'Maybe somebody has something in store for me. I don't know if that is going to be bad or good.'

PSD: *Is this a hard job to leave at the office?*

ET: No, it's not hard. It is impossible. (He laughs.) You can't leave this job at the office. We have roughly 1,165 police officers in an operation that runs 365 days a year, 24 hours a day. I am lucky if I can get through a weekend without getting a call about something. Being in the position I am in right now, there is a lot of demand for me to do different things. You have no private life. The positive side to this is that people come up and give you words of encouragement.

PSD: *An officer was recently killed in the line of duty. Is it different when you are the chief and it happens on your watch?*

ET: I think it is. From my personal experience, you feel like you have lost someone that is part of your family. I think that holds true throughout this department. It is hard. You never get used to it. When you look at the particular situation you're referring to, it was a waste of two lives. It affected the gentleman who got killed. It affected the police officer and his family.

PSD: *It all seemed so senseless.*
ET: It was senseless.

PSD: *Despite all of the crime and violence, are you still optimistic when you come in every morning?*
ET: I am always optimistic, because if I wasn't, I couldn't come to work. Some days are worse than others, but every time I come in here it is with a positive attitude. If you change one or two lives ... if you change a couple of things ... if you help people in this department ... if you help people in the community ... then I feel good. You have to look at what is going to happen down the road. You have to look at what you are doing today and what you will do tomorrow.

PSD: *How would you like to be remembered?*
ET: "He made a contribution to society. He made things a little bit better than they were prior to him coming along."

Betty Larsen

Yoga Instructor/Owner, Yoga Room

"I think if we all live long enough, we will eventually come to the under-standing that God exists, that there is a supreme power, and that we are a part of God — the Divine power shines within each and every one of us."

PSD: *How did you first get started in the practice of yoga?*
BL: I moved to Nashville to attend graduate school in 1980. I had been living in Asia for a while and came back to the States not having any idea of what I wanted to do. A good friend said, "You know what to do when you don't have any idea what you want to do." I said, 'Go back to school?' And she said, "Yes, of course!" So I did. I entered into a Master's of Social Work program.

PSD: *What were you doing in Asia?*
BL: I was just hanging out doing some volunteer medical work in Sri Lanka. This was a very solid seat of Buddhism.

PSD: *So you came to Nashville for school?*
BL: Yes. Once here, I wanted to diversify the circle of people I was meeting, so I took a yoga class that I stumbled upon. I had actually done yoga back in my early days of college. So yoga helped me get through graduate school. After I had been taking the class for about a year, the teacher asked me if I had ever thought about becoming a teacher. I liked her lifestyle. She wore exercise clothes and didn't seem very stressed, plus there was the element of working with people. But I worked in the therapy field for a few years first at the Dede Wallace Center and Family and Children's Service.

PSD: *Did you dive right in with the Yoga Room?*
BL: No. I started to take some more serious training. I took leaves of absence from work and traveled around the country to study with different teachers.

PSD: *Has teaching yoga been an easy path?*
BL: Yes and no. I get to wear what I want, set my own schedule, work for myself, and work with people. I feel like the work I do is something profound in their lives. In social work, we always talked about being change agents. With yoga, I realized I could speed up the process of being a change agent by being more specific and more directive in terms of taking a positive path. In therapy, people have to meander about to find the answers to where they are going. Yoga speeds up that whole process by doing the breathing and the physical exercises.

PSD: *I have experienced a lot of emotional release in my brief exposure to yoga. I was quite surprised by how it works.*
BL: Doesn't it? It is both body-mind and mind-body. Yoga became a creative way to work with people and do what I love and enjoy. It is also said that we teach what we need to learn most. How true that is — I needed it a lot. In teaching yoga, you learn in a deeper way to be adequate and have integrity.

PSD: *You have to do your own work?*
BL: You have to do your own work.

PSD: *That's a never-ending process.*
BL: It is not supposed to be. When you are younger, you think you will reach a certain point and then be able to coast — free sailing. But it is not the case. You soon find out you have yet to begin.

PSD: *The further you get along the path, the longer the path gets.*
BL: Yes.

PSD: *What was the downside of teaching yoga? The business aspects?*
BL: Yes. Nobody told me what it meant to run a business.

PSD: *What motivates you to want to help other people?*
BL: Even as a child, I was a social worker at heart. There were elderly people I visited in my neighborhood. I would use my wagon to help them bring their groceries home.

It probably came from my grandmother and my parents. Somehow, I grew up with this way of being, so it was very natural for me to go into social work. I never felt comfortable in the corporate environment. It wasn't natural for me.

PSD: *Service is almost inherent for you.*
BL: I think it is for a lot of people. You don't choose it, it picks you.

PSD: *How did you know you were chosen? Was it an inner knowing?*
BL: Eventually. Yoga was what I was most comfortable with. Someone told me, "As soon as you talk about yoga you come alive. You're animated. It is obvious that you could sit and talk about this for days." I realized, 'Yes, this is why I am really alive'.

PSD: *Joseph Campbell calls it "following your bliss."*
BL: Yes, but there are days when it is really a job like any other job. On those days I am not Suzy Sunshine. I would rather go out and look at a flower. There is this beautiful dove who is nesting on our windowsill, and I realized I could probably sit here and watch her all day. Just watch the mother and father dove, who mate for life, care for their young.

PSD: *There are not many people whom I have met who have that sense of calm. There is such an urgency these days just to be moving, and I see a lot of extraneous movement.*
BL: Too much extraneous movement and sound. Radio and television, loud speakers, all the time.

PSD: *What is success for you?*
BL: I would define it as a lack of pain, stress, and unpleasantness. In yoga, one of the main priorities in life is to avoid future pain. That says it all. By adulthood, we should be awakening more and more, opening like concentric circles lighting outward

from the center. As we keep opening ourselves, we become more knowledgeable, more enlightened, more experienced. Through all that, we should be seeing the behaviors that cause pain in our lives. Pain, confusion, contusions, strain, pressure, ugliness, whatever.

If you accept the philosophy that we create our own reality, collectively we create 100% of our reality. Individually, I believe we create some percentage of what the collective is sending out. Once we begin to believe this and understand it — and I don't mean just academically — we begin to see how pain is created and the ways we can avoid that pain or do something that changes the course that we are on.

PSD: *And success?*
BL: For me, success is being able to engage in this philosophy within my self, my family, and my students. To be a change agent. These are not exercises, they are 'inner-cises.' Yoga is inner work. Through the inner-cises of yoga, I can help people find pathways to avoid pain and suffering, even though they are a part of life.

PSD: *Pain and suffering are part of the Buddha's noble truths.*
BL: Noble truths cause us to grow and mature. Some things are always going to sneak up behind us and slap us in the back of the head.

PSD: *Usually it all happens in the same week.*
BL: It does, doesn't it? (She laughs.) When it rains, it pours. Soon after, we usually learn a valuable lesson. I think success is being more in command of our lives, directing the course even if the course takes us off a cliff sometimes. Whether we make a lot of money or a little money. Whether we change the course of humanity or not. At least we are in command and staying as whole and healthy as possible through it all. It isn't about just

trying to live more years, but the quality of life while our soul exists in this body here on earth. We can really improve the quality of our lives.

PSD: *Tell me how.*
BL: Yoga is my personal bias because it has worked for me. There are many other ways for people, but I think the main thing is to think and to be introspective. Take a good look within yourself. Look at areas of your life that are not comfortable for you, where the quality is not as high as you want it to be. We all have these areas. I know I have areas where I can be healthier. Perfection is impossible. I finally understand this.

PSD: *That's a hard one.*
BL: That is a very hard one. We can get hooked on perfection. Just look at the areas that don't feel comfortable. Be thoughtful and seek practices and ways where we can be in command and have the tools we need to work on those areas of our life. We also need to nurture the parts we feel good about. Like a nice garden, we need to cultivate these areas so we reap the benefits. Look at how any particular action that we take affects others, the environment, whatever. Serious Yogis are vegetarians because they understand what it is to slaughter another animal and eat it. They understand that we don't have to do this in order to survive. Once you really get this, you realize you can live a non-violent life.

PSD: *Being raised in this culture, it takes a while to get into this way of thinking.*
BL: That's true, but the idea to avoid future pain and violence starts by first considering these things. Before you put a bite of food in your mouth, think of the ramifications.

PSD: *What are the ramifications of dessert?*
BL: (She laughs.) They are all good. Yogis love their sweets. As adults in America, we need to understand the cruel treatment of ani-

mals. The information is available to us. If we don't look, then we are sticking our heads in the sand and denying reality.

PSD: *You see yoga as a way of life, not something one does an hour a day?*
BL: It becomes a way of life with practice.

PSD: *We are almost taught to shut down. The job is then to wake up.*
BL: Yes. I feel yoga is one of God's greatest gifts to humanity. It gives us all the tools we need — spiritually, physically, physiologically, all of it. I love teaching Yoga.

PSD: *I have a deep knowing about this.*
BL: There are people in yoga we refer to as old souls. If you talk about karma, then you have to talk about reincarnation. Yoga is not a religion or a cult, there is no credo, there is no one or nothing you worship. When you bow, you are surrendering your ego to a higher power or whatever you want to call it. I think if we all live long enough, we will eventually come to the understanding that God exists, that there is a supreme power, and that we are a part of God — the Divine power shines within each and every one of us.

PSD: *What you are trying to describe will ultimately always exist outside the realm of language.*
BL: But we keep trying to capture it.

PSD: *What is your biggest challenge?*
BL: Doing what I am supposed to do. Doing the practice even when I don't feel like it. Staying focused, especially on the business aspect. This is hard for me.

PSD: *What makes a successful marriage?*
BL: Good question. Commitment and being constantly open to really hearing each other. We both feel responsible for 100% of this marriage. Not in a co-dependent way, where

one leans on the other all the time. It goes back and forth. Sometimes we both just surrender to the outcome. We work together and run the business together. We were friends for 6 years before we got married, even though the spark was there from the beginning. In a word, the answer is responsibility.

PSD: *Responsibility is a beautiful word, though it seems to be an anathema in today's society.*
BL: You can only have freedom through responsibility. Freedom never comes from being cut loose. You can only direct a situation — the way you act and react — when you are responsible.

PSD: *How would you like to be remembered?*
BL: She was able to transmit yoga in a clear and compassionate way. She served as a conduit to the teachings.

PSD: *And as a person as well as a teacher?*
BL: That is very difficult to answer. I would like to leave something behind to the collective that brings clarity and understanding. To be someone who contributed to the collective karmic pool in a very positive way. This comes from a gut level, not from the intellect. Karma is both individual and collective to me. I want to help clean up some of the karma. That the general intent of my life was to contribute to good karma, that I was a caring person.

Joel Solomon

President, The Joel Solomon Company

"**Effortlessness is about becoming more and more at peace and relaxed amidst all the intensity that is around us all the time. I am choosing to activate as much as possible that is around me while staying at peace and relaxed. If I can do this, then I can become a channel for the values that I care about. And the main value for me is our planet Earth.**"

PSD: *What is important to you?*

JS: What is important to me about my work here is to support and encourage independent, creative, progressive business projects and not-for-profit projects. And through that, to build a healthy community, a community that comes back around to support other creative and progressive success stories.

PSD: *Are you talking about your company, or about you personally?*

JS: Both. More importantly why Joel, the human being, is here. The company is one of the multiple structures I use to pursue this.

PSD: *What is it that the Joel Solomon Company does to promote this philosophy?*

JS: The company is 12 years old and comes out of my inherited assets. My father was a shopping center developer, and in his time, that was an important contribution to make. In my time, I want to convert the benefit of those assets into a different kind of infrastructure for the values I care about. It is about relationship and values. I like to use the word infrastructure in terms of small businesses, ways that people can make a living, ways that people can interact, and ways that people can think independently and freely.

PSD: *Right now our culture seems to be moving in the opposite direction.*

JS: I believe that we are at a time in history where mono-culturing is happening. I believe that the biggest raw material or resource is human attention, and human attention is being harvested globally and being trained and cultivated to think the same things and want the same things — to buy into the same paradigm. I see McDonalds about to hit 10,000 locations around the globe in 60 countries. Mono-culturing is a really powerful and important force in society and one I think there needs to be alternatives to. What my work and my life is about is being a gardener, sowing seeds that will grow diversity.

PSD: *You mentioned the word 'community'. Are you familiar with M. Scott Peck and his definition and work in establishing community?*

JS: Yes, his work is about relationship. I would put it this way — all of what I'm talking about extends as deeply as we can carry it and as deeply as we can open up and receive it. So what that has meant for me and my time in Nashville, as well as what I have used this company for, is to create jobs, credible financial abundance, businesses that succeed, non-profit companies that can pay their bills, and an environment that encourages the interconnectedness among people.

I like to create business ventures that have multiple partners. I only do business with friends or people I would want to be friends with. I believe that if you cannot do business with your friends, then whatever religion you are participating in is telling you the wrong thing. I am very happy to be a non-controlling partner, but I believe in a strong leadership model. In all of our entities, there is someone and some place where the buck stops.

PSD: *Are you more of a catalyst than a hands-on manager?*

JS: Yes. I decided a long time ago that I wanted my freedom, and if I built an empire below me, I would be the slave. If I can find people with whom I share enough values and a mutual agenda, then I want to find out how I can support them.

PSD: *So you are creating synergy?*

JS: What the company does is pretty much focus on a one mile radius from Hillsboro Village. We do very small projects and a lot of rehabilitation of old buildings. We have worked very heavily in Hillsboro Village because we think it is very critical to the future of Nashville. It is one of the last pedestrian, accessible, mixed-use areas, and it is in the heart of a creative center. There's Belmont, Vanderbilt, and Music Row. Hillsboro Village has always been threatened by demolition and the construction of high-rises. We have been doing what we can to preserve this area.

PSD: *You are also active on a national level.*
JS: Out of town, I am attempting to steer the flow of sleeping capital into progressive and social impact business ventures and projects. In other words, I am a partner in a venture fund based in Vancouver, British Columbia that focuses on British Columbia businesses that have a positive, ecological, and social impact. So we do a lot of natural and organic foods.

The vehicle in which I try to do what I do is a rather neutral substance, which is money. I am trying to learn how to steer the flow of it more towards the kinds of things I am talking about. If you are going to put money in the stock market, try to invest in the companies that are being the least destructive. You might want to refrain from investing in multi national corporations that are bleeding the planet of its resources. Maybe you can put money into a local revolving loan fund that supports low-income housing. Maybe you can buy bonds that your city is issuing to build schools. In other words, politicize your money. Whatever amount of money you have, think about everywhere that you spend a dollar. Every dollar you spend can be a conscious choice.

PSD: *Is apathy your biggest enemy?*
JS: I'd call it sleepiness. We are carefully and systematically trained to be obedient consumers.

PSD: *Where did this philosophy come from?*
JS: I was trained to become a shopping center developer like my father. For a number of reasons, that did not make me very happy. So the first place that I went to was politics. I got heavily involved and was fortunate enough to become Jimmy Carter's National Youth Coordinator the year before he was elected President. I ended up helping to elect Jimmy Carter. That got me into a too powerful world at too young an age, and I wasn't ready for it. At the time, I was also diagnosed with a hereditary degenerative kidney disease. That helped me think about what I really wanted to do with my time.

PSD: *Where did you go from there?*
JS: I ended up getting trained in a school of gardening called French Intensive Bio-Dynamic. The basic messages were about building the soil, diversity, and paying attention to the cosmos, because it has impact you cannot always see or understand, and you cannot control it. You can only be a steward and steer it, no matter how small your garden is. You can never control it all. Plants will teach you a lot about planting. That metaphor is how I do my business.

PSD: *Where does your sense of service come from?*
JS: I come from a cultural and religious tradition, and a specific family, that values service. I am Jewish, and both my mother and father were very civic-minded and involved with the community. On top of having this illness and working on the land for seven years, I decided to live every day of my life from the vantage point of my death bed. Each decision was predicated on what I would feel when I looked back on it.

PSD: *Is your health in good shape?*
JS: I have had great health. I never have had a problem yet. But the disease is something I live with.

PSD: *We all have a terminal disease in the form of our mortality.*
JS: My diagnosis helped me awaken to that fact. I am a fairly intense guy, who works with great enthusiasm and gusto. Every time I get a little lazy, I think I may not have a lot of time left.

PSD: *Why did you end up living in Nashville?*
JS: My father lived here and died here. He also had his business interests here after he had gone into the Carter Administration. So I came back to Nashville from British Columbia because I realized what he had built here and left for me was a real treasure. It was a neutral tool that was here for me to apply my values to. So I have been gradually pulling out of new shopping center construction and doing rehab whenever I do real estate. I think that rehab is a huge environmental contribution, instead of helping to encourage more suburban sprawl.

PSD: *Rehabilitation also flies in the face of our cultural obsession with newer, better, faster.*
JS: There is more money to be made in urban sprawl. The real religion in this country, where church and state are totally aligned, is the religion of maximum return and personal accumulation.

PSD: *At any cost.*
JS: At any cost, at any cost. Now I am a capitalist, a person who works in the free-market system. I think it is by far the best market system for this species, but you still have to apply values to it. And you do not have to have maximum return, this week. If you are going to think about your descendants and your community, this will have to change. There are people with hundreds of millions of dollars who are the heroes of today. They are like the saints were to the church. Bill Gates is a hero today. This is the religion of the country.

PSD: *And it is happening at the expense of the planet.*
JS: We lost our connection, in my view, with what is actually important. I really feel that our institutions — the corporate sector and the religious sector — are letting us down.

PSD: *Do you take personal time to help keep you grounded?*
JS: Absolutely. Nature is my primary balance and I still garden. I like to sit out and pull weeds or prune and just be. I get absorbed there. I paint and do some hobby artist work which is a great release from my mentally focused world. I walk a lot. I try to blend business and my life. I do not really see a separation between business and my life's work, which is about being here as fully and dynamically as possible. So I have many of my business meetings on foot.

PSD: *What advice would you give to someone trying to access that most inner part of themselves?*
JS: The simplest thing that I know to say, given the direction that I see the world going, is to get out on the land and be quiet. Look inside as deeply as you know how, and find out what is really true for you. Be fiercely dedicated to it.

PSD: *How would you define success?*
JS: Good relationship.

PSD: *Good relationship?*
JS: There is probably a better way to say that. It follows from the premise that everything is connected, it is all one big soup. Everything. Right relationship is probably a better way to say it than good relationship. That will mean that I have been successful in caring for my body, caring for the people I care about, caring for my business relationships, because I will be at peace. There will be energy and life rippling all around me in every activity.

PSD: *Is it a great challenge to juggle all of this?*
JS: Absolutely. And anyone that says 'no' is probably not asking the question deeply enough. I believe what I am practicing is

effortlessness. Effortlessness is about becoming more and more at peace and relaxed amidst all the intensity that is around us all the time. I am choosing to activate as much as possible that is around me while staying at peace and relaxed. If I can do this, then I can become a channel for the values that I care about. And the main value for me is our planet Earth.

PSD: *We really take our sacred planet for granted.*

JS: At all times. While we sit here right now, we are on the land. That is why real estate became such an interesting karmic thing for me and that my family was involved in real estate. I went off and became a gardener, which is really a kind of real estate developer. So now the reason I work in this neighborhood and do the deals I do is because the land is here. There may be deed lines down at the courthouse, but the land is here. This philosophy permeates everything.

PSD: *Is this a kind of Taoist approach?*

JS: I am a product of the later part of the twentieth century and we have access to much of the deepest spiritual and sacred teachings. This is one of the more positive aspects of the amazing communication that we have access to. We no longer grow up in a village where there is one church, so I am a product of all these influences. If you open yourself to it, you have access to a huge diversity of teachings, understandings, and wisdom.

PSD: *Are you optimistic in terms of the planet and its survival?*

JS: I am always an optimist and always equally a pessimist. I am not even smart enough to know what the right direction would be, much less whether we are going there.

PSD: *So you don't have a gut feeling about it?*

JS: I believe it is still possible to lead a very deep and meaningful life, not only as a luxury for the affluent. But it is impossible to do on large parts of the planet for many, many people — a number that seems to be growing at an accelerated pace. And that is what makes me pessimistic. The tools are all here for us to awaken to a consciousness that would make it possible for more people, but I am not smart enough to know if this will happen.

PSD: *You recently did a conference in Seattle along these lines.*

JS: I am a partner and President of the Board of a place called Hollyhok, which is on an island in British Columbia and puts on retreats and workshops in the practical, creative, and healing arts. We have just started a larger forum conference in partnership with *New Age Journal* magazine. We bring together some of the leading presenters, teachers, and authors, so people can come for a weekend and be exposed to these folks. We just finished our first one, which sold out, and are now working on our second one.

PSD: *You must love to be involved with this sort of project.*

JS: I love it. In this day and age where we don't really have villages anymore and we don't really have tribes, coming together for a few days with a shared purpose and shared attention, in a thoughtful structured way, is kind of like an injection of that community experience. So that we can keep it alive in us.

PSD: *Do you feel that the need for community is primal? Are we suffering on some inner level because we lack it?*

JS: Yes. The way we get it is through football stadiums and watching something on television in our arm chairs. I feel this is unfortunate.

PSD: *What gives you the most pleasure in your life?*

JS: The creative process gives me the most satisfaction, especially when there is a high level of play involved. When all of these creative, independent people come together and learn how to work together and trust each other, something magical happens.

PSD: *You touched on your mortality earlier. How would you like to be remembered?*

JS: "He was good compost. He was good fertilizer." I mean it metaphorically. That I was really able to help nourish other people's success and helped the values that I care about flourish and grow.

Jane Jones

Founder, Jane Jones Employment Services

"The harder the challenge, the more I am inspired. I do not like the word 'no'. When someone tells me 'It cannot be done,' that really fires me up. There is always a way."

PSD: *You must love people to do the kind of work you do.*

JJ: Absolutely. In fact, I have been in the human resource field over the last 26 years of my life. Jane Jones Enterprises placed at least 150,000 people in full-time jobs. That was very rewarding. We helped people get employment who could not overcome the interview process. Some people just don't interview well. We would select them for the jobs, send them in as temps, and they would get hired in record numbers.

PSD: *How did you get involved in this profession?*

JJ: I got a job as a receptionist at a small company that later became a national company called Norrell. One day, they lost both of their managers, so the boss asked me if I could keep his office open. He didn't know it, but I had already been running it. Then I went to Commerce Union Bank and was the first woman to become an officer in human resources. I used to go lunch with Ed Potter, the founder, who used to say, "Miss Jane, how do people like my bank?"

PSD: *When did you start Jane Jones Enterprises?*

JJ: In 1977, with a thousand dollars, I started Jane Jones Enterprises. My Mom and Dad and an Aunt all borrowed money to help me get started. I was scared at the time, but I had never seen so many people who needed help. We were profitable in the first month, which was phenomenal. I had two children, a two-year-old and a seven-year-old, so I was doing lots of juggling.

PSD: *Why do you think your business worked so well? Did you have a plan?*

JJ: Having already worked for a temporary service, I knew what to do. We very much believed in Mary Kay Ash's famous formula: God first, family second, job third. I think it worked so well because I really tried for this balance. Whenever things got difficult, I relied on a higher power. So it was our basic religious beliefs and our ability to pull together as a family. My Dad and Mother both worked there, my husband came to work there, my son, too. We were a very good team. All organizations have to have someone who knows how to make money and someone else who knows how to invest and take care of it.

PSD: *What happened to the company?*

JJ: It was sold to Randstad Staffing Service, because small businesses have trouble growing due to lack of capital.

PSD: *Was there a personal reason, too?*

JJ: Yes. I felt like I wanted better balance in my life. Also, the stakes were getting higher. It got to the point where I couldn't go somewhere to eat without someone saying, "Could you get my son a job?" Fame was not something I wanted, because the cost is so high. I was losing my own identity running after the business.

PSD: *You have a lot of energy, so it is hard to imagine you back home, just laying around. What are you doing now?*

JJ: I have another business idea called Creative Training Solutions. It's where I think the market is headed — using interactive, multi-media, computer training with TV quality to help people grasp educational tools.

PSD: *Where does all your energy come from?*

JJ: I'm not sure. I have always been high-strung. It takes me about 30 minutes to wake up, but once I do, this burst of energy comes — then look out!

PSD: *What advice would you give a young person about being successful?*

JJ: First of all, business success is not a monkey on your back. You are not running from something or running to something. You are trying to cause something to happen, but that's not all there is. Find balance. Success can be all-consuming. People try to be what others expect them to be, instead of being who they are. It is unfair to put expectations on children. If children find who and what they are, then they are successful.

PSD: *How do they find that certain something, that clarity in their inner voices?*

JJ: Once again, I go back to the basics. Nothing ever makes you happy except the right relationship to God. When you leave this old world, what can you leave behind? One is the things you do for God. Another is the heritage you leave for children, your own or someone else's. And the third is what you do for your fellow man. If you put your contributions into those three areas, you will ultimately be successful.

PSD: *Money is not even in your top three.*

JJ: Don't get me wrong. I like to have money, because you can help people who are down and out. If I can take this creative training approach and help one child, then it is worth it for me. This is my passion. This is what is fun.

PSD: *Do you take time to get in touch with God?*

JJ: My husband is very structured, but I am more free-flowing. I get up and thank God for another day. I ask for the strength to try and help somebody, to do something good. It is easy to get consumed with self, so I try to remember to give.

PSD: *What do you do when you get down?*

JJ: Usually I work. Work helps. When I feel down, it is a form of depression. When it gets really bad, I overeat. You can look at my size and tell that. (She laughs.) This is something that I faced a long time ago. I am my worst critic. When I am in a bad mood, I tell everyone to stay out of my way. But this is rare. I found out that I am a diabetic, so a lot of my mood can be related to blood sugar levels. I am basically a happy person.

PSD: *Are you a perfectionist?*

JJ: Not really. I just have a quest for knowledge. I like to share and I like to teach. I think we made a big mistake in this country in that there is no honor in getting old. There should be! Because people really hit their stride around 50. They are fairly settled and have a lot of experience. So when you get to that level, you should be able to teach other people your wisdom. But we don't.

PSD: *We are one of the few cultures in the world that do not honor the elderly and their vast amount of knowledge.*

JJ: And it is wrong.

PSD: *You had some personal struggles recently.*

JJ: My daughter had open heart surgery. Talk about bringing your world to a halt. As far as we know, she is OK.

PSD: *What was that like as a mother?*

JJ: If I had known it was going to be so difficult, I might not have wanted to live. My mother had colon cancer at the same time, then my father had a massive heart attack and died 5 weeks later. My whole world was falling apart.

The night my father died, he had not been ready. When everyone had left the room, he came out of his coma and asked me, "What am I gonna do?" I said, 'Daddy, you are going to die.' And that is what he needed. He needed permission. Once I said it was OK, I held him and loved him, then he moved on. I wouldn't trade anything for that.

PSD: *Was there a metaphysical quality to the whole experience?*

JJ: Oh, yes. Instinctively, I knew immediately what to do for him. And where does that kind of wisdom come from? I know that he is in a much better place.

PSD: *Was your faith tested?*
JJ: Surely, it was pitiful. But I never asked God, 'Why me?' Whatever the conscious will of God, we must accept it.

PSD: *How have your priorities changed through all of this?*
JJ: One of the things I have been doing is noticing the color of the sky again, and the smell of the rain. I am still working hard, but I am not completely without balance. One thing I am good at is being a good time manager. Being organized helps to reduce stress because you have more time.

Also, I am really involved with giving my time to welfare programs. I believe that if someone doesn't help these women come off welfare, we are going to force them into a horrible situation. I don't have any answers, but I am working desperately with agencies to try to find some. I believe Randstad can help find them employment. There has to be a natural connection. If there can be job brokers for rocket scientists, why can't there be brokers for welfare recipients? It is just different ends of the spectrum. I have also gotten a church involved to help minister to the faith needs that these women have. We have to give them pride.

PSD: *You are obviously optimistic. Do you get discouraged by the enormity of the challenge?*
JJ: The harder the challenge, the more I am inspired. I do not like the word 'no'. When someone tells me "It cannot be done," that really fires me up. There is always a way. People's circumstances are not always their fault. They don't always start on the same level playing field.

PSD: *One of the things that inspires me is the great miracle of love. I have never seen a human being not respond to unconditional love.*
JJ: I haven't either. I have seen these welfare women respond to kindness. People respond to kindness in kind. I think that human dignity is important. Even when I had to let someone go, you could still let them maintain their dignity.

PSD: *Are you insatiably curious?*
JJ: A better word is nosy. Even as a little kid I was always wanting to know everything.

PSD: *How would you like to be remembered?*
JJ: I would like to be remembered as a person who carried a banner that said "If she can do it, anybody can!" I am serious. My life has been the all-American dream. "If she can find the beauty of her dream, anyone can."

PSD: *What has enabled you to do that?*
JJ: It all comes back to that simple little thing called love. I have a compassion and need for people from all walks of life. To meet a total stranger, no matter where they are in the world, and just love that person. I love because I was loved.

PSD: *How would you define success?*
JJ: Giving everything that God enabled you to give and expecting nothing in return. Throughout your entire life.

PSD: *I get the feeling that you are just getting started.*
JJ: Oh yes, I hope so. I am here for a purpose. I am here because I have something to give. Not a day goes by where you are not given an opportunity to give something. Even if it is just a kind word. A smile and enthusiasm are two of the most contagious things in the whole wide world. It can light up an entire room. This is the kind of person I want to be.

Joe Calloway

Motivational Speaker

"I have become a real believer in doing what your gut tells you to. I say try it, go for it. You may fall flat on your face, but who cares? Don't be afraid of failure because, ultimately, you're not playing it safe at all. That is just guaranteed failure. Be bold!"

PSD: *You must hear people talk about success all the time. How would you define it?*

JC: I define success as being happy. It's simple. Some people would say that my definition is rather shallow. But being happy means different things to different people. For me, being happy entails making a contribution to the planet, living your life in balance, and knowing who you are in terms of values and integrity. If you're not happy, then something is incongruent. Now everybody has a bad day now and then, but I generally aspire to be happy, and for me, a big part of that is to grow. I try to remind myself to be like a tree sometimes. I'm just supposed to grow.

PSD: *So you use happiness as one of your barometers?*

JC: How can anybody who is not happy claim to be successful? I don't care how many yachts or houses you have. If you are not happy, something didn't work.

PSD: *How did you get started as a professional speaker?*

JC: I have been speaking professionally for 15 years. I actually started as a real estate salesman, then an office manager, then a director of marketing for a real estate company. My duties included designing and conducting all the sales meetings that we did for the agents. I left the company to go independent, doing customized training programs for businesses. That evolved into speaking. I had no idea there was a profession for speakers.

PSD: *Was it a difficult field to break into?*

JC: Starting out, it was a major financial struggle. It is so hard to break into this business, for 3 or 4 years I was just hanging on by my fingernails. Then, little by little, it started to pick up. I started getting jobs and it was really fun. Every time a new job came along I would be high-fiving my wife, Annette. All of a sudden, it started to become work and I wasn't high-fiving anybody. A big part of that was my inability to say no. I had been so hungry for so long I couldn't imagine turning down a job if I could physically get there.

PSD: *Is speaking still your passion?*

JC: Not really. I am in the process of looking for the next thing. I think what I do is slowly becoming, to some degree, obsolete. People have changed the way they learn. People have changed the way they like to listen to things. I am currently exploring going back into training and facilitating. So it has kind of come full circle for me.

PSD: *That strikes me as walking away on top.*

JC: It is really easy in business to get stuck in doing what works. You think, 'Well, this works. Why change anything?' Then one day you wake up with cobwebs all over you and you say, 'What happened?' It is a huge trap. I like to say in my speeches, 'If I'm successful, then to me, that means I know what worked yesterday.' So I'm continually trying to start over.

PSD: *What are your programs about?*

JC: I talk about change and how it affects people in organizations — how they can move from change being a threat to change being an opportunity — because most people are still afraid of change, especially when it is forced upon them. Certainly most big corporations, the kind of companies I work with, are going through massive change. What I try to do is get people to take a new approach to change.

PSD: *Many of us think of corporate America as a cold, heartless place. How do you find the corporate world at this moment?*

JC: I hear people say "It's a cold, mean place." Maybe it used to be, but it's warming up! More and more corporations are paying attention to the concept of the whole person, in terms of their employees. It is not enough just to pay them. We have to consider the

95

whole person and what he or she is trying to achieve as an individual. People need to have a sense of family where they work. This is spreading like wildfire through corporate America.

PSD: *It is warming up despite the downsizing?*

JC: A lot of companies are finding that downsizing didn't work like they thought it would. They didn't achieve all the economies of scale and the efficiencies they were looking for just by laying a bunch of people off. They are starting to realize that maybe they should look for long-term growth.

PSD: *Can you talk more about change in terms of your programs?*

JC: In my presentation, when I talk about change, I have come up with this model of it. People have boundaries on what they consider to be normal. For instance, I travel a lot. So when I go to the airport and see my flight has been canceled, it doesn't bother me, because for me it's normal. Flights get canceled all the time. I'm immediately thinking, 'What's my next step? How do I get to where I need to be?' People who don't fly much go to the airport, see their flight canceled, and sometimes go crazy.

PSD: *So people can become more flexible with training?*

JC: I think that people can expand their parameters, expand their borders of what's normal. Which is not to say that what's normal is acceptable. Sometimes there are things that happen that I am not going to put up with. But it is still normal.

PSD: *The rate of change is sometimes both scary and exciting.*

JC: There is this wonderful quote I use, "You think you understand the situation, but what you don't understand is that the situation just changed." Which is always true. If you look at a relationship, it is always changing because people are always growing to one degree or another. I think you can learn to say that change is a lot more fun than things being static.

PSD: *This is not a passive approach, though, is it?*

JC: No. The paradigm of 'everything is normal' is not a roll over and lay down attitude. It is a very proactive position that isn't going to tear me up because I am going to handle it. This is what I get paid for — to help people deal with difficult situations. There isn't much of a market for people who can handle easy situations because anyone can handle it if it's easy.

PSD: *Is perception reality?*

JC: My belief is that we all make up our reality. My real world is made up of the way I 'interpret' what happens.

PSD: *Who influenced you in your formative years?*

JC: When I first went into the realty business, I worked for a guy who was very much into the positive thinking thing with books, tapes, and such. I had never been exposed to it. I was one of those people who considered myself to be a realist. I pooh-poohed it all, rolled my eyes and thought 'Yes, let's just sugar-coat the world and pretend like everything is great and then it will be, right?' What I realized was I wasn't a realist as much as I was a wimp because whenever things didn't suit me or got tough I would say, 'There you go, the world's a lousy place.' The people I knew who got what they wanted said, "Oh, this has happened. OK, how do I deal with it?" They would just keep going, and say "There is always another way to look at it. There is always another way." What I finally learned was that it's not about sugar-coating, or being naive, it's quite the opposite. It is about being tough, smart, resilient, flexible, and being able to persevere.

PSD: *Isn't experience sometimes a hindrance to accomplishment because we feel there are preset rules and barriers when in fact most of the walls we face are self-created?*

JC: Oh, yes. I draw a circle. You start out at the top of the circle which represents ignorance, where you just don't know any better. Then you work your way down to expert, where you know everything. If you are lucky, you work your way back up to the top again, to ignorance. But it's what I call enlightened ignorance where you wake up every day not assuming you know what works.

PSD: *Has balance been difficult for you to achieve?*

JC: Balance was hard for me. I hit a wall. I was doing a massive amount of work with a massive amount of travel where I was in a different city every day. Some people thrive on this, but I don't. I want to be at home with my wife and friends. I was struggling with the concept of, 'Am I willing to be happy?' Then, I thought, this is absurd! I am going to do this business on my terms, not everybody else's. If the marketplace says to me, 'Joe, you're fired, you can't do it this way,' then so be it. I will find another way to make a living.

PSD: *Did your goals have to change for your life to change?*

JC: I used to set goals every year and the number one goal was always financial, to make more money. Last year, I actually set a goal to make less money, and I did. Yet I was infinitely richer because I stayed home and got to play. I started living rather than just making a living. I heard a great line once about a successful person, "He never let his career get in the way of him leading a good life."

PSD: *What matters most to you?*

JC: My marriage is very important to me.

What works for us is we are constantly in communication. We talk about everything. We have worked really hard at putting everything on the table, not letting resentments build up. We stick with each other knowing we will come out closer on the other side. She is my best friend and I am her best friend.

PSD: *What is challenging for you?*

JC: My biggest challenge right now is regaining the sense of enthusiasm for everything that is going on in my life. I could continue doing what I am doing and the bills would be paid but I get bored. I am going through a process of figuring out what I really want to do.

PSD: *What brings you a sense a fulfillment?*

JC: For me, it feels really good to do things for the community. We work with the Triangle House program. We are involved in a wonderful little church that is service-oriented. I also like to meet with people one on one who are interested in getting into the speaking business and try to help.

PSD: *Are you a spiritual person?*

JC: I love simple ideas. Abraham Lincoln was once asked what religion he believed in. He said, " When I do good, I feel good. When I do bad, I feel bad."

PSD: *Do you have any sort of mission statement?*

JC: For my business, my mission statement is, 'To joyfully and creatively communicate ideas that help people feel better about themselves and their work.' Personally it's 'Be happy,' though as I said, that runs deep with me.

PSD: *Sometimes we can give so much of ourselves there is nothing left for us. Where do you draw the line on personal service?*

JC: I think there are a lot of people out there who feel you almost have to be a martyr to be a truly giving person. But if you can't give without attachment, that's not a good thing because you end up resenting it.

PSD: *Any advice for becoming successful?*
JC: I have become a real believer in doing what your gut tells you to. My gut is seldom wrong. I say try it, go for it. You may fall flat on your face, but who cares? Don't be afraid of failure because, ultimately, you're not playing it safe at all. That is just guaranteed failure. Be bold! I have made some bad decisions and some bad choices in my life, but I don't regret any of them because, ultimately, they led me here. I have always learned more from my mistakes. Just don't make the same mistakes over and over.

PSD: *How about in business?*
JC: If you are going to have successful relationships in business, you have to create win/win situations. You can't make people lose and expect to survive, because they won't play with you anymore and you will be out of business. Business is about helping people win. You have to treat people well.

PSD: *I heard you once use a great Churchill quote.*
JC: Winston Churchill said, "If you are afraid of something, the worst thing you can do is turn your back on it and run because it will most certainly defeat you."

PSD: *What type of impression would you like to leave behind?*
JC: I would like people to say, "You know, he was a good guy." Even the people who just knew me professionally And you know what else? "He was a gentleman. He was kind and he treated people respectfully. He was OK. He was a nice guy."

Jane Eskind

Political Activist/Philanthropist

"There are all kinds of ways to succeed. One is to win the election. Another is to lose the election, but win the debate. Success is raising a family that is happy and well-adjusted and doesn't mind living in the same city as the parent. That is a great success and a great honor."

PSD: *What motivates you to get involved in community service?*

JE: One was the way I was brought up. My parents were involved in the community in which I lived. They thought that you not only took from the community, but you had an obligation to give something back. They were involved with civic things in one form or the other. So I guess it was my birthright.

The other thing that motivates me is that public service, whether as a volunteer or an elected politician, is getting a very bad name at this time of our lives. I believe in public service, in doing for my community. My commitment is heightened because everybody else is cursing the public servant. I want to make sure we still talk about public service and we still do public service, that we still think about doing good for our communities, either on a very small or a very grand level.

I have often talked about what would happen in our community if the volunteers stayed home. You begin to think about your public school system, your public and private hospitals, and the volunteers that work there. You realize that a community cannot afford to replace that kind of help and enthusiasm, not only on an emotional level, but also on a fiscal level.

PSD: *Why has public service gotten such a bad rap?*

JE: We believe that someone who volunteers is more noble than somebody who is not a volunteer. We became very cynical back in the 1970s with Richard Nixon. We began to distrust anyone who wanted to be in public office or public service. The minute you say, "I want to run for office," you are suspect and lay yourself open to being vulnerable, to having the most impertinent questions asked of you and of your family — things that have no basis in public discourse. So I can time the shift to that point.

The tragedy from my perspective is that we all know 20 people who would make wonderful public servants, people who would make wonderful contributions to the community. But we don't know one who would run for public office.

PSD: *The press takes the rap for its tabloid mentality. Do you think that mentality might just be more of a reflection of the general electorate?*

JE: People get most of the information on which they base decisions in a 30- to 60-second sound-bite they see on television. They certainly don't have all the information they need to make good decisions. We are turning most of our newspapers into a form of tele-journalism. You'll only find either heartbreaking stories or sensational stories that make the front page. You have to work pretty hard to find news of the world in current journalism unless it is specifically a magazine or periodical that speaks to that subject alone.

We have gotten lazy as a society. But in that 60-second sound-bite you could have substance instead of gossip. You could talk about ideas instead of personalities. You could talk about issues instead of whole numbers. Deciding what to put in that sound-bite is the media's responsibility. It falls back to the editors and the people who make decisions about content.

PSD: *Despite what could easily be called a depressing political landscape, you strike me as quite optimistic.*

JE: (She laughs.) I am optimistic, because I am not going to give in. I am still going to talk about it and mention it. I hope that someday you will hear me and say, "Yes, by George, you are right, and I am going to be part of the answer, not part of the problem." I believe in democracy.

One of the most wonderful lessons I learned was from a woman I worked with when I first moved to town way back in the early '60s. We had just lost the vote on a project we had been working on. I was ready to say, 'Well, if that's the way they feel about it, they got what they deserve.' But she said, "We will just have to start all over again." She made me realize that you are only defeated if you think you are defeated. You can be deferred, you can be delayed, but you can't be defeated unless you agree to it.

PSD: *If you sit on the sidelines, it's easy to be cynical and feel hopeless. People like you, though, have a sense of enthusiasm and optimism because they are on the cutting edge and can see things affected by their own energies. Do you find that involvement breeds enthusiasm?*

JE: If you are active and involved, you certainly wouldn't want to think it useless, because that would be self-defeating. It would be depressing to think that expending your energy wouldn't have a positive result.

PSD: *How would you define success?*

JE: There are all kinds of ways to succeed. One is to win the election. Another is to lose the election, but win the debate. If I felt strongly about something and lost an election, but the person who defeated me picked up on my issue and pushed for it, that is success. Success is raising a family that is happy and well-adjusted and doesn't mind living in the same city as the parent. That is a great success and a great honor.

PSD: *What brings you the most satisfaction?*

JE: Just about everything I do. Conversations with my grandchildren are terrific. Raising money for the President is terrific. I am blessed in having the time and the option to do what gives me pleasure. And what gives me pleasure is doing what I feel contributes to the community, both small and large.

PSD: *You mentioned raising a family. There was a little piece in the* Nashville Scene *in which the paper tipped its hat to you and your husband Dick for doing such a fine job as parents and role models.*

JE: It touched me deeply. Had somebody said, "Write anything you want — it can be anonymous and nobody will know where it came from," I could not and would not have been as generous as they were.

PSD: *What was your philosophy as a parent and mother?*

JE: What I mostly tried to do was listen, to hear what my kids were saying, and to remember how I felt when I was their age. To understand how important the issue was on a scale of zero to 10, and see if we needed to make an issue of it.

PSD: *What advice would you give to your kids as they prepared to go out into this world?*

JE: The main thing I hope they take with them is a sense of humor. That way, when everything is absurd and awful, laughter can be very therapeutic. It is a warm, embracing kind of thing. Whatever strikes your funnybone opens you to other people and lets them into your world.

I would talk about compromises. I would also hope that they knew their own center, that they knew who they were and where they lived. So when people were mean, they wouldn't be. Or when things were unfair, they always were. They were neither disheartened by the negative any more than they were inflated by positive reinforcement. You need to have your own focus and your own center, so you maintain a balance.

PSD: *How do you remain grounded?*

JE: If I am not grounded by now, I am never going to be. (She laughs.) When I was running for office, I would drive into a town and there on a billboard, bigger than life, would be Jane Eskind. Then there would be a newspaper column that said what a scoundrel Jane Eskind was. And I was neither of those things. I wasn't bigger than life, and I wasn't a low-life. There isn't any Zen philosophy or any meditation, I don't think I have the time. Some days, when everything seems out of whack and nothing is the way that it should be, I will go for a ride in the country. I will just get in the car and turn right or left as the mood strikes me. I'll do some back-road driving and by the time I get back, everything is back in place. Call it free association.

PSD: *You are very well off monetarily. Do you have a mind-set about prosperity and abundance separate from Jane on other levels?*
JE: Again, it goes back to knowing who you are and staying focused. It is a great gift to be able to do certain things that other people would like to, were they able. It might sound as if I'm gloating, but I don't mean it that way at all. There are certain times in our lives when we have been able to do things that have turned out to be terribly important to other people's lives. And it has been an honor to do it.

PSD: *I happen to know people close to me that you have helped a great deal. You were very quiet about it.*
JE: It is a very private thing. We haven't done anything that 100,000 other people wouldn't have done if they could. We are just lucky to have that privilege.

PSD: *You see it as a great honor to give to another human being.*
JE: According to the scholar Moses Maimonides, there are nine stages of charity. He says the highest form of charity is to remove the need for it. The lowest form is to humiliate the recipient in the giving.

PSD: *Was it your parents who instilled this attitude in you?*
JE: They both thought that community participation not only included the tea-and-crumpets organizations that were easy to join, but the rough-and-tumble organizations of political action. My father managed campaigns for candidates. My mother was involved in issues. I couldn't avoid it. I swore I wouldn't do it, but then I came to Nashville and decided I wanted to learn about this community. The avenue to learn was to participate in the issues of the community.

PSD: *When did you arrive here?*
JE: Forty-two years ago. We've been married for 42 years.

PSD: *Are you happy?*
JE: If not now, never. (She laughs.) This is a good community. We just met some people who recently moved here, and I told them they needed to know that this town is full of people who came here for one reason or another, and now you can't pry them lose.

PSD: *There is a real sense of community here, a real warmth.*
JE: That's why Nashville succeeds more than Memphis. Memphis is a very unhappy community that is not reaching its potential because of the competition within.

PSD: *You were a kind of pioneer as a woman in politics. Was it a pleasant experience?*
JE: Sometimes. (She laughs.) I've said with some humor that somebody had to be first, and I was happy to do that. Not having women in politics was depriving the state, the country, of half the talent. It's like a bird flying with just one wing — he can't soar nearly as far or as high. We are not so wonderful that we can afford to waste half our talent pool. One of the problems in Tennessee is that we elect so few people. We are unique in how we elect the Attorney General and the Lieutenant Governor.

PSD: *How would Jane Eskind like to be remembered?*
JE: A friend of mine once said she was

going to put on my tombstone, "She Cared."
You know, that's good enough. She cared.

Gen. William Moore, USAF (Ret.)

Chairman, Nashville Airport Authority

"The first thing we need to do is have faith in the human being. The help you can give an unfortunate person to get on their own feet and take control of their lives is a hell of a lot more benefit to them than any amount of money you can give."

PSD: *What was it like to win the award for Nashvillian of the Year?*

WM: It was quite an honor and one that I accept with a great deal of humility. Someone once wrote that "no man is an island." When I think of all that is represented in Nashvillian of the Year, it transcends Bill Moore. I am grateful for the support of a lot of people and the accomplishments of others, for which I am being awarded. I am very proud of this community. I have lived here now for 17 years, long enough to see Nashville grow and achieve. More and more people are taking greater pride in what Nashville represents and are working to make it better. One of the things that brought me to Nashville when I retired from the Air Force was that the values of this community are representative of my own.

PSD: *There seems to be an intangible special feeling with regard to this community.*

WM: I agree that there's magic here. I sensed it years ago before this community was anything like what it is today.

PSD: *How did you end up running an airport?*

WM: Aviation was my whole life in the military. I ended up out here because the Chairman of the Airport Authority, Bob Matthews, and Pat Wilson were looking for somebody to run this airport. They called me up one day and asked if we could talk. We talked over a three week period, and I decided to accept because the job is challenging and it is a dynamic operation. The whole aviation industry is dynamic, especially the commercial aviation operation.

PSD: *What is the most challenging part of the job?*

WM: Getting Nashville the airport service it needs to sustain our growth and to support our community. Also, convincing the airlines that we are a strong aviation market that is

worth an investment, for any kind of business. Nashville is a wonderful place to live and raise children.

PSD: *How did you feel when American Airlines pulled back its hub operation and direct flights to London?*

WM: Very regretful. I felt then — and still feel — that we are a good marketplace for international operations. We exceeded all of our parameters in terms of the application that we submitted to the Department of Transportation. We exceeded load factors by a considerable amount, but according to American, they were not filling enough of the premium seats. So the flight was not producing the yield that they needed.

PSD: *Do you think they might have acted prematurely?*

WM: Yes. Normally, you could expect at least a couple of years for an international route to fully develop, but they pulled out of this one after sixteen months. American was trying to provide maximum return to their shareholders so they decided to consolidate. They stated that, "The problem is not Nashville, it is American." I can't quarrel with their business decisions, but I can quarrel with the fact that I think it was premature.

PSD: *The lack of corporate patience seems due to the constant concern with shareholder profits.*

WM: I think so. We are a fast-paced society. Some years ago, it seems our corporate organizations went to a quarter-by-quarter bottom line, as an indication of how strong they were. In so doing, long-range planning — charting your course of action and sticking to it — sort of went out the window.

PSD: *Yet isn't that long-range paradigm the only way to achieve any real results?*

WM: I have long felt that putting so much emphasis, quarter by quarter, on the bottom line is really not the best way to judge what is happening because it is happening too fast. I suppose this is driven to some degree by the way earnings are reported in the stock market. If, in one quarter, your earnings don't reach expectations, then your stock falls.

PSD: *There seems to be more emphasis lately on safety issues. The FAA has taken a lot of heat.*

WM: Commercial aviation is safe, in my view, understanding that everything is relative. You are going to have exceptions to the rule. So no matter how safe aviation is, you will always have accidents. When you have a catastrophic incident with an airplane, it gets everybody's attention because they can see themselves sitting in one of those seats. People wonder if the accident could have been prevented. It only takes one thing to go wrong, like in the ValuJet crash, to have an accident.

PSD: *How many years were you in the service?*

WM: I was on active duty for 35 years and spent 4 more years in the reserves. So I really spent my whole life in the military.

PSD: *Did Vietnam veterans get a bad deal?*

WM: I believe they were the first group in history that ever came home from war and were disrespected. And this was a terrible thing because these people did nothing but what their country had asked them to do. In some areas, a Vietnam veteran had a hard time just getting a job. I hope we are over that now. But the short answer to your question is that they were badly treated.

PSD: *How would you define success?*

WM: Success for me personally is peace of mind. It is not about material things, though everybody, including myself, wants to have material things. People want comfortable lives for themselves and their families. If you can attain that with the peace of mind that you have been true to yourself, that you have accomplished at least a good percentage of your goals, and if you have satisfaction in whatever you are doing, that to me is success.

PSD: *Are you a person that goes on gut feelings?*

WM: I have learned over the years that my first instincts are usually right. There is something about the human makeup that pulls a lot of information and data together, and rings the bell without you knowing it. I learned in the military that every man can do more than he thinks he can do.

PSD: *What advice would you give a young person to better cultivate a sense of self in order to be successful as you define it?*

WM: I think the most important attribute that a person can have is integrity, because a person without integrity doesn't know who he is, nor does anybody else.

Anyone can accomplish 'something'. But if you are going to accomplish more, you have to develop relationships. You have to work with others. If you have enough integrity to merit the trust of others, you can start leading them to do things that need to be done. When you undertake a task, you commit yourself to that task and you meet your commitment. That way, you can earn trust as an honest, whole person, and demonstrate reliability so that others are willing to follow your lead.

Along with that, you have to develop knowledge. You have to understand what you are doing, and as much as possible, the world around you. That doesn't mean you have to compromise your own values to exist in an environment. If you can demonstrate your values under any conditions, then you can successfully exist in any environment.

PSD: *You do a lot of charity work. What do*

we need to do as a society for the underprivileged?

WM: The first thing we need to do is have faith in the human being. The help you can give an unfortunate person to get on their own feet and take control of their lives is a hell of a lot more benefit to them than any amount of money you can give.

PSD: *The gift of self-esteem?*

WM: The unfortunate or the indigent person has to have two things. The first is assistance in learning who he is, where he is, what is possible, and how to do it. The second is enough money to sustain him through this process. He has to be brought to the point where he can see there is more to life, so he can get some enjoyment out of what he can do. If we can accomplish something like that, we could really do a lot to help these unfortunate people.

PSD: *Why do you do a lot of charity work?*

WM: If you have the ability to do something and there is a need out there, you just need to get involved. You need to participate in a constructive way, not like a gadfly. I really enjoy it because I feel like it is accomplishing something. It is a contribution that I can make to the community. I love being part of a community, after so many years of being transient through many communities where you never stopped long enough to be a real part of it.

This is my home. I want it to be as good as it can be and I want to contribute what I can to make it that way.

PSD: *Who influenced you to think so outwardly?*

WM: My parents. They were very strong on values and generally devoted to their children, all six of us. They provided a good home, a good education, a good sense of values, and taught us to be honest. They were very careful how they raised their children, demanding that we use the right kind of language and respect our elders.

PSD: *What advice would you give someone who had just become a parent?*

WM: I would say that you have taken on a responsibility that is as important as any that you have. A father's responsibility to his children is to be sensitive to them, know what they are doing, and help them to develop their instincts. Place a lot of importance on being a good role model, which is especially hard when a child spends a good portion of the day in child care. Many kids come home to an empty house and are left unsupervised for long periods of time. I think that hurts the child and the family. Fatherhood has to be taken very, very, seriously.

PSD: *Did you have any children?*

WM: I have one daughter that I am very proud of, and she has a little boy that she adopted. He is a great young fellow. Being a grandfather is a lot easier than being a parent.

PSD: *Was it a difficult transition to be a commander of men by day and a parent to a little girl by night?*

WM: Actually, it was not at all difficult. I think it depends on what type of person you are, and the type of commander you are. I have seen some commanders who were simply pompous asses, the type who might come home and try to be like a king in his own household. Fortunately they were in the minority.

A man does not have to be a martinet. He does not have to be pompous. He does not have to do anything except use good judgment and common sense, and be sensitive to people. The guy who wants to have unquestioned authority is going to lose a lot of feedback from his people, and he is going to make mistakes because he is not that smart. I always thought that leadership is not about ordering people around, it's about making people want to do what needs to be done.

PSD: *How do you take time to regenerate?*
WM: I like to read. When I was a youngster, I was an avid reader. I read everything in sight. Television is an instrument that takes all the rest of us for idiots. I don't really take any quiet time these days. I really think that what I am today is just what I am.

PSD: *What brings you the most pleasure?*
WM: So many things bring me pleasure, I think I may be really easy to please. First of all, there's my family, including my daughter and her child. I get more of a charge out of that than anything else. Number two is my job. I really love it. I think the two worst things that a man could have is a wife he didn't like and a job he didn't like. I have never had either, thank the Lord.

PSD: *Are you a spiritual man?*
WM: I don't really know how spiritual matters might affect other people, but I can talk about how they affect me. To me, spirituality is the feeling that there is a greater presence. Various religions call that presence different things. I call it God, that is almighty and is governing in both a benevolent and autocratic way. I believe each of us are given some talents and an opportunity to use those talents. Then it is left up to us how to do it, and how to achieve the benefits that are available.

PSD: *How would you like to be remembered?*
WM: If you were to sum it all up in one word, I would like to be remembered as a patriot, because I believe in this country. I have fought in three wars. To me, the meaning of patriot takes in so many attributes. General MacArthur defined it as well as anybody, "Duty, Honor, Country." Country is much more than land and territory, it's about values, family, the things a man works for. So if I am known as a patriot, that would be a very satisfactory definition.

Carol Orsborn

Author

"I believe that we have defined human potential wrongly. The western paradigm tends to think of human potential as the will and drive to achieve a goal. But it leaves out the potential to daydream, to love, to cry, and to feel compassion for others. That, to me, is the true human potential."

PSD: *How did you get involved in writing books?*

CO: I have loved writing all my life. I never thought I would be in a position where I would be able to get a book published, because the odds are so greatly against you. What happened, though, is that I had this incredible pressure building up in me while I was running a business in San Francisco where we had hundreds of clients over a 20 year period. I began to see trends and things that all of our clients were doing that were really making them miserable and creating unnecessary stress. Sometimes I could talk to them about it, but most of the time I couldn't. The wonderful thing about being a consultant is that you get a bird's eye view of a whole lot of industries and lives, and you start to see patterns.

I realized there were a lot of people I couldn't talk to. My job was to help them market their companies, not have them look at their spiritual beliefs. So I decided to release the pressure building up inside me by writing my ideas down. That was really the beginning of my serious career as a writer, although I realize that a whole book came before that.

PSD: *Was that* Enough is Enough*?*

CO: Yes, that was my 15 minutes of fame and it was really what made all the other things possible. That book came out of my founding the group 'Overachievers Anonymous'. You see, I had been one of those unhealthy business people I was just talking about who have really destructive beliefs. I had been stressed out and anxious, with a really poor concept of success which was killing me. I had convinced my husband, Dan, who was a partner in the business, to make really huge changes in our business — to get off that fast track where we were worried what other people thought about what we were doing. We were going to reclaim our own inner experience, instead of being successful in society's terms. We made some fair-ly radical changes. We moved from a big house to a small one, got rid of our fancy cars, pulled our kids out of private schools, and just cut back to bare bones. We cut our staff from 23 people to just 7 so that we could get some quality back into our lives. And we did it all by choice.

PSD: *How did that go over with your business peers?*

CO: The rumors started to circulate that we were in trouble because we had downsized. In defense, I started a little group called 'Overachievers Anonymous' for people who were already too busy, so the group would never meet. We were founded on a platform of no meetings, no fund-raisers, and no classes, in perpetuity. The *New York Times* got hold of this information and did a feature on me, which led to a whole bunch of other press. I was on the *Today* show, I sold the movie rights to my life, and I went out on the lecture circuit. This all went on for about a year, and while it was an exciting year, it was also an awful year. Though I was sincere about wanting to simplify my life, every success fantasy imaginable just dropped on me, and I fell for them all — hook, line and sinker.

PSD: *You took some time between books.*

CO: It took me 7 years between that first book and the second one, because I did a very courageous thing and stepped off the fast-track. There is really something seductive and unhealthy in succumbing to fame if it is not inwardly driven. I found that everyone had agendas for me, and I was trying to please them all. I ended up dealing my life away in little pieces until I was empty again, and when I realized I was empty, I got back off the fast-track.

PSD: *What was the initial catalyst that made you change directions when you had so submerged yourself in pursuit of the American dream?*

CO: I had this idea that there was something higher on the human scale than coping. If you look up 'coping' in the dictionary, it means 'to hold your own in a battle.' I am just a stubborn son-of-a-gun and I wanted to have joy, I wanted to have freedom, and I wanted to have fun. I also wanted to have enough time and space to be of service to the community. I felt as if I had created this creature that needed feeding, and I just didn't want to feed it. I had been really hungry for freedom, and even if people thought that we had it all, I really didn't have what I wanted.

PSD: *You were unfulfilled and unhappy?*
CO: Happiness doesn't work for me as a concept because I feel there is something much higher up the scale than happiness.

PSD: *What would you call that high point?*
CO: I call it 'wholeness'. I believe that we have defined human potential wrongly. The western paradigm tends to think of human potential as the will and drive to achieve a goal. But it leaves out the potential to daydream, to love, to cry, and to feel compassion for others. That, to me, is the true human potential. There is a lot of emphasis right now on 'exceptionalism' and the perfection of human capabilities to solve all of our problems.

PSD: *You are currently enrolled at Vanderbilt's Divinity School.*
CO: Yes, because I feel that if human beings rely only on direct communication to God and the Divine, and the perfection of self-knowledge, devoid of any kind of discipline or some grounded community of tradition, it is possible to go wrong — even if you are well-meaning. A lot of times, people define spirituality as what makes them feel good, so in the short-term, they may come up with some decisions and turn them into teachings. They may integrate those teachings into their lives or share them with other people

without really having the benefit of knowing that there is a history of implications with those thoughts, and eventually, that well may run dry.

PSD: *Regardless of what path you take, there will still be life with all its suffering and inherent problems. We cannot control everything, no matter what our form of spiritual practice.*
CO: That has been my experience. When we were in California, everybody had direct and wonderful relationships with God, but you couldn't borrow a cup of sugar from your next-door neighbor. Nobody was ever home — they were always out there competing and proving themselves. When we visited here for the first time, we thought that people had this incredibly rich sense of community, that people really cared about one another.

PSD: *Nashville is truly a friendly town.*
CO: I was a bit suspicious at first. The funny thing about Nashville is that one of the first things people ask you is, "What church do you go to?" You don't hear that question very often in California. People might ask, "What is your sign?" but they wouldn't ask what church you go to. (She laughs)

PSD: *Talk about your books a little.*
CO: My books had really represented eclectic spirituality. I had a lot of Zen stories, Sufi stories, stories from our Native-American culture, but there was a huge hole — I had no Christian and Jewish stories. I knew what I didn't know, so I was afraid to quote something out of context. That is what drew me to divinity school. I wanted to be able to include some stories about Jesus and rabbis to round things off a bit.

PSD: *According to what you have learned, how does a person improve the quality of his life?*
CO: The paradigm shift is really quite simple. For many people, just hearing the con-

114

cepts is enough for them to shift their whole lives. The Western paradigm says that the goal is the most important thing and you should sacrifice everything to achieve the goal. So you push through your feelings, you push through your fears, you don't stop to take care of yourself or your family or your concerns or your values. You just get to the goal. But there's another model.

PSD: *What was the model for your own breakthrough?*
CO: My big breakthrough came from the I-Ching, which is a 3,000-year-old book of wisdom from China. It held a completely different model of success, which I found to match my personal experience very closely. In this philosophy, you pay attention to the growth and character of your spirit; your greatest success comes as a by-product of that. It turns the Western paradigm totally upside-down. People who hear this will experiment with nurturing their spirit and taking time for love. Ironically, they become more successful — with less effort. But there is a caveat, in that they judge success by a whole new definition.

PSD: *So success is not achievement-oriented.*
CO: Achievement can come as a by-product. If people really get in touch with their inner-most, authentic impulses, in my view, that is where the unfolding of the Divine occurs. Generally, people who are in that space want to make a contribution. There are also people who say they have broken through to that inner place and withdraw to go live on a mountainside or in a cave. The I-Ching would say that is fine — that is one path — but it can also be fairly self-indulgent. That is one reason I love the Jewish tradition. Basically, the Jewish tradition teaches that when you are into that special kind of place, you really want to make a contribution. You want to be merciful, to be just, and to do what is good and what is right.

PSD: *So the model you are describing is for one's energy or love to be flowing outward.*
CO: There is a balance, because I know people who give and give and give, but they mostly do it for the external strokes. I don't think it's a matter of how much time and energy you are putting out in the world, as much as it is the source of your motivation. I am probably as busy and effective now as I used to be, but I don't feel drained or exhausted. It seems the more I do, the more excited I get. It is inner and Divinely directed, it is being in the flow.

PSD: *How does one get more in touch with that inner element?*
CO: I am going to say something really strange. I would have said before that if you are way out of balance and took some time to nurture yourself, like taking a walk in nature, you would replenish yourself. While that might be true for many people, I have some new advice, because to tell those who have been in the rat race for so long to just stop and collect themselves doesn't really cut it. I have noticed something different that is also very close to the Jewish tradition. I would say to go ahead and act like your higher self, start giving to your community, make a contribution to others, pretend like you are caring, pretend like you are loving.

PSD: *So in an odd sort of way, start from the outside-in. Assume the posture of one in alignment.*
CO: These might be two extremes, but different personalities and spiritual orientations require different ways.

PSD: *Don't you still need to get quiet?*
CO: Well, I certainly do. But I know some people who thrive on going, going, going, and giving to the community. They seem frazzled, but they are sacrificing to society to make a contribution. Even if they have lost their peace of mind.

PSD: *Is that healthy? I'm not so sure that it is, because you owe it to yourself and to the world to be the healthiest 'you' possible. What you're describing seems more like martyrdom.*
CO: I would agree. Being in the middle is an ideal. The way balance works is at various points of the day or week, different things call to us. Balance is sequential. The *I-Ching* says, "Even moderation needs moderation." Our lives need seasoning. I was saying before that happiness and peace are not the highest states for me. I prefer a sense of the bitter-sweet and the dynamic tension. I like the struggle. I can't operate in the world and see the pain in it, the bombings, people starving, and then think about happiness and peace as being the ultimate goal. To me, it is about asking the big questions and feeling the big feelings, including joy, peace, and happiness. But not exclusively.

PSD: *You need to be present and experience the world.*
CO: I would say that I want to be fully alive.

PSD: *How would you define success?*
CO: Far from the normal definition! What I strive for is to feel that I have a faithful relationship to God. If I am in a faithful relationship to God, then it doesn't matter what is going on in my life. I feel like I am doing what I ought to be doing, what I should be doing, or the very best that is possible for me at any given time. And that is enough.

PSD: *So it is completely within?*
CO: (She laughs.) If you think that God is within.

PSD: *You're saying that success is measured by inner parameters, not the daily stock exchange numbers. Is it intuitive?*
CO: If I am in right relationship, do I feel it intuitively? Yes! But the word Grace has to come into this somehow. Is that an external or an internal word?

PSD: *I don't think you can define it.*
CO: Some people confuse good psychology with good spirituality. A psychologically healthy person is individuated. They have somehow found who they are apart from other people. Spirituality is about surrendering to the Divine, and the two things have to go on simultaneously, which makes for an incredible paradox. That is why I say it is dynamic tension. I would say that being both psychologically and spiritually balanced are my goals. If I am both of those things, then I am going to have a rich connection to community. I am going to be serving and making a contribution on a level that is appropriate with my abilities.

PSD: *It's important for you to give something back?*
CO: I think it is key. People who don't give back may be spiritually healthy or psychologically healthy, but probably not both. My most basic level of giving is ordinary kindness, just to my family and the people who cross my path. I get disillusioned with people who become famous for their spirituality, but are grouchy when you meet them. The way a lot of my books have been written, you could say I have been in the soul-saving business. I have really wanted to get my books in as many hands as possible, especially business people at the top of their companies. Maybe they would treat their employees better as a result, and could show that it is feasible to have an element of spirituality in the workplace.

PSD: *There is a bit of the missionary in you.*
CO: There has been, and I have devoted almost 10 years in that martyred way we spoke of earlier, though I don't regret it. Quite honestly, I see that there has to be some ego involved. But it has become less important for me to stroke my ego than to have my freedom. I would like to be able to write books that take more risks. I would like to live my

life in such a way that if I can't make a living selling my spiritual ideas, then I would be just as happy to work in public relations.

PSD: *What advice would you offer young people to deepen their life experience?*
CO: Being young is the time to dream big and to put your muscle power behind it. Don't be afraid to really go at it. At the beginning, there is always a lot of excitement and adrenalin. You need to give your life a kick-start and go after a profession and a way to contribute. Keep those high-minded books you read in college on the bookshelf. Have the humility and the wisdom to let yourself be in conflict. Allow yourself to be in dynamic tension. Realize the paradox. Let yourself be in a struggle about things.

PSD: *How important is integrity?*
CO: I think it is everything. Integrity really means wholeness. If you are going to be whole, then you are going to be fully alive. You will be aware of your capacity for joy and sorrow. You are going to be aware of both the conflict and the peace. When you are out of integrity, you are blocking something that doesn't need to be blocked.

PSD: *What is your parental philosophy?*
CO: Give your kids lots of love, know that you are going to make lots of mistakes, and hope there is more love than mistakes. I have also learned to apologize a lot. I didn't grow up in a family where I was ever apologized to. I have realized that apologies are very empowering and honest. All I can really be is honest. I share as much as possible about what is going on inside me. If I am relating to my child in a repressive way out of fear, I may not be able to stop, but I can communicate this to my child if I am aware of it.

PSD: *There is something happening here in Nashville in terms of a convergence of some sort of progressive energy.*

CO: I recently started an 'Inner Excellence Round-Table' and 45 people showed up for the last one. There is a sweetness to life here. The size of the community has a lot to do with it. You can know people with similar interests and bump into them from time to time around town. We seem so grateful for each other. The kindness and sweetness is somehow built into the fabric of this community. When we come here from New York or California with our attitudes, it seems to soften us up.

PSD: *What brings you the most joy?*
CO: The very first thing I discovered when I moved here is still my favorite – a walk around Radnor Lake. I prefer to walk it alone, it really is my sacred time.

PSD: *I believe that lake has some magic.*
CO: There is something going on there. Part of it is that people greet you there as you walk. That blows my mind. I am so used to living in places where you don't make eye contact and greet one another. At Radnor, the ritual is to gently nod, say hello, and then pass on by. You might even see someone a second time around, and by then, you have a relationship going. (She laughs.) I really like to be alone there. It is really important for me to be able to walk somewhere and Radnor is close by, it is free, it is gentle, and it is magnificent. One of my most exciting experiences since I've been in Nashville was the day they lined the trails with recycled Christmas trees. Here in the middle of winter was this path of fragrant, green Christmas tree needles. I could feel everyone's joy. I was so thrilled, I cried.

PSD: *How would you like to be remembered?*
CO: I solved that issue when I wrote my first book. I remember thinking that it would be nice to be immortal and have something live on after I departed. I remembered the

books in the trunk of my car and thought, 'I don't have to do anything else the rest of my life. (She laughs.) My greatest contribution will end up being my children. It is so important to be present and participate in your children's life. I believe in evolution. If you actively participate in your children's lives, they can look at your strengths and weaknesses and build on them, showing some improvement for the next generation. I feel like I have done my piece, and now the pressure is off. There is some Grace there.

PSD: *What does the word 'Grace' mean to you?*
CO: It is a sense of not being in 'this' alone. That there is Divine support, and guidance and gifts that are beyond what I may deserve or have merited. When I was on the fast-track, it seemed like the more I gave, the less I got back. It felt like diminishing returns all the time. Since I made the shift and have been practicing a new paradigm over the past ten years, it feels as if that whole ratio is completely turned upside-down. Now, whatever it is I do is met by energy, support, and love beyond what I had imagined for myself.

PSD: *One could call Grace God, even though it transcends language and explanation.*
CO: I call it God because I finally just surrendered.

Henry Ponder, Ph.D

President, National Association for Equal Opportunity and Higher Education

"To care is the thing. To care about the plight of people who are in some difficulty, people suffering from AIDS, people who are starving in Africa. I would like to believe that any time a human being hurts, I hurt."

PSD: *What is the greatest challenge facing today's universities?*

HP: The university is a part of the whole cosmos of higher education, which is suffering from a loss of prestige and importance in the eyes of the public. The general public has been turned off to higher education. They think we are all fat cats who are making a lot of money and doing very little. When you look at what some of our graduates are doing, it gives cause for that. I think we have to do something to change that.

PSD: *Then you have the fierce competition for students and resources.*

HP: Public institutions are going to corporations and foundations asking for funds, where they used to go to state government. I think one of the challenges for private institutions will be getting the state to support them.

PSD: *Is the lack of education in our society alarming to you?*

HP: We tend to take it for granted that 'everybody can get an education.' You don't even think about supporting it, because it is just there. We have to let the general public know that if we are going to constantly maintain our leadership in the world, then we are going to have to have an educated population and put more money into our institutions — all the way from kindergarten through graduate school — so that they can perform.

We have to decide that if "NFL Yes" will get the Oilers here, then we need to have signs in our yard that say "Education Yes!" We have to become as emotional about education as the people who wanted to bring the Oilers here. Educators feel that it is not professional to do this sort of thing, but I feel we are going to have to.

PSD: *It can no longer be a passive approach.*

HP: It can't be, not any more. We've gone that route too long.

PSD: *Aren't government priorities distorted in terms of commitment to education?*

HP: The only reason that leadership is apathetic about education is because they don't have to worry about their voters. You can't make an issue out of education and cause somebody to get kicked out of Congress.

This is what I was saying about having to start a grass-roots movement. Any politician who was against the Oilers was in trouble. What we have to do is let every politician know that if they are not strongly for education, then we will see them next time at the polls. The people who build Stealth bombers scare the world by saying, "If we don't have these things, something really bad is going to happen to us." We need to tell our congressmen that we don't need that many bombers. What we really need is some scholarships to make it possible for talented kids to go to school. We need to make it possible for every youngster who finishes high school with a B average, and who stays out of trouble, to go to college free. Now that is worth something. Try that today and politicians would probably laugh at you. But if we can get enough people emotional about it, politicians will do it.

PSD: *You see our leadership as reactionary rather than visionary.*

HP: That is correct.

PSD: *What do you think of the idea of giving a free college education in exchange for a few years of community service corps work?*

HP: I have no problem with that. In fact, I think it would be a great idea. However, if you educate your population, you get your money back in taxes anyway. A person who finishes college and gets a Masters degree pays much more in taxes then someone who has just finished high school. So it is not necessary to have that service corps in terms of recouping the money. The good thing about the service idea is it is important for youngsters to know they have to give something back for this free education. Very few college graduates are burdens on society. They are tax payers rather than tax receivers.

PSD: *You recently retired as president of Fisk University. Were there any challenges unique to Fisk?*

HP: It is the same for any of the small, private liberal arts schools. It is money. In our society, we have come to accept as fact that the larger the institution, the better it is. So when you say you only have nine hundred students, people think you cannot be doing very much. Which is not true, because that is where you can really give students more attention.

PSD: *Talk about your new job.*

HP: This year, I became the president of the National Association For Equal Opportunity and Higher Education, which is the umbrella organization for 117 African-American colleges and universities.

In that role, I will be a spokesperson for a subset of higher education where it pertains to African-Americans. However, I want to broaden my role to talk about all of higher education. It is always necessary to have subsets, because what is good for one is not always good for the other. So you need to be there to protect the integrity of different organizations, like Hispanic and Native American groups. We need to be sure that we are all working together for the same cause, and that cause is to improve higher education for the masses of this country.

PSD: *What a great job. Are you excited?*

HP: Very excited. I will do a lot of work with Congress trying to get bills passed. You have to make them understand that education is high on the agenda. Just imagine if we organized the alumni of all of the colleges and universities of this country and had them flood Washington, saying we need to do more for higher education.

PSD: *Are you the kind of person who needs new challenges?*

HP: Not really. I just enjoy being active. I don't have to have a challenge. I don't even look at my job as a challenge. When I came to Fisk, I looked at it as a job I thought I would enjoy, and I did. I am going to this new position not because it is a challenge, but because I think I will enjoy doing the job that needs to be done — and I have some ideas on what needs to be done. That ought to be enough to keep the adrenalin flowing.

PSD: *You stay very focused.*

HP: One of the problems with society today is we are not very focused. If we decide what the priorities are, and zero in on those, you will get farther than if you are all over the place.

Here's an example. This trash can here, as I clean out my office, is full of letters from charitable organizations asking for donations. There are probably two or three hundred letters just from the first six months of this year. All of them are good causes, there is no question about it. I wish I had enough money for all of them. Now I could lose my focus and try to do something for all of them — the scatter-gun approach — and not accomplishing much of anything. I want to concentrate instead on something for the NAFEO that is really good. That does not mean I will not be a good citizen or will stop going to church or participating in the PTA. But I will put most of my energy into my job and only help with these other things when and where I can.

PSD: *Staying focused and accomplish one thing at a time is a good model for young people.*

HP: The more you accomplish, the more chances you will have to do many things. Every time you succeed, someone is going to ask you to do something else. Then you get more choices. But always choose something you can focus on. Bring that to conclusion, then move on to something else.

PSD: *Talk about discipline.*
HP:　What keeps most people from succeeding is they don't have the discipline to stay with it until they get it done. It is too easy to go watch television or read a newspaper or go have lunch. You know, every time you sit down to work the gremlins come out of the wall with all kinds of distractions.

If people have discipline, they will be more successful. I think that any youngster, as long as he wasn't dropped on his head as a baby, can graduate from high school if he has the discipline to do it. And I think that every youngster can graduate from college with discipline.

PSD: *When one is disciplined, it seems to permeate every area of your life.*
HP:　Definitely. You are either disciplined or you're not. Discipline is hard work. You will only get gratification from discipline if you are a disciplined person.

PSD: *How can one cultivate discipline?*
HP:　I don't think it is inherited, it is an acquired trait. You have to come to a realization at some point that if you are going to be successful, you are going to have to stick with it until you get it done. Start out with something you like to do. Most of the management manuals will tell you to pick something that will produce quick results, to give you enthusiasm and confidence. Some youngsters can ponder (he laughs) — no pun intended — a math problem for two or three hours and enjoy it. Then when they get the answer there is an "Ahhh!" You have to then think, 'If I put in that kind of work in English, maybe I will get the same results.' Discipline becomes habit. Most people are unhappy with an undisciplined life.

PSD: *You have an interesting view as it regards success. You like to use the term 'effective'.*

HP:　Most people will ascribe success to you when something is accomplished. I don't start out trying to be successful. 'Effective' means you get the job done, whatever that job is, even though people might not always consider you successful. You must have an inner satisfaction in getting it done. To be effective means that you have set some goals, you have worked at them, you got some people to buy into them, and you were effective in bringing them about. Perhaps later on, people will judge you as successful. If you start out trying to be successful, you may stop short of your goal, and history will show that to be unsuccessful. I think that it is poor management for a person to start out by saying "I want to be successful." It is better to start out thinking "I want to be effective."

PSD: *This paradigm seems based more on inner validation, whereas success is more of a perception from outside.*
HP:　That's right, and I know when I have been effective. I would like everyone to like me and see me as successful, but if I think I have been effective, I can live with that. I will listen to your feedback because I may have thought I was effective, but upon hearing you, realize that I could be even more effective. I listen, I let other people have their say, then I pick and choose those things I can use to benefit my life.

PSD: *What works for you in terms of leadership?*
HP:　I let people know up front that I have confidence in them. Then I give them the responsibility and hold them accountable. I don't embarrass people if I disagree with them. The real thing in leadership is not to embarrass your people, and keep showing you have confidence in them. When you do have to let someone go, do it with the same grace as when you praise someone. Respect has to be there.

PSD: *Did you raise your children the same way?*

HP: I tried to. My office staff knew if my kids called to put them through. My family always came first, and I made sure my two daughters understood that. Anything that they wanted to deal with, I was never too busy for. My daughter recently told me how much she appreciated this and how important it is to a child's sense of security. I always tried to convey to my children that 'You are somebody, and I expect you to act like somebody.'

PSD: *This is a form of success.*

HP: I suppose so. All that I went through with my daughters suddenly jumped into perspective when she said, "Daddy, you don't know how much security it gave me knowing that I could get a hold of you anytime I called you." I was just doing the best I can. There is no roadmap for being a successful parent. When she said that, the effective nature of what I did came through.

PSD: *Was that one of the more beautiful, priceless moments of your life?*

HP: You cannot put a price on what it felt like to hear that from a grown woman.

PSD: *There is a magical feeling to those kinds of personal moments that transcends so much of what we do.*

HP: That's what is so important to me. That is where all of my feelings of being effective come to fruition. It lifts you up and you think, 'Hey, I really did something right.'

PSD: *These are the moments we will take with us to the other side as we take our last breath on this plane of existence.*

HP: If you remember, I think it was Vassar College who had invited Barbara Bush to be the commencement speaker and some students demonstrated because they said she had not accomplished anything — she was just the wife of the President. One of the state-ments she made was, "I will tell you right now that twenty years from now, or at retirement, you will never regret the times you did not go the office. But you will regret all the times you did not spend with your family and kids."

That is what I am talking about. There are things you cannot undo once you have screwed them up. If you don't raise your kids right from the ages one through five, you don't get a second chance. With your job, you get a second chance every day. Family is tremendously important, and it's the most important thing in my life.

PSD: *I hear in your words the acknowledgement of personal responsibility, in choosing to bring life into this world.*

HP: This is part of what's missing today. Kids don't believe that their parents love them or were happy when they were born. My kids have never complained about the discipline I unfolded on them because it helped mold them.

PSD: *Was love the great motivation in terms of being a parent?*

HP: A tremendous motivation, and you cannot fool your children. They know when it is genuine and when it isn't. That is part of the problem in our education system. Teachers have ceased to love children, who can tell when a teacher is just tolerating them. Little things like putting your arm around a kid and saying, "You are doing all right today" go so far. Most kids don't get hugged anymore.

PSD: *So often, love is the missing ingredient.*

HP: Love is the missing ingredient, the magical thing. That is what you need.

PSD: *What was it like for you during the 1960s with all the civil rights turbulence?*

HP: I was a part of it and tried to give leadership to the movement without being an

active participant. My thinking was that someone had to be in the background trying to get
things done.

PSD: *Even though they were the worst of
times for civil rights, there was beauty in the
pro-activity, the passion, the levels of involvement.*

HP: They were beautiful indeed. Go back
to what we talked about earlier. The reason
politicians don't do things is because people
are not moved. Politicians did not want to
change things back then, but when they saw
people marching in the streets, they had to
act. That is what democracy is all about. I
would like educators to come forth with that
kind of passion, saying we are going to sit in
the legislature until a bill is appropriated for
education. If all of the teachers moved into
Washington, things would change. We are
ripe for the right leader.

PSD: *How would you like to remembered?*

HP: I would like to be remembered as
someone who cares. You can add whatever
you like after that. I care about people, I care
about Fisk, I care about the maintenance
workers who clean this office. I care about
everybody. As Kipling said, "Walk with kings
and lose the common touch." You might go
to a party with President Clinton, but you
have to understand that the man who cleans
up this office is also somebody.

To care is the thing. To care about the plight
of people who are in some difficulty, people
suffering from AIDS, people who are starving
in Africa. I would like to believe that any time
a human being hurts, I hurt. Even if I don't
know them.

Frances Preston

President & CEO, Broadcast Music International

**"It is a genuine love of people and God that is my center.
It makes for a happy life."**

PSD: *You're the President and CEO of BMI. How did you end up in that seat?*

FP: Hard work and long hours. I gave up a lot of my personal life. Determination, drive, involvement, being enthusiastic, loving what I do. Basically, that sums it up.

PSD: *How many years have you been at it?*

FP: I have been with BMI about 38 years.

PSD: *Obviously an overnight success.*

FP: (She laughs.) I worked my way up through the ranks. I started out opening BMI's first office in Nashville and I was just a one-person office for a year. Then I had a secretary and built from there. I started out with just Nashville as my territory, and grew it into everything south of the Mason-Dixon line.

PSD: *As a woman in upper level management, you were a pioneer of sorts.*

FP: When I started in the music business 38 years ago, there were no women executives in the music industry in Nashville. The Governor at the time used me as an example. There were some women who were vice-presidents or board members of companies because they had inherited stock. Our New York office had two women, because the President of BMI at that time strongly believed in us.

There were many doors to open. If I had not succeeded, then I don't think it would have been quite as easy for women to come along. The doors of opportunity might have been closed if I had failed.

PSD: *You have a sense of satisfaction in seeing this.*

FP: When you see that other women have come along and are being accepted in executive positions, you feel like you have accomplished something and it does give you a sense of satisfaction. It makes you feel proud when you see them succeed.

PSD: *Do you feel any extra pressure being the first woman who is President and CEO of BMI, or just the normal pressure of being on top where the buck stops?*

FP: All along, I never thought of myself as a woman in business, but as a businessperson instead. I took this job as 'head of the Nashville office', not as a 'woman who was head of the Nashville office'. You were often reminded by others as you were put on boards that you were the first woman on the board. People would say, "Let's come to order, gentlemen. Excuse me, gentlemen and lady."

PSD: *So you were just a hard-working executive trying to build an organization.*

FP: When I took over as President of BMI 10 years ago, my thought was, 'I have to make it happen.' It had nothing to do with being a woman. I also never demanded things because I was a woman. I don't think anyone ever heard me say, 'I am not treated like a male executive because I am a woman.' Now that could be because I worked for a company that believed in women. I believed in women's rights, but I also believed that you had to work for what you got. There were many women who believed that being an executive meant you came in at nine and left at five and you had an expense account.

Any man that I ever saw in my life who was successful never had a nine-to-five pattern. Anybody who is successful lives and breathes their job. My father had long hours, as did my grandfather. That's what I saw growing up. So when I saw people thinking an executive job meant they didn't have to pour coffee anymore, those sort of things aggravated me because I did believe in women's rights and equal pay for equal work. But some of the excuses I heard made me angry. Besides, I poured coffee all the time for my own employees.

PSD: *So the whole woman executive thing was externally projected onto you. It was not something you dwelled on.*

FP: Exactly. I knew that being an executive was hard work.

PSD: *Did your father have a big influence on you?*

FP: Yes, he did, and my mother did, too. My mother was a homemaker but she was very driven. If she was in the Garden Club, she had to be President of the Garden Club, or President of the PTA. I guess it was part of our German background because my grandparents and great-grandparents were all hard-working people. It was a way of life we were brought up with as children.

PSD: *How would you define success?*

FP: Success is usually what other people feel that you have. I don't know if you ever feel successful inside because you are always striving to do more. So what you gauge as successful and what other people on the outside gauge as successful may be two different things.

PSD: *What brings you inner gratification?*

FP: A lot of it comes from how people perceive you, if you have friends, and you feel that you have helped people along the way. One of the things that I enjoy most is having the cancer research lab at Vanderbilt, which is a division of the T.J. Martell Foundation, named for me.

I feel very good that I could bring funding for the lab about and make it happen. It makes me feel that I am doing something to help other people. Also, there are now-successful songwriters that I might have helped along the way. That I believed in them in the beginning gives me a sense of achievement.

Constructing this building in Nashville, my hometown, going from a one-person office to now having almost 500 people, makes you feel good. I feel I have brought something to my hometown and the music industry here. That I have three healthy children and six

grandchildren makes me feel good. It is a nice balance.

PSD: *It's interesting that everything you named is centered around helping other people.*

FP: That is where the joy is for me. I think that most people, who are what other people would call successful, feel that way because you have to love what you are doing. Mine is such a people business. I take great pride in the people that work for me and that I have helped. Now I haven't developed them, I gave them the opportunity, and they really ran with it. I think that is what success is all about.

PSD: *Helping others is where your inherent joy comes from?*

FP: I love giving, I really do. It is part of me. Sometimes it is to my own detriment, but it helps someone else or the company.

PSD: *What was your philosophy as a parent?*

FP: Many times I wonder if I was too driven, and maybe my children are not as driven as I am. Their father also worked hard and was successful. We had a good life and a fun life. My children always had responsibilities and I tried to bring them along as good citizens, to teach them about involvement in the community. My family means a lot to me. Sometimes my children would say, "I wish I had a little old mother who sat in a rocking chair and baked cookies all the time, but when you get me front row tickets at a concert, I am glad you are who you are."

PSD: *Was the balance between work and family hard to strike?*

FP: It was a hard balance to strike, I must say. My theory was that it was not the amount of time you spend with your children, but the quality of the time you gave them.

Fortunately, when I was home, I was with my

children totally. Come Friday afternoon, that was a time for my family and we were together all weekend. My children knew that on Friday afternoon we went to the lake, and we were family until Sunday night. We did that for most of their young lives. When we traveled, we took them with us. We had quality time together. We always had sit-down breakfasts and sit-down dinners where we could talk and share.

PSD: *Is discipline a key to your achievement?*
FP: Hey, listen! I'm a Virgo. Everything has its place. I always pictured my life like the old-fashioned mailboxes at the post office — lots of cubicles and everything and everybody in their own little cubicles. It would be hectic when things would start coming out of those cubicles. I always wanted everything in it's own little spot. But you have to have discipline to succeed.

PSD: *Can discipline be developed?*
FP: I think so. You know, it still bothers me that I travel constantly with a suitcase full of papers. I can never get to the bottom. Even on vacation, what could be in those papers is always on my mind. There is never a moment when I don't think about 'those papers'. (She laughs.) But I realize that if I ever got to the end of them, it would all be over.

PSD: *You've traveled a lot. Any observations?*
FP: We can be different in many ways. In India, where there is so much poverty, you see people crippling children in order for them to be able to beg and make more money. Our poorest people here are rich compared to the average people there, where they live out in open fields and gather sticks all day to light a fire for their one bowl of porridge. It is a totally different culture. In China, everybody is working and everybody seems happy.

All my travel has given me a better understanding of what we face in the world and

how unusual we are and how unusual this country is. The masses out there are not like people in the United States and Europe, where we have everything in abundance.

PSD: *What advice would you give to a young person starting out in the world?*
FP: Have patience. So many people want to jump from job to job to job. They never really learn anything that way, and never have the patience to grow within a job. Granted, if you hate what you are doing, you should move on, because no one should go to work every day and hate what they do. But you have to give a job and a company a chance.

Now I look at résumés all the time where the person has changed jobs every two years, probably for more money, but no one can say whether that person has done a good job or not because they don't have a track record. Somewhere along the line this will catch up with them. They never will accomplish anything like that.

PSD: *No footprints, so to speak.*
FP: You might gain a little knowledge about a lot of things, which is OK, but it will never get you to the top. You need to have a lot of knowledge about something. People today are so impatient. They go to work and think they should be president of the place in five years.

It is also important to think of the big picture. Everybody is usually prone to only think about their own little section, but you need to see the bigger picture. You need to think about all the things that go on in a company or a situation in order to advance and do well.

PSD: *You could apply that paradigm to being a better human being.*
FP: It's like people talking about what is going on in China and never having been there. How can you know if you haven't

actually been there? We are very prone to think we are the most important people in the world and that everything we do is right. Sure, we are big and successful in this country, but we are not the happiest people on earth because we don't appreciate what we have.

PSD: *Why do you think there is such a void in this country?*
FP: People are always wanting more, more, more, and you can't get it from the outside. I think that one of the things we are suffering from right now is a lack of appreciation in the arts — reading, good music, painting, all of that. We are missing it in a lot of the schools. I took music classes all through school even though I knew I wasn't going to be a musician. We have a generation growing up without this. If we are not training people to have an appreciation of art, theater, dance, and things that are beautiful, then who is going to pay for it? The symphony is not paid for by musicians but by people who appreciate what the musicians are doing. We are lacking a lot of that in our school systems. We are not teaching our children to read. There are kids who graduate from high school who are unable to read. Children have problems in school because they can't read and write. It is alarming if you look at the statistics, and it is happening all over this country.

PSD: *Is this due in part to a short-term gratification paradigm?*
FP: Exactly. Short-term return, just moving people along.

PSD: *What is your greatest challenge?*
FP: On the personal side, to watch my children and grandchildren continue to grow and hope that in some way I am able to help them have a good life. Trying to strike that balance. Professionally, to make sure that writers and publishers are protected and compensated for their work.

PSD: *How would you like to be remembered?*
FP: I would hope that people would think of me as open, warm, feeling, and caring. That I left a little something behind in my career. That the people I helped along the way or brought along will be helping others as I did or as they saw me do. I would like people to have a warm, fuzzy feeling when they think of me.

PSD: *Why is it so important for you to give?*
FP: It is the joy of life. It is much more exciting to buy someone a Christmas gift than it is to receive one. I remember my first job, when I was able to buy my mother and father a Christmas gift with my own money. That was the most exciting thing to me and it made my whole Christmas. It is so much more fun to give things to other people than to get things. I would much rather hand out an award than to receive one. I am almost embarrassed to receive a gift. Giving is just the greatest thing for me.

PSD: *There is a spirituality in that?*
FP: There is, there is. It is a genuine love of people and God that is my center. It makes for a happy life.

Ed Temple

Track and Field Coach, Tennessee State University and the U.S. Olympic Team

"You have to be able to accept rejection because you are always going to have setbacks and you must have the will to persevere. Some people can't accept rejection, because they think it is the end of the line, but it doesn't have to be. You have to keep on pushing. This is what athletics instills in people — what you put in is what you pull out."

PSD: *Athletics sure have changed.*

ET: I remember when Wilma Rudolph came back from the Olympics and someone wanted to give her a little black and white television set. She couldn't accept it because she wouldn't be considered an amateur anymore, even though there wasn't professional track at the time. After she had won three gold medals, Adidas gave her two pairs of track shoes. We were really happy about that. It started to change after the 1984 Olympics in Los Angeles. Carl Lewis really opened up some doors with the medals he won.

PSD: *What do you look for when you work with an athlete?*

ET: Having been in the field now for 44 years, I know that each individual is different. You can't make a racehorse out of a mule. You have to have some natural ability. You can improve a person's running, but you can't make a person fast. The individual has to have determination and perseverance, a desire to achieve.

PSD: *How would you define success?*

ET: I always thought of success as how bad <u>you</u> wanted it, and how much <u>rejection</u> you can take. I underscore both you and rejection, because you are always going to have rejection from the time you are born to the time you die. How you look at it is always up to you as an individual, though other people can help.

You have to be able to accept rejection because you are always going to have setbacks and you must have the will to persevere. Some people can't accept rejection, because they think it is the end of the line, but it doesn't have to be. You have to keep on pushing. This is what athletics instills in people — what you put in is what you pull out.

PSD: *What a great metaphor for life! How did you first get into coaching?*

ET: I came to Tennessee State in 1946 on what was supposed to be a track scholarship,

but when I got here, there was no track. We had to have all of our track meets away. I graduated in physical education and sociology, and was waiting around to get a job in football or basketball at the high school level, while I was doing some part-time construction.

So I got started at $150 a month coaching track, going to graduate school, and running the post office. My first budget was $300, we had one track meet, and this went on for about three years. The thing that really got us started was when Mae Faggs came here from Bayside, New York. She had already made the 1942 and 1952 Olympic teams. We almost lost her, because in 1953, there was a whole lot of difference between Nashville and New York. We call her the 'mother of our program.' We won our first National Championship in 1955 in Oklahoma.

PSD: *That didn't take long.*

ET: No, it didn't. That was when Wilma Rudolph was in the tenth grade and on our junior team, which also won the National Championship.

PSD: *I know you have won 34 national titles since then, which is rather incredible. Was the first one special?*

ET: That first title was the first integrated title that the school had ever won. After that, we won about fourteen right in a row. I put six girls on the 1956 Olympic team, the only time that had ever happened. Then we put eight girls on the 1960 team that went to Rome. No one has ever done that before or since.

PSD: *What is it that appeals to you about working so closely with people?*

ET: People said that I was crazy to work with women because they would be too temperamental, but I have never found that to be true. The key was that these women wanted to be given an opportunity. Our university president, Dr. Davis, believed — even in those days — that women should be given an equal opportunity. We didn't even have an athletic scholarship until 1968, and I had to go to the Governor directly to get it. I got really disgusted when the president told me we didn't have enough scholarship money for the women, so I went directly to the Governor. The Governor was just shocked. He said, "Ed, I can't believe you don't have any scholarships." He picked up the phone, and by the time I got back, I had six scholarships. Right after that, they fixed up my track.

PSD: *Wilma Rudolph was pretty special.*
ET: She came from a family of 22 and could hardly walk until after she was eleven. She was the only one in her family who had graduated from college. Wilma was the greatest thing that came out of Tennessee, there was no doubt about it. She had charisma and a great personality. She was tall and had a very joyful, pleasing personality with a beautiful smile. She really loved people, and loved to be around them.

PSD: *Do you miss her?*
ET: Yes, I do. There is no doubt about it. The Olympic flag sitting in a chair in my office is the one that was on her coffin. She was a very good person. The only harm Wilma ever did was to herself. She was always doing something for other people — too many things for too many people — and I believe that this is one of the things that caused her death. She really forgot about herself, she hated to say no to anyone.

PSD: *She had a very big heart.*
ET: She certainly did. She was 54 when she died, but she covered an awful lot of territory in those 54 years, no doubt about it. She was the first person ever from Tennessee to win the Sullivan Award. She was a caring and sharing type of person.

PSD: *Did you ever feel like a father to all these women?*

ET: Oh, well, I am. (He laughs.) They always considered me a father because a lot of them had their fathers pass away at an early age. I was there as a father-figure.

PSD: *Do you keep in touch with a lot of your girls?*
ET: I see them all the time, though Wilma was the glue because she traveled all over the world and would keep everyone in touch. I used to always tease them that they would only call when they wanted something.

PSD: *What advice would you give a young person looking for success?*
ET: 'How badly do you want it?' and 'what sacrifices are you willing to make for it?' I will never forget the biggest rejection I ever got back in 1960, when we won six gold medals — that was more than 83 countries! I just knew that the next year I was going to get a raise. Here I was, the Olympic coach. That alone should have done it, not counting all the gold medals. I thought what a nice Christmas present that raise would be, but nothing came. I didn't get one cent, and I was really hurt.

When I look back, I realize that it had to be jealousy because we went too far and got too big, and on top of that, it was the women. They couldn't accept that. It is rough when you get to the top, because everyone is shooting at you.

PSD: *You went overseas during the 1960s while representing this country and did extraordinarily well at the Olympics. What was it like to come back home after a 'high' like that and not be able to sit at certain lunch counters merely because of the color of your skin?*
ET: That happened to me back in 1958. The question also came up when I was in Russia at a press conference when they asked me, "In your democracy, does everybody have equal opportunity?" It tickled me when one of the white coaches answered, "We don't know, we are all just Americans here." Then the

134

Russians asked me, "Can anybody marry anybody else?" I was thinking, 'My goodness, why do they have to ask me all these loaded questions?' (He laughs.)

To answer your question, though, it was real hard. I had to go away to Russia to be able to sit down at a lunch counter and eat a hamburger. At that time you could not do that here.

PSD: *Isn't that sad?*
ET: No doubt about it. When we used to go to our one track meet a year, we got in the car and drove down, but we couldn't even use a restroom. The girls had to go out into a field. There was nowhere we could stop and get something to eat, so we carried brown bags with us. At the time, we decided there was no other way to do it, so we just did it all through those years. It was sad. It was awfully hard, too.

PSD: *Ultimately, your success opened a few doors.*
ET: Yes, one thing it did do was open up doors. When Wilma came back from the Olympics, they wanted to have a big parade for her up in Clarksville. She insisted that the only way she would do it was if the parade was integrated. Of course, it had never been integrated up until that time. She also said that if you are going to have a banquet, everyone will have to be included and allowed to mingle with the guests. At first they didn't want to do it, but she would not have done it any other way. So they opened up and did it.

PSD: *How much better is it these days than before?*
ET: We have come a long way, but we still have a long way to go to really have an even field. I have always had the philosophy which I shared with my athletes, 'Athletics can open up the doors, but education will keep them open.' That's why we have put 40 girls on Olympic teams. Thirty-nine have graduated with their degrees. All but three received masters' or doctoral degrees.

PSD: *Do you have any children of your own?*
ET: A boy and a girl, both graduated from college. I have been married for 46 years.

PSD: *So you must have some secrets on a successful marriage.*
ET: Once again, it's how badly you want it and how much rejection you can take. (He laughs.) We have worked hard together. There have been ups and downs, but you have to keep on pushing.

PSD: *Do you have a spiritual philosophy?*
ET: I believe in helping other people, and in people helping themselves. I go to church, but I am not very religious. I was raised by my church-going grandparents. I was always a strict disciplinarian with my teams. Structure and discipline are important. I wanted my girls to be young women first and track athletes second. Class was important.

PSD: *Any regrets?*
ET: There is nothing I regret because I accomplished more than I ever dreamed was possible. I have been all over the world and met all kinds of people. I had no idea I was going to get that kind of exposure.

PSD: *Are you hopeful for the world?*
ET: I am. The main thing with all different cultures is respect. You don't have to like it, you just have to respect it, the same way you want them to respect what we do. We learn from them, and they learn from us.

PSD: *How would you like to be remembered?*
ET: Just that I made a contribution in helping other people. That is all anybody can do.

Dave Ramsey

Financial Consultant, Radio Host, Speaker, Author

"**What gives me hope and puts the light back into my eye is when you talk to a group of a thousand people and then come back a year later to find literally hundreds of them coming up and saying, 'There was something inside of us you touched, we paid off all of our debt and we are saving money.'**"

PSD: *I have listened to your program,* The Money Game, *on the radio and read your book,* Financial Peace. *What has really struck me is how much you love what you are doing.*

DR: If you do something that you hate doing, I don't know how you could call it a success. If you make 100 million dollars and hate every minute of it, what's the point? You lose your wife and kids or die early. This is not success. You have got to have fun. In fact, it is in our corporate policy manual that you will either enjoy what you are doing, we will help you find something you enjoy doing, or you will leave. I am having a blast and I refuse to hang out with people that are not also having a blast. Consequently, we have a great team.

PSD: *Who influenced you to think along these lines?*

DR: Don't do something you hate doing? My parents taught me that growing up. Your creativity is down, you don't have energy, you don't want to get up, you lose your focus. If you just want to chase dollars, there are a million ways to do it. Very few people have the blessing of a meaningful life.

PSD: *What does 'meaningful life' mean to you?*

DR: Doing something that will matter five hundred years from now.

PSD: *By taking something that people generally have an aversion to, like personal finance, and making it fun, you are opening up a lot of doors and a lot of minds.*

DR: People shift their beliefs based on emotion, not logic. This is an old persuasion tool from Sales 101. People buy on emotion. When you try to inspire someone, you do it with emotion — with tears, laughter, and hope. Sometimes with a little touch of crusade-based anger. This is what moves people. People are moved to do something differently either by pleasure or pain.

PSD: *What is your financial doctrine?*

DR: If you had your retirement well underway and you do not have any debt — no house payment, no car payment, no credit card debt, no student loan — then most people in our society would fall asleep, they would be so peaceful. The idea that your family is secure and you don't have to kill yourself this month just to make it is such a foreign concept to most people right now.

A lot of people would quit their jobs and go into business for themselves because they hate their jobs. A lot of people would do things differently. A lot of people would give more than they have ever given before. A lot of people would do more volunteer work than they do now. It would really change things.

I am living proof, sitting here right now. I don't have any debt, I have an emergency fund, and can fully fund my retirement. We are able to do almost whatever we want to do and we don't have to make a lot of money to do it.

PSD: *Sadly, most people will never experience that level of freedom in their lives.*

DR: They won't, but a lot of people around middle Tennessee are starting to. We have sold over 120,000 books!

PSD: *You are a bit evangelical in your style.*

DR: No question about it. The principles we are teaching are biblical-based, but the bottom line about changing your finances is changing the way you think about finances. You have to understand that material stuff doesn't amount to anything, and that very few things you do with your money will last five hundred years. But the way you impact the next generation, the way you impact the people around you, and how they in turn impact society, all have lasting effect. Yes, it is evangelical because you never have any real peace from stuff, any more than you do from alcohol or drugs.

We try to find peace in a lot of different categories. Some of it is socially acceptable, some of it is not. It is not a hype thing or a religion thing with me, but there just is no real peace except in Jesus Christ. When you do find real peace or contentment, then it is easy to save money. Because you are not buying all this stuff to feel better or impress people you don't even know.

Then it becomes easier to pay off debt and avoid further debt, because you're saving money. Personal finance has a whole lot more to do with who we are than it does with numbers.

PSD: *Have you always been so deeply spiritual? Or did this come about later in life?*
DR: I like to say I met the Lord on the way up and got to know him on the way down. (He laughs.) Spiritually and maritally, it was the only way we could have survived. I don't know how couples get through it otherwise. I am a real pragmatist, so for me it is practical. It is not ethereal and mystical. Fog doesn't have to roll in the room while we talk about this. God is a practical thing to me. He is who He is. He has a real simple study guide that you can follow. When you jump off a building, you find out He has a law called gravity. I crashed and burned because I wasn't doing stuff correctly. I did some stupid stuff with money.

So I haven't always been like this. I grew up heathen. I was a wild animal. These biblical principles are the crux and the center for everything we are.

PSD: *Didn't you have a metaphysical experience?*
DR: All things spiritual are kind of metaphysical. Yes, I have gone through a lot of spiritual experiences over the years, including being saved and those kinds of things. It was a series of events, not a one-time thing. But every time I get confused or full of pain, I

sure learn to pray again.

PSD: *Do you take time for your spirituality every day?*
DR: My wife and I spend every morning together on the deck watching the sunrise, reading scripture, praying together, and talking. I will keep her up to date on all the things that are happening down here at the office. When we don't do this, it affects our marriage. Also, it takes me two hours just to wake up. I am not a morning person, so I have to force myself to get up.

PSD: *When I was reading your book, I had the thought that if we taught these principles from grades one through twelve, the paradigm about the way things are done would be vastly different.*
DR: Yes, it would greatly affect it. It's truly amazing that this is the way it used to be! This financial philosophy is common sense, but common sense is not common any more. Debt used to be sinful back in 1898. It is amazing how we have eroded away from common sense and have called it sophistication. We invented none of the principles that we teach, none of them. They are all creatively stolen and differently packaged.

Sometimes people need repackaging in order to penetrate the information. They have to hear it first for them to respond to it. You have a delivery style first for people to hear you or the message doesn't matter.

PSD: *When it comes to spending, is the government's lack of discipline a reflection of our own lack of personal financial responsibility?*
DR: It has to be a reflection, because we voted them in. Change will only come from a grass-roots level. Washington won't get it until we fire enough of them.

PSD: *Unless we can personally have fiscal responsibility we will be unable to elect people with fiscal wisdom.*

DR: Just like the counselors here in the office, they have to believe what they teach. The problem is you have people in Washington who believe overspending and debt are a good idea, that it is the way it has always been. But it is not the way it has always been.

PSD: *There is an element of denial involved that the debt will somehow never come due.*
DR: Yes, denial is not just a river in Egypt. It is laziness and irresponsibility. Our spoiled Congress is a reflection of our spoiled selves.

PSD: *One thing that really called out to me from your book was that so much of the problem comes from a simple lack of discipline — the inability to delay gratification.*
DR: We have an overweight population and an over-debt population. Success can kill people. In a sense, our society has been very successful. Self-denial and learning to delay pleasure are character qualities that have gotten to be very rare. It is sad and scary, but the neat thing is I still see it inside a lot of people.

What gives me hope and puts the light back into my eye is when you talk to a group of a thousand people and then come back a year later to find literally hundreds of them coming up and saying, "There was something inside of us you touched, and we paid off all of our debt. We are saving money." It is still down inside of us. It just needed somebody to come along and reawaken it.

PSD: *How would Dave Ramsey define success?*
DR: That is a hard question. For me, it is finding God's will and staying in it. I find peace and fulfilllment there, I find I am impacting the most lives there, including my children and my spouse. I find that money is never an issue there. I heard a guy once define prosperity as having the money to do God's will.

PSD: *How do you know what God's will is? Through your inner voice?*
DR: I don't think you do. It is trial and error. I find it in a three-way check system — scripture reading, prayer, and circumstances. If I resonate to only one of those areas, maybe my timing is off. But if all three are lined up, you are probably already there.

It is not just something narrow that you can fall off all the time like a balance beam, it is more like wandering down the interstate. You have plenty of room to stay in there and still accomplish what He has in mind for your life. I feel He is a lot more concerned with how we react to our circumstances than to our circumstances themselves. In general, it is the broad scope of having a personal mission statement and staying within that.

PSD: *What is your mission statement?*
DR: The company mission statement encompasses mine. It states, "To provide biblically-based common sense and empowerment which gives hope to everyone from the financially secure to the financially distressed." If it doesn't have to do with transferring the Financial Peace Principles, then we don't do it. We know this will encompass a healthy level of discipline.

PSD: *What are your views on happiness?*
DR: I am such a goal-oriented person that, years ago, when I was an immature man, I tried to find happiness when I got there. My belief was 'When I get to that point, I will be happy.' What I have learned in my maturity is that the process is the most fun. I almost hate to get there now, because then you have to line up another goal.

PSD: *Do you feel called to be doing this?*
DR: This is what I am supposed to be doing. I don't know if it is what I will be doing the rest of my life. I am willing to change and do other things, but there is not any question this is what I am to do right

now. We are about to be nationally-syndicated with our radio show.

PSD: *Do you read a lot?*
DR: Not enough. I wish I could do more. I really like John Maxwell's stuff on leadership in the marketplace and the *Chicken Soup* books are wonderful. I have read all of Steven Covey's books. I don't think you can achieve and not read. I see people's income change just by reading a book a month, non-fiction of course. Television has done us a great disservice.

PSD: *What is your greatest challenge right now?*
DR: Learning how to be a better leader. Twenty-six months ago, it was just me working out of my house with a beat-up car and a cellular phone. By the end of the year, we will have over forty people working here.

PSD: *Is it frightening to grow so quickly?*
DR: What is really scary is all of the people and their kids who now depend on me to have a roof. So every decision we make, we take a little more time with. I'm learning to slow down. I'm learning to be a better team-builder.

PSD: *What would you tell your children if they were about to go out in the world alone?*
DR: Find something that you really enjoy and are gifted at, and do it with all of your heart, mind, and soul. Make sure you are helping people in the process, and you will always be happy doing that.

PSD: *Your life is based on service?*
DR: It is selfish in a sense, but this is where I get my psychological income. How many times do you have the opportunity to have someone come up to you and tell you that something you said helped change his life for the better? How many times could people tell you that before you got tired of hearing it? *Never!!!*

PSD: *What do you like best about being a father?*
DR: Watching my children grow spiritually and seeing them unfold and see the Lord. The thing I like least is that it goes so fast, in a blink. I have a ten-year-old who is going to be a teenager in a minute. I am enjoying it a lot more now that I am not so intimidated by being a father.

PSD: *Any advice for couples?*
DR: Do a budget together. The only way that Sharon and I have made it work is when we are not selfish, and we are more concerned about helping the other. The irony of being selfish is that it actually robs you of what you were after. That is ego, but you can let go of that and trade ego for confidence. We have been married for fifteen years.

PSD: *How would you like to be remembered?*
DR: He loved God and led others to Him. It is not that money is spiritual, it is how people handle it. I can look at someone's checkbook and tell a whole lot about them. Jesus said, "Your treasure is where your heart is."

140

Gayle Ray

Sheriff, Davidson County

"I am a strong believer in developing the inner life and listening to what subconscious messages, or God, may be telling you in silent moments."

PSD: *You took a risk running for the office of sheriff.*

GR: You have to take risks in order to get to the next plateau. I haven't always known this, but I learned it later in life. To have any kind of personal growth, you have to try new things, regardless if you succeed or fail. It is the only way you are going to learn anything.

PSD: *How did you end up in this position?*

GR: I never dreamed I would be here. It was never one of my career choices or possibilities when I was a child, young adult, or even in my 40s. My whole pattern has basically been one of gradual evolution. There are things that I did and tried that you would not expect to have a connection to the next thing, but it really turned out that way. Being in acting and public speaking helped, also being an English major and doing a lot of writing. It is amazing how well these things transfer into the political world, because it is all about communication.

PSD: *Talk a little about your past.*

GR: I had been a college English professor for about seven years, then I got married and had babies. I was fortunate enough to stay at home with the kids, but I needed other challenges, so I got very involved with the church and the community. I founded Bread for the World from Nashville and became a big advocate for public education. As the children grew older, I knew I wanted a different kind of career, so I enrolled at Belmont and got my MBA. When I graduated, my goal was to get a job, to be a real, full-time working person. I had been dabbling in a lot of different things for a long time.

About this time, there was a Metro Council seat coming up in my district. I was actually trying to get somebody else to run when one of my best friends said, "Gayle, if you will run for council, I will give up six months of my life and devote it to you. I will be your campaign manager and I will do what you need."

That put me over the edge, because if she was willing to do that for me, I was willing to run. So we were the dynamic duo for a few months. We had a grass-roots, well-organized campaign, and though it is hard to knock off an incumbent of 24 years, we were successful and won 60% of the vote.

One of the first things I did after being elected was to ask the Vice-Mayor to put me on the Budget and Finance Committee, because that is where most of the important decisions are made. By virtue of just having received my MBA, I wanted to use it. Lo and behold, I got put on the committee.

PSD: *'Ask and ye shall receive.'*

GR: Exactly. I wasn't obnoxious about it, just persistent. At this time, I still had no inkling or desire to be Sheriff. Being on the Finance Committee, I was not happy with the way the Sheriff's Office was being run from a business perspective. Once again, I tried to find someone else to do the job, and it was the same story. We started late in December when the primary was in May, which is really unusual to do in such a tight window and win. We had to get it together very quickly. It was very hectic, a lot of 14-hour days. Also, it is harder for female candidates to raise money, though I knew I would get some money from a group called Woman in the '90s. I ended up putting in over $20,000 of my own money, a lot of which I have gotten back.

PSD: *Were you ever afraid at any time?*

GR: I was never afraid, and really felt that I could win. I was also comfortable with the fact that if I didn't win, I would be happy that I had done it. If you lose, mark it up to experience and move on.

PSD: *Are you in an age of self-discovery?*

GR: I am learning about who I am. I am a more mature person. From experience, I have learned that I am happiest when I am learning new things, taking chances, meeting new people, making connections, and putting things together.

Sometimes you can feel like, 'That is so much work. How will I ever be able to do it all?' But another thing that I have learned is that if you are willing to step out for something you really believe in and for something that really needs to be done, there is a kind of energy created. That energy starts attracting like-minded people who want to help you and be part of the action.

PSD: *It's almost magical, isn't it?*
GR: It really is. It is all about one person with an idea, some will, and some enthusiasm, who can communicate the vision and the idea in a way that is exciting to people. It is almost a miracle.

PSD: *'Miracle' is the word that came to my mind, but it is interesting to hear the Sheriff say it. Many of us are aware of what you're describing, but it is not always politically correct to say it.*
GR: That's true.

PSD: *What strikes me is the fact that you are only one Sheriff removed from the days of Fate Thomas.*
GR: I am definitely a new kind of sheriff, and Nashville is a new kind of town. Look at Phil Bredesen. The people who live in Nashville want a new kind of leadership — a more professional, well-educated leadership.

PSD: *And honest leadership.*
GR: I went to a seminar recently where Ken Kragen said, "Honesty works." People are hungry and starving for someone who will tell it like it is, and that's not a gimmick with me. I think people find it refreshing.

PSD: *Even if you don't agree with the position, you can still respect the truth.*
GR: Exactly.

PSD: *Respect is so important. Do you like the job?*
GR: *I love the job!!!!!* Obviously, I didn't have a real idea of what I was getting into. I have a great team here, and that has been key. It makes it fun to come to work. There are wonderful people who have worked at the sheriff's office for 20 years or so. I value their ideas and input.

PSD: *What is the most challenging part of your job?*
GR: Having over 500 employees and handling the various personal problems. Employees are people with many skills and virtues, but because they are also human beings, they have many, many problems. We have discipline situations, especially with people who are working with inmates and get tempted by the opportunity to make a fast buck.

PSD: *If you were going to define success, for you personally, what would that be?*
GR: That is hard. Really, really, hard. This is not anything earth-shattering, but for me, success is having meaningful work to do — something that has a greater influence on the community or policy. Beyond just running the sheriff's office, I am very interested in all the problems of society, of crime and punishment and also early intervention with children.

In a sense, I have the perfect job and that is part of success. Yet your life is not your career, so success also means having balance in your life. You have fulfilling work, you have a spiritual life, and meaningful relationships with people — in my case, both family and friends. And you have some *fun*!

PSD: *That is a pretty good definition. Is this a difficult job to leave in the office?*
GR: It was almost impossible the first year. I was working 60 and 70 hours a week, and thinking about it every second when I was

not here. Gradually, as things have gotten better organized and I have responsible people I can trust, I can definitely leave the job behind. Especially on weekends. I have recently taken up golf. I also really enjoy gardening, getting my hands dirty digging in the dirt. I find this very therapeutic.

PSD: *You seem to have a strong spiritual side. Can you talk about it?*

GR: I am a very spiritual person, though I haven't devoted as much time to developing it lately as I probably should. I am a strong believer in developing the inner life and listening to what subconscious messages, or God, may be telling you in silent moments. I am a great reader and I think you get important messages that way. I also believe that certain people appear in your life at certain times to bring you messages. You really need to be an open and active listener, because it may not be an important or impressive person who brings the message. It may be the person who cleans out your gutters. There is value in all human beings. I am a very strong believer in that.

PSD: *What would you tell a young person in pursuit of self-discovery?*

GR: I have two children, and right now, the 20-year-old is asking these kinds of questions of exploration. When I was their age, I felt like I was really off track because I had no clue as to what I wanted to do. If you read a lot of these success books, they say you need a plan. Yes, you do need to think somewhat of what you like to do and be good at it. But to me, the key is to make every experience valuable. I learned a tremendous amount waiting tables at Yellowstone Park. I think I learned more in that experience then anything else I have ever done in life.

PSD: *What I hear you saying is, "It is good to have some vision, but go with the flow of things, too."*

GR: Going with the flow and listening to your inner self has worked for me. There will always be authority figures telling you what to do, but you have to listen to your heart and your soul. Listen to your gut. Later in life, I want to do something totally artistic.

PSD: *Like what?*
GR: Paint.

PSD: *Teacher, mother, MBA student, Councilwoman, Sheriff, painter ... you're sounding more and more like a new renaissance woman.*

GR: One thing that makes me sad is that I am 50 years old. There are so many things I want to learn and do, I don't think I am going to be able to do them in my remaining years. I will have to wait for the next life. I will take it as it comes. Live life to the fullest and appreciate the little things.

PSD: *What is it that makes you happiest?*

GR: The thing that makes me the happiest is when I have made a positive influence on another person's life. That gives me a little thrill and a high like nothing else. Going to schools and talking to young people, seeing in the eyes of a little girl that maybe she can do anything because of my career path.

PSD: *Who has had the greatest influence on you in terms of being so outward in your thinking?*

GR: I don't know. I didn't have the greatest relationship with my mother. She was very negative, and I knew I never wanted to be like that. I did have a wonderful relationship with this aunt of mine. Her caring for me has had a great influence. She is very outward in her thinking.

PSD: *Are you hopeful despite all the suffering you deal with in this brutal world?*

GR: Everything you would know about the facts would tend to make you a non-hopeful, depressed person. But I think you are either an optimist or pessimist, and I have always felt that things will improve. It is part of my spiritual belief, too. I do believe that God is in charge of the world and has a plan that we cannot see or understand in our short, little window of time. I don't know how people can live if they do not believe that.

PSD: *What is it about your character that has allowed you to achieve?*
GR: I can get pretty intense, anyone can tell you that. I may not be an easy person to live with. I also have a controlling side that is not always pleasant.

PSD: *How would like to be remembered when all is said and done?*
GR: 'She really cared about me and other people. She was someone I could always count on when I needed her. She was there.'

Rev. Carl Resener

Director, Nashville Union Rescue Mission

"I have taken drunks, put them to bed, and watched over them. I have helped old men take showers because they were too feeble to help themselves. We have done unusual things to help these people. The impact comes from doing a lot of things that we don't have to do. They notice it, and this is sometimes a turning point."

PSD: *How did you become a minister working with the homeless population?*
CR: In 1949, I was attending Purdue University and my life was all out of kilter. I had had three mothers, two fathers, and two homes. I was at a point where any strong wind could have taken me, vulnerable to life itself. Fortunately, I started going to church and a Sunday school teacher gave me words and knowledge of things that I had never heard before. It made sense that God could do more for my life than I could do myself. So I yielded to the Lord and experienced salvation.

PSD: *Was there a specific event that brought you to the chair in which you sit?*
CR: Coming home one night from a long walk, I came by a beer tavern where some drunks were coming out. It reminded me of what my past life had been like. Not me personally, but my past environment. There the Lord indicated that He wanted me to be a preacher, and I asked 'Who do you want me to preach to and reach?' The drunks coming out were the answer.

I believe with all my heart that God called me to this type of ministry. We had to deal with alcohol in my family, and we lived on the periphery of skid row for years. So I was familiar with drunks and people who were destroying their lives through reckless living. For that I accepted God's call. It was something that God put in my heart and hasn't taken out since 1949, so that is why I am here.

PSD: *When you actually had the experience of salvation, was there something unnerving about it? Or was it very matter-of-fact?*
CR: It was a very impressive experience that I have only known one other time. The first time, it seemed like God was just overshadowing me and talking to me. The second time it occurred, I was a senior in college determining where I wanted to go, and at that time, I really committed myself to this kind of ministry. I think the Lord overshadows you at times where He speaks and there is no doubt in your mind. It is an unusual experience, but I think that every minister called by God knows what I am talking about.

PSD: *My theory is that a lot of people have this experience, but do not share it because it carries a great deal of baggage in our culture.*
CR: If people would just be willing to listen to the Lord, they will find the Lord talking to them. I am not charismatic to any degree and do not cater to these types of practices. But I do know the Lord talks to His people, and when you are willing to do His will, He really opens up to you. Those were the two greatest experiences in my life regarding the Lord and that is what keeps me here.

PSD: *How many years have you been doing mission work in Nashville?*
CR: My wife Laura and I came in 1957, when the mission was three years old. I stayed as Chaplain until 1961, when the funding went down and they had to let me go. But I couldn't leave Nashville. I tried, but I just couldn't leave. So I started a little Baptist church to keep me going and worked there for 9 1/2 years until I thought it was time to leave. I tried to leave Nashville again and still couldn't. So I went down to the mission, told them I was leaving town, and asked if I could just help out until I found something. They said, "Carl, we need you here," and about three months later, I became the director.

PSD: *What is the mission about?*
CR: The mission is the fulfillment of the Lord's word, "The spirit of the Lord is upon me because He has anointed me to heal." To take care of the poor and the needy and preach the gospel. The mission is actually the fulfillment of what the Lord said that He himself had come to do.

PSD: *This is what Jesus came to do?*

CR: I believe with all my heart that the rescue mission is probably the fulfillment, in the closest way we know, of what the Lord had come to do. Feed the poor, bind up the wounded, release the captives, and preach a little gospel. Rescue missions are closest to what Jesus said is the calling of why He came into the world. We meet physical, material, mental, emotional, and spiritual needs. We don't have an agenda beyond that.

PSD: *What is the hardest part about this kind of ministry?*

CR: Making sure that spiritual needs are on the same level or higher as the physical and material. We do not consider ourselves a social service agency. We meet social needs in order to provide spiritual remedies for problems. It used to be that 85% of the people on the street were there because of their lifestyle — drugs, drinking, you could name the reasons. Today, there are a lot of other problems that put people on the street. Many of our donors say, "We like you feeding these people, but why worry about religious aspects?" The government won't supply us with provisions because we maintain a spiritual atmosphere here. That is why we don't ask the government to help us.

The uniqueness of the mission is this — not only are we able to help a man make a living, but we are also able to help a man know how to live. That is the key element. I am not content to send fat sinners to hell. We want to help people know how to live. That is the missing element in the agenda on dealing with mankind today.

PSD: *Why do you think there are so many problems with chemical dependency in this culture?*

CR: Chemical dependency is an attempt to replace God. The chemical will do for the drug addict what I get from prayer time with the Lord. In other words, Christ and whiskey do the same thing.

PSD: *Fill a hole?*

CR: Fill a hole. Drugs and whiskey are a substitute for a man who has no living God. They reinforce a man who feels he is nothing. I differentiate drinking and certain drugs, though both are about escape. A man who drinks is running from his life, while someone using cocaine is trying to find a new life. But the whole issue is escape from reality. We use drugs to fill the void in our lives created by a separation from God when man fell into sin.

PSD: *You have been working with people a long time in many ways. How would you define success?*

CR: Success is being able to do what you feel is your calling, and getting others to believe in you so that they become partners in what you are doing.

PSD: *To have success, you have to have some relationship with a higher power?*

CR: To be successful, you have to have something to live for and to live by. You have to have someone to stand by you. Jesus makes all of those things possible. I have heard people say that salvation by Jesus is too simple, but this is the way God has made it.

PSD: *How much time do you spend each day for prayer?*

CR: I have a morning hour to prepare and get myself in shape. I get up about 5:30 every morning, and have seen many a sunrise. It is a wonderful hour of the day. I have often said, 'Before you meet man, you better meet God.'

PSD: *Do you ever get discouraged?*

CR: I am not discouraged by the ministry God gave me. The discouraging aspect is that you sometimes cannot get these people to believe in themselves and see themselves as worthy of God's love. I know men who have been here at the mission for as long as I have. At times I have felt guilty and felt like a failure because I couldn't help some of these men. I have buried too many fellows who, with a little bit of effort, could have been alive or have died in a home, not in a flop house. That is the greatest discouragement. It is not because of lack of food, the Lord has blessed us abundantly in that aspect. It is simply that they won't see the light for one reason or another. For some of them, it is one continuous day, one continuous mile — they never get out of it.

PSD: *Even though you have been doing this for a very long time, I can see it still affects you when a soul falls by the wayside.*
CR: That is part of the fire that has never gone out. The bottom line is, will the guy take what we offer? You have to wait for him. That is why time is of no relevance here at the mission. Someone can stay as long as it takes for God to deal with him. The mission door is open every day because I believe God comes down here and talks to people every day.

PSD: *I sense an optimism in you. Do you see the saint through every sinner? The potential for salvation?*
CR: There is a man inside every man, even you and me, and with the right kind of help, especially from the Lord, we can become the kind of man that God intended us to be. Every man that comes to this mission is a potential candidate for God's Grace and help in this world, and the promise of eternal life.

PSD: *Do you think that it is our calling to get closer to God, wherever we may be on the cultural food chain?*
CR: The ministry of rescue is God giving man another chance to become the man he is supposed to become. I believe that men are called to come here rather than it happening randomly. This is why I have an open-door policy.

PSD: *What is it like to see someone come in here at the bottom and turn his life around?*
CR: We've seen a lot of that. We have a young man studying at Dallas Theological Seminary who was a former alcoholic from Brentwood who God called upon to preach. I also had a 16 year old boy from South Africa that turned his life around. He won a scholarship to law school and went back to Africa. We also have three fellows working on construction of the new arena.

This is proof that the mission is not a dead-end street. This type of program really recovers lives. It is rewarding to know that we are not wasting our time here, that the time we spend in a man's life is not in vain.

PSD: *Do you have any children?*
CR: I have two daughters.

PSD: *What advice would you give them to help them be successful?*
CR: There is no success unless you are rightly related to God. Because success is going to be based more upon what you take out of this world than what you leave in it. You have to determine which world you want to be successful in. The tragedy for Christians today is believing that the world is the prize for Christian living, when in reality it is the price. If you want to live in the Lord's world, you let the Lord's will direct you.

PSD: *How would you advise one to seek the Lord?*
CR: Humble yourself before the Lord and ask Him to come into your life and take over.

PSD: *Salvation can occur in any moment, even the last moment.*
CR: True enough. The end of your life is more important than the beginning, like the thief on the cross. There are some people who have considered my life wasted because I went into the rescue mission. I have been criticized greatly for my choice.

PSD: *When we reach our highest level of humanity, is life about service?*

CR: I would say ministry instead of service. I don't consider myself a servant to these people, although I make sure they get enough to eat and drink and have a place to sleep. But I minister to them in a way that a doctor practices medicine.

PSD: *Your energy flows outward towards others, it is not self-oriented. I call it service, you call it ministry — but it is all about giving.*

CR: That call I received from God indicated to me that whatever it takes for a man to hear the gospel from me, that is what I need to do. I have taken drunks, put them to bed, and watched over them. I have helped old men take showers because they were too feeble to help themselves. We have done unusual things to help these people. The impact comes from doing a lot of things that we don't have to do. They notice it, and this is sometimes a turning point.

PSD: *Like the good Samaritan.*

CR: Everything around here is a ministry where we are giving in many ways. We are showing God's love for man. Our meals are exceptional. I tell the cooks to stack it high because God is approving the meal.

PSD: *You treat people with love and respect who are unaccustomed to it.*

CR: This is where we are successful, too. We gain their attention through what we do and how we do it. A good meal has turned some people around here. What we do for these people really rings their bells.

PSD: *Is it the magic of love?*

CR: Well, if it is magic, it is based on hard work. When they realize the cook got up at 5:00 a.m. to make them gravy and biscuits, they sense it. Poor people have a difficult time saying thank you.

PSD: *How would you like to be remembered when you finally do 'leave town'?*

CR: Someone once said, "There is no success unless there is a successor." I want to be known as a man who provided a ministry that really helps people, and that it is a type of a ministry that can continue even without me. Some men want to be known as being fruitful, but I want to be remembered as a man who was faithful.

PSD: *Faithful?*

CR: Faithful to what I know God wanted me to do, and faithful to the provisions that people provided.

PSD: *You are fortunate to be living a life that has such tremendous personal resonance.*

CR: I have had sense enough to do what God wanted me to do and He has never changed the orders or let me change the orders. The ministry is something God places on you. It is humbling but also restrictive. You don't mess with God's plan. I have simply tried to do the best I know how with the resources I have been given, to do a work that God said needs to be done.

Ron Bombardi, Ph.D

Professor of Philosophy, Middle Tennessee State University

"You must learn to think for yourself. No one else can do your thinking for you. You must have your own reflective life if you want to capitalize on this sense of a difference between being knowledgeable and being wise. Wisdom is the way you live, not the things you say."

PSD: *Were you a philosophical kid?*

RB: I was a pretty dorky kid, not very athletic, kind of egg headed. While most kids spent their summers improving their physical skills, I was in a basement with my nose buried in a book. I read *The Rise and Fall of the Third Reich* when I was 11 years old. I had that sort of temperament, so I was very self-sustaining.

PSD: *How did you become a teacher of philosophy?*

RB: I thought I would always wind up, in one way or another, being a professional philosopher. I didn't always know that would mean the kind of commitment to undergraduate teaching, which sort of came my way. I was 16 or 17 years old when I realized I was really good at this.

When I was 17, I had a certain formative experience. I was not a popular kid, I wasn't used to other kids seeking me out. I was usually running away from them because they were bullying me. We had this place where we would hang out that was part of an old movie theater where you could go have Cokes if you were a teenager. One evening we were thinking about whether any object could be an object of aesthetic appreciation or not. I took the latter position and made short work of the opposition, but from there, I started going off on a theory. It was the first time in my life I had ever done this, really thought for myself. Before I realized it, I had 15 people looking up at me sitting on a counter. There were my peers, the athletes, the good looking people. And they were looking at me. I realized at that moment I was good at this teaching thing. So I knew one way or another I could do this. If I really went to town with an idea, people would listen.

I always knew I would learn, but I didn't know I would get an advanced degree. I was pretty active in the civil rights movement, so I thought I might take my talents into politics.

This was back in the '60s and a lot of things were going on. I was also active in the Peace and Freedom Party, seeking racial and social justice. I was involved in early feminism.

PSD: *Who had the greatest influence on your formative years?*

RB: I had a great English teacher who made Shakespeare come alive. His name was Fittipaldi and he had passion for the material. He embodied an emotional response to literature I had never seen before.

PSD: *Though the '60s were a difficult time, it was also a magical time of passion and involvement.*

RB: It was a very exciting time compared to today.

PSD: *There wasn't as much apathy.*

RB: No, and there was a sense of purpose and potential for change. We really believed we were on the edge of a cultural revolution. We thought we were the generation going to bring about cataclysmic change. We were revolting not just about policies, but a way of life — a way of life in which some oppressed others. We could see it, but just seeing it somehow wasn't enough.

PSD: *What do you think happened to that dream?*

RB: I think it got co-opted by the engines of capitalism. I think it was cooking along pretty well but the promise of easy money was very seductive. It wasn't some sort of conspiracy or anything. I think the way in which that disillusionment occurred has been kind of a 'divide and conquer' thing. Interests got subdivided. We got fragmented. I think in some sense there might have been a loss of collective vision.

PSD: *You work on campus. Do you see anything remotely like it used to be in terms of involvement, passion, and commitment?*

155

RB: No, nothing like that, and not since the '60s. The willingness on university campuses to shut the administration down, not only the belief, but the will to bring it off — there isn't anything like that.

PSD: *Why do you think you approach teaching with such a passion?*

RB: Because I see the classroom as an environment of mutual inquiry more than an environment for the transmission of inherited wisdom. I don't see the classroom as a vessel for the wisdom of the ancients. So I am not as concerned with whether I have succeeded or failed in communicating these eternal truths to the students. I see the classroom as an opportunity where the student can also educate the teacher.

PSD: *Socratic in nature?*

RB: Well, I do conduct my classes in a very Socratic style. We try to put our heads in a certain place and inquire as to the nature of this thing together. I can learn from 'you' because any set of joint inquirers can learn from each other.

PSD: *Is it hard for you to use a grading system with students?*

RB: One of the things I try to come to is that grades are not everything, but it is the process. The whole relationship with the instructor is based on trust and I hope to use the fruits of my experience and personal inquiry in a responsible way — to help other people to improve and to mature their own abilities and skills. So the grading process allows me in a very formal way to interact with you as a student, so that you may benefit from my experience. Grading can really be helpful in this context.

PSD: *What do you try to develop in your students?*

RB: Intellectual health, in a very broad way. I am using that notion, which is ancient and goes back to Plato's dialogues, that analogy between physical and intellectual health. This reminds us that health is not something you achieve once and then put in a drawer. It is an activity which has to be constantly maintained. Why use a model like that? So often in modern education we tend to think of the course work that you do as having a beginning, a middle, and an end. You put it in a box and file it in the cerebral cortex, almost like the standards of currency exchange. It is something you possess, but not something you actually use anymore.

PSD: *Like a degree?*

RB: Like a degree. But health is not like that. Health is not something you possess, it is something you practice. Health is something you have to live every day, which means you have to live a certain way. You have to have a certain sense of attitudes or habits you want to cultivate. As a teacher, I'm much more interested in helping people cultivate good habits that will be effective for them, rather than saying these are the truths or the facts that you should know.

PSD: *Shouldn't one question everything to see if it has inner resonance?*

RB: Oh yes, of course. Of course. You may know all the classical disciplines and what Plato said, but it doesn't mean you will be able to think your way out of a paper bag. Part of the role of an instructor is to give students basic knowledge, but you also have to train them to acquire skills so that they will be healthy. That something we all have, the thinking life, can be healthy or unhealthy. Just like your body.

PSD: *Metaphorically, you are supplying software tools.*

RB: Yes. What are your needs and what are your projects? Well, then, you will need tools that are appropriate to those projects. So you need to be tolerant and open minded, not just of beliefs, but of techniques. Techniques for thinking are not all the same.

PSD: *Then there are experiences of instant awakening and spiritual enlightenment, satori!*
RB: And those are amazingly more common as one gets older. It is an interesting sort of thing I have been thinking about. How many of these things were understandings of the world that I knew by phrases? They were there to be had, but now they are living things for me. I am beginning to understand why the earlier thinkers, at least in the western tradition, made such a distinction between knowledge and wisdom. They insisted that it was experiential.

PSD: *What advice would you offer someone with less experience than yourself?*
RB: The old Socratic notion that you must learn to think for yourself. No one else can do your thinking for you. You must have your own reflective life if you want to capitalize on this sense of a difference between being knowledgeable and being wise. Being wise is something you can only have as an experience, you can't write it down. And don't stop when the phase makes sense. Maintain curiosity and a sense of tolerance of other views. Maintain a willingness to change your mind. Sometimes you will have insights that are worth keeping.

PSD: *How about for a senior in high school or a college student?*
RB: I would guess at that age you already have a very healthy distrust of your elders and the best thing you can do is enrich it, maintain it, and feed it as best you can. Question authority, even the authority that tells you to question authority. This is a very special gift that human beings have. To be able to look at the inherited wisdom of the race and to question it. To suspect that it isn't any good unless it is my experience. To be able to do that means that we are more than instinctual beings, we don't have to behave like those who came before us. We can change the future of our culture, but we can't do that if we can't question.

There is a big difference between inherited knowledge and real experience. I think Thoreau said, "You cannot learn what you believe you already know." So a healthy disposition to have is a sense of your own ignorance. I find that the older I get, the less I know, although I am wiser. I am amazed at how much I do not know. You realize that wisdom is a way you live, not the things you say.

PSD: *How would you define success?*
RB: Continuing the experiment. Life is a grand experiment and to be successful is to continue it. Of course that means to continue to have an experimental spirit. To have lost that spirit would have been to be a failure. When you see life as a thought and as experimental, you are free to just keep trying different things. You are always learning. I engage in projects because I have questions.

PSD: *For you it seems that the process is everything, that there is no big payday.*
RB: That is what is meant by 'virtue is its own reward.' It is the activity that matters.

PSD: *Are you a spiritual man?*
RB: That is a pretty big question. Sometimes I am so intoxicated by the beauty of music made by a composer like Bach, that it would be very difficult for me to say that I was not having a religious experience. That you became rapturous over something that was beyond you, something that is much, much bigger. If you are willing to extend the language of religiosity and spirituality to those sort of experiences where the hair on the back of your neck stands up and you are in awe, intoxicated, rapturously infatuated with something incredibly beautiful and incredibly big. If that is what religious experience is,

then certainly, I cultivate these regularly. They are some of the biggest kicks that I have. This is sort of non-standard talk.

PSD: *Hopefully, this book will be full of non-standard talk.*
RB: Also, I get really blissed out over mathematical ideas. I find them entrancing.

PSD: *As I am sure Stephen Hawking has on occasion.*
RB: Yes. A kind of awe. Spirituality is passionate for me, it is not intellectual. It is not a matter of having true belief. For many people that is what spirituality is. It is involved in organizing, systematizing, and appreciating their beliefs. Whereas for me it is in the expression, the focusing, the concentration of passion. One can have a passion for ideas and have a spiritual kind of experience. I often think that many people are wrong in believing that they are spiritual when they are really looking through a window at spirituality wishing they were. But they don't know how to do it.

PSD: *Was it not James Joyce who said, "Religion is a defense against having a religious experience?"*
RB: Yes. You are imagining what it would be like to have the experience and mistaking imagination for actually having one. Religion is closer to what it is to be spiritual, and theology is closer to what it means to be knowledgeable. To be spiritual is to have a certain kind of experience. Those who have experienced the passion of ideas have a responsibility to their descendants to communicate that passion. Because if they fail to do so, it could come to an end and all it takes is one generation. It tells us how fragile culture is. Part of what we call spirituality is a recognition of the fragility.

PSD: *You are a father. How about a personal definition of parental success?*

RB: I think you know you are successful as a parent if you can still have deep, intimate, meaningful conversations with your children when they are 20. If you can still have a trusting, open, inquiring, relationship of how you see the world, with the people whose diapers you changed, that is success.

PSD: *What has worked for you in raising children?*
RB: I think the most important thing as a parent is keeping a healthy attitude rather than making a new rule. "I need a new rule and then everything will be fine." This is a way that a lot of parents solve problems. This is pretty much the control model. My sense of having children is I invited them into the world. My wife and I took parts of each of us and invited this being into the world. This acknowledges the child as an autonomous being. Suppose you threw a party, invited people over, and started telling them how to live. You probably wouldn't have many friends.

PSD: *Would you call that love?*
RB: Sure, it is a kind of love. Love is a word in English which is about as vague as you can find. But it is interesting, given that vagueness is so attractive to philosophers, who love vague things. One needs to remember the games played with that word are very multifarious, and we need to be careful.

Amy Kurland

Owner, The Bluebird Cafe

"Never be too proud to do the small stuff. I know how to run the dish-washer and bus the tables. In the beginning, you have to be willing to do any facet of what it takes."

PSD: *How did this legendary place ever come into being?*

AK: I wanted to be in the restaurant business and went to cooking school for a while in Washington, D.C. before dropping out. I came back to Nashville and worked in the kitchen at Dalts. With a small inheritance from my grandmother, I started looking around for a place to open a restaurant. I was a 26-year-old who thought she knew it all and could do it. At the time, I was dating a guitar player who hung around at a lot of the musical clubs and bars. Some of the musicians we were hanging around with said, "Why don't you open a music club and let us get involved?" So I had people encouraging me with my dream.

I found this place in the neighborhood I had grown up in. When I started out, I built the place not so much like a music club, but more towards what the room lent itself to. We opened as a lunch counter, a tea place for blue-haired Green Hills ladies, with music on weekend nights. People came pouring out of the woodwork to hear music. In July of 1982, someone came to me asking if they could do a writer's night that would be a benefit. It was a great night, one of the best we had that summer. I wasn't booking the music, but I told the person who was to get me more writers.

The big news in the fall of 1982 was that Kathy Mattea was out looking for a record deal and needed a place to play. So, almost every Saturday night, Kathy played down here with her band. Soon after she got the record deal, *Good Morning America* was coming to Nashville to broadcast for a whole week. One of things they wanted to film was an up-and-coming young star.

They got in touch with Kathy, who said, "Let's do it at the Bluebird, where I always play." They filmed here and it was shown on national television. That little piece of fortuitous luck was the beginning of the mythology of the Bluebird. People saw that segment, which gave a face to the name of Nashville. "If I go to Nashville, I need to play at that Bluebird place." Come June of 1997, we will have been in business fifteen years.

PSD: *This place has a magical feel.*

AK: The magic of the place comes from the shape of the room, the color of the walls — really nothing that I created. It is a room with ambiance. It is small, tight, and carpeted. It just works for music.

So there is a combination of magical elements, though in a city like Nashville, songwriters would play at the city dump if three people would come out there and watch them. (She laughs) When other people started to play here and got record deals, we got credit for it.

PSD: *Was the business element challenging?*

AK: Somewhere along the way I realized how little I knew about business. So I signed up for adult education courses at Nashville Tech. The marketing class in particular absolutely changed my life. At that point, I had been doing the lunch business and the music for about four years. In the class, I learned that you have to figure out your one mission and just focus on that. No one succeeds in business trying to do more than one thing. I have believed that ever since. Within three weeks of being in that class, I shut down the lunch business. But our income never went down.

PSD: *The Bluebird has had a charmed existence.*

AK: Oh, yes. Almost every other thing that has happened has been good fortune and Grace from God, combined with my ability and the ability of others, to notice when good things were happening and to follow them up.

Around 1988, Garth Brooks was in town looking for his record deal. This is where he mostly played and where he got his deal. He is an honorable and wonderful man who talked a lot about the Bluebird. He chose to have the Barbara Walters interview right here, so we got more national publicity. The biggest piece of publicity was when the CBS News show *48 Hours* taped a nice segment about the Bluebird during their show about Nashville. While the show was airing, the phone started ringing. Seven years later, I still get calls from people who have seen that show.

PSD: *What about Garth? I have heard many people say, in a positive way, that he is a different kind of guy.*

AK: My feeling about Garth, who I don't see very often — actually Garth and Vince Gill — is that both are true, honest, wonderful, giving, humble people. How good they are doesn't even begin to show in how good they look in public. Which is saying a lot, because both of those guys look like very good people in public. It is absolutely true. They are both human, but they believe in what they do and they do it honestly.

PSD: *You had no idea that this phenomenon would have come out of such humble beginnings?*

AK: I didn't even intend to have a music club, but for that guitar-playing boyfriend. A screenwriter wrote a movie about Nashville called *A Thing Called Love*. It was a box-office disaster, but we did a lot of press about the Bluebird. I'm holding my breath when it's released on network television.

PSD: *In the past couple of years, has the club gone to another level of popularity?*

AK: Yes, I think the whole movie thing put us over the top.

PSD: *Do you have a business philosophy?*

AK: No, not really. Every time I have tried to make something happen, it never happens quite that way. So I guess my business philos-

ophy is to let good things come, pay attention, and try to honor them. If I have a mission, it is to present a forum for songwriters to get their music heard.

PSD: *Are you a music lover?*

AK: I guess so, but I probably don't listen to as much music as my customers do. Remember, I have been at it for a long time.

PSD: *So your passion is more to help the writer find a means of expression.*

AK: Right. From a marketing perspective, I need to market the club to the writer. If this is a good place for the writer to play, he or she will bring in their own audience. I say 'Play here, and the public will come.' One of my goals is for the place to have a strong enough reputation for good music that people will come here even if they don't know who is playing.

PSD: *I'm sure people have approached you about expanding.*

AK: People ask me all the time when are we going to expand. The last thing in the world I want to do is run a place where I have to hire more people as waitresses or dishwashers. I want to expand the reach of who I am touching. I would love to do that.

PSD: *Who influenced you to channel your energy into helping other people?*

AK: Both my parents, but mostly my mother. She believes in doing good things for other people. My father is actually a musician. The Bluebird does a series of concerts for children and senior citizens that are purely non-profit. I am on the Alcohol and Drug Council and an organization called Book 'Em that tries to get books to children who otherwise would not get them. We do a tremendous number of benefits here for causes like the St. Patrick's Shelter that helps homeless families.

PSD: *How would you define success?*

AK: I probably should have thought about this before. The ability to be comfortable, both physically and emotionally, while you participate in adding to your world. Not just your world, but the whole world. Is Mother Teresa a success? Obviously, in what she creates. Does she live comfortably? I'm not sure. People consider her to be a saint. I am not enough of a saint to do things for the world and live in uncomfortable surroundings. So, for me, part of success is being able to live comfortably. I don't think you have to be a martyr to be considered a success.

PSD: *Do you enjoy the personal notoriety?*

AK: I remember in high school taking one of those tests designed to show you what you want to be when you grow up. One question gave you a choice about whether you wanted to be rich, famous, or powerful. At the time, I didn't know the difference. One of the things I know in my life is that I am fairly famous, kind of a low-level celebrity. Most people around here know what I do. So I can say that fame is the most useless of the three.

People think that I have a lot of power, and I certainly do have a kind of negative power. I certainly have the power to make sure that somebody has a bad day. If I saw a person who had the ability to be a star, I could make a few calls for them and open a few doors, but I could not get them a record deal.

PSD: *How do you stay grounded?*

AK: Some self-help groups and some individual counseling. I have three dogs and I like to exercise. I had a good upbringing, I try to stay humble. Sometimes, I have a hard time accepting that what I do is important and good.

PSD: *I guess there is always that sense within us that we are only human.*

AK: And being human gives you a lot of humility, because human beings are full of the capacity for mistakes and unpleasantness, to make bad judgments no matter who you are. It is very hard to be public with that, but it is also very hard to be private with it. Every single one of us is afraid of going out with a green thing on our teeth, whether it is me, a star, or someone you never heard of.

PSD: *What advice would you give on how to find more meaning in this lifetime?*

AK: Make sure that whatever you are doing you would do for free. You do it because you love it. I would also say to try out a lot of things. I hope I don't go on living until I'm eighty with the Bluebird being the only thing I ever do. I would like to get on a bicycle at some point and ride across the country. Or get into an RV and drive someplace. Maybe move to Vermont and sell books at the corner book store. I would say that any of those things would be nice to do early on in one's life.

PSD: *What else?*

AK: Take your time. Do a bunch of different things and if something sticks, put some more energy into it. Don't be afraid to ask questions or to ask for help. But be careful who you ask. Find somebody smart, somebody who knows, who is willing to talk to you. Don't forget you are a human being, so you can't know everything. It's OK not to know. Pay attention to what is right in front of you. Work hard for things, but if you have to really fight for it and it doesn't feel right, let it go.

When you get involved with a lot of side projects, just remember what your main mission is and don't ever put that aside for the little things you get interested in. Never be too proud to do the small stuff. I know how to run the dishwasher and bus the tables. In the beginning, you have to be willing to do any facet of what it takes. Down the road, you will have to be able to get some perspective on your life and not become a total workaholic. If you do, what is the point?

PSD: *It is nice to see you with plenty of dreams in your heart.*

AK: There is so much more I can do. I have recently hired someone to manage the place so I can stay home at night and not worry. I still have a little guilt, but at least I don't have a lot of worry. I would like to be able to come down here and listen to music because I want to, just for the fun of it. Not because I have to.

PSD: *What do you see as your biggest challenge?*

AK: Transforming myself from a person who is synonymous with the Bluebird to someone who can go home and bake cookies, or reacquaint myself with friends. You do sacrifice family dinners and lunches with friends for an operation like this.

PSD: *What has been the most fun about the Bluebird's evolution?*

AK: Watching the success of other people, the lasting satisfaction of watching their careers take off. Not just the likes of Garth Brooks, but all the people I have seen struggle and then make it. I have had a lot of fun doing this.

PSD: *You seem to have a love for people.*

AK: I'm not very social, but I do love mankind. I think that people are basically good and should be given every opportunity to make the most of themselves.

Walter Knestrick

Builder and Contractor

"I think if more people were involved in the arts and listening to their own souls, the world would be a better place to live. You'd find some relief from the rat race of work, providing for your family, and all the political things."

PSD: *What is it that you love about building?*
WK: I guess creating something. It's not that I like construction — the highest paid person in our company is always the guy who has to go out and do it. My wife can't even get me to paint the kitchen or hang a picture. I'm the worst. (He laughs) But I really get a thrill out of closing a deal, making a sale.

PSD: *How would you define success?*
WK: One of the first things you have to do is decide for yourself what is meant by success. What success is for one person may not be what it is for another. If you are really going to be content and successful, you have to know your limits, what you feel comfortable with. I always thought that I could do anything I wanted to do as long as I was willing to pay the price. But success for me is wanting to be financially successful enough where money is not a concern. Therefore, to be successful, I want to have a little extra money to do the things that I want to do. And that means filling in the holes of my life so I am exposed to a lot of different things. I basically turned over Walter Knestrick Contractors a couple of years ago to other people. My idea of success is to have the afternoons of most days free to take on the challenge of playing golf.

It is easy for me to say that I am not chasing the dollar anymore because I have enough of them. So it is sort of a cop-out to tell some poor inner city guy, 'You should not be so interested in money,' when he is working two jobs to support a family and to send a kid — the first in their family — through college. What he is doing is also success. I am not saying I have done everything I wanted to do. At this time, I get a lot of satisfaction over seeing things develop, whether it is a museum or a program or working with kids. That is real inner satisfaction.

PSD: *Your personal success is internal?*
WK: I find myself happiest when I am the busiest. I stay busy, but not for the sake of being busy. I'm always after something, even if it is a lower golf score. You can't be driven by money. Money has to be secondary. When a youngster can find something exciting, that you want to be doing fourteen hours a day, where you sleep so you can get up and do it again the next day, that's success. Figure out what that is. Success is doing what you really love and being good at it.

PSD: *How long have you been involved with the arts?*
WK: Since I was probably 12 years old, along with Red Grooms, though it was Charlie Grooms back then. Our mothers took us over to the old Children's Museum on Second Avenue every Saturday morning, my mother on one Saturday and his mother the next. That was where we first learned pastels, water colors, and even oils and charcoal. That was the first time that I had any formal education in the arts. From there, Red and I went all through grammar school and high school together. In high school, Red and I spent almost all of our weekends painting around Nashville. We were known at Hillsboro as the two crazy guys.

Based on that, I have always had an interest in the arts. I took piano as a youngster and my sister has a large school of dance. My parents played in the symphony, so I think you inherit a lot.

PSD: *Was painting your first love?*
WK: Yes. I really zeroed in on water colors, because oils seemed to take so long and I didn't have the patience. It's tough. I have again given up painting for golf. Five years ago, I was painting all Monday afternoons and preparing during the week for things, producing a couple of works a week. Someone like Red, with all that raw talent, probably likes the process. For me, it was only fun when I got to the end result. Art is hard work and I couldn't do it for a living. I

have never spent the time to make it feel really natural.

PSD: *How did you go from the art world to the world of contracting?*
WK: Red and I both had scholarships to go to the Chicago Institute of Art. I won the high school national scholastic award, but for some reason, I ended up at Vanderbilt in engineering school and have never really been sure why or how. I always thought that my Daddy must have pulled some strings. He leaned on some people to get me in, and I really didn't want to disappoint my Dad.

PSD: *You were probably just a young guy who did what was expected of him.*
WK: That's right. I went to Vanderbilt with no advanced math, no chemistry or physics. In my first semester, the only B grade I got was in was ROTC, but by my senior year, I made straight A's. I got out in four years, by some miraculous feat, with an engineering degree and went to work as a draftsman for an architectural firm. I then went into the army. When I got out, I went to work with a fraternity brother in a firm for 9 years. Then I started my own firm in 1969. I always loved the architectural and real estate business. There is nothing else I would rather be doing.

PSD: *You and Red Grooms have a rather unique connection.*
WK: Very unique. When we are together, it is just wonderful. It reminds us of all the years we have been together. He is moving back to Tennessee. Back in the '70s, when he would run out of money, I would send him a check to keep him going. We have always kept up with each other. I am doing all the research for a catalog résumé, a book to chronicle all of Red's work. I am in my second year on this book, and am fortunate to know all these people. It has been a real thrill to research this.

PSD: *Is Red your best friend?*
WK: No, because artists need space. I have never burdened him with a close relationship.

PSD: *You seem to have a very easy time fluctuating between the two different spheres of your brain.*
WK: It is one of the reasons I feel like I have wanted to be successful in dealing with art organizations. You have to deal with a committee and the board on the artistic side, but it is also important to be able to deal with the business side. Usually the businessman has a hard time understanding why some goofy guy wants certain things to happen in his gallery. And the art guy can't understand why the businessman won't spend $5000 to change the color of the walls. So I have always found myself as a mediator, since I had a strong sense of both sides.

PSD: *You don't put yourself in one box.*
WK: No. Sometimes I wonder if that is a cop-out, and whether I should take a stand. But I would rather accomplish a goal. If it takes compromise on some people's part to reach that goal, I am good at bringing different personalities together.

PSD: *In an age of specialization, you are a bit of an oddity.*
WK: Yes, I guess so. The arts are a very, very important part of everybody's life, whether you realize it or not. In small ways, too. You don't have to be real knowledgeable. Just walking through an art gallery — getting away from the reality of life — can make you feel good, too. Whether you understand the pieces of art or not, your mind is questioning why the artist did that. It just makes you feel good.

PSD: *Isn't there an element of magic, too?*
WK: You can't really explain it. People ask me all the time, "Why do we need to put all this energy and money into art? What is the

return?" That is a hard one to answer. I've seen several articles where people have tried to put this into words but haven't captured it.

PSD: *Throughout history, the arts have always needed the financial support of the general populace.*

WK: There is something about every culture in an industrial country where people feel they have to become knowledgeable about the arts. Of course, that's only after they have made all the money they think they want. I am more interested in art in a grass roots sense than the man on the street.

PSD: *You are currently very active in bringing a museum to downtown Nashville.*

WK: I am involved in bringing the Visual Arts Center down to where the post office is because it is such a great location. It would be so accessible, you could ride the bus or trolley to get there. We are trying to work a deal with the State to make it free, like the Metropolitan Museum in New York. It would be open to accept donations. This is a perfect example of what I talked about before in terms of serving as a mediator. I am dealing with a lot of egos trying to bring this together.

PSD: *What makes you unselfishly give of your energy and time?*

WK: I have an ego, too. I probably decided that unless I do it, there is a good chance it won't get done. They have been working on this museum thing for two years.

Red and I were really lucky that we had a full time art teacher in high school. Her name was Helen Connell. In the bottom two or three grades of our public school system, the number of art teachers is pathetically low. There was some funding made available through the State which allowed schools to decide whether to have assistant athletic coaches for sports teams or a music or art teacher. Less than 10% decided on spending the money for an art teacher.

PSD: *That is sad.*

WK: Nelson Andrews did an eight-year study on a state-wide level and came to the conclusion that some kids are not going to be doctors and engineers. These are the kids who are going to drop out, if you don't focus on their special needs. Once they drop out, you have lost them. These kids are going to the magnet schools but it is a real struggle. Helen Connell was always telling Red how good he was and how refreshing his work was. Maybe he would have been a successful artist anyway, but I don't know.

PSD: *Because Helen Connell was there for you and gave you the opportunity for artistic appreciation, do you now feel a sense of responsibility to bring the arts center to downtown Nashville for all the youngsters who aren't fortunate enough to have the exposure you were given?*

WK: I don't feel a sense of duty. Every year I go down to the Performing Arts Center where they do theater. This year, they did *Fiddler on the Roof,* and bused in 1,200 school children a day. To see these junior high school kids, all dressed up to come to Nashville from everywhere across the state ... to see their interest, how quiet and respectful they are to something they have never seen ... if there is just one kid out of a thousand who says, "That's it! I want to do that!", it opens up that creative element in his soul that needs to be brought out. If you don't bring it out when they're young, you miss out.

PSD: *Why do you care about such things?*
WK: I think if more people were involved in the arts and listening to their own souls, the world would be a better place to live. You'd find some relief from the rat race of work and providing for your family, all the political things. I heard a survey once say that 75% of all people do not enjoy their jobs. Why are they doing it? We now have a 55-

169

year-old guy down at the State Museum who was once Vice President of Finance for the Bridgestone Tire Company. Because he worked in a museum when he was going through school, this was something he always wanted to do. He was deprived because he felt an obligation to support his family. He took early retirement and said that we only had to pay him a little something, because "I want to spend the next ten years of my life doing what I really want to do."

Maybe in some cases you can't do all you want to do. But wouldn't it be nice to be able to get away from the rat race and sit down and hear poetry? Or just something that you enjoy. It can be any one of 20 different art forms, as long as it appeals to you.

PSD: *The thought that one kid in that audience may be affected is quite powerful.*
WK: Or one teacher. All of my children went to Brentwood Academy where they had one really good music teacher named Ron Huff, who could really motivate the students. He was so good, he was a threat to the school.

PSD: *How would you like to be remembered?*
WK: As you get older, you start to think about stuff like that. I plan to give my entire collection to a museum to be displayed. I want to be remembered as having the love to spend a lifetime putting this collection together. And a one in ten million shot that I would know an internationally renowned artist as a 12-year-old. What were the chances of that? And to have believed in him? I want it to be a little, simple thing but I know deep down that this collection would have never happened without my commitment.

Muhammad Omar Ali

Declined to have picture taken
for religious reasons.

Street Merchant

"Once each of us recognizes that we need to try to do what is right, then at that point we begin to advance towards each other. You may be in India and I may be in Honolulu, but we are moving toward one another. Ultimately, we will all be gathered together in the end."

PSD: *When did you first embrace Islam?*

MOA: Sixteen years ago. I had existed in this world for 34 years, and had reached a point where I was walking down the street over near Meharry — I can show you the exact spot — when these questions came straight down into my mind and frightened me. "Who are you? Where are you going? Who is God?" These questions stopped me right in my tracks with a fear I had never felt before because I didn't know the answers, and these were some serious questions.

From that point on, my life began to slowly evolve around the pursuit of the answers to these questions. I couldn't do anything else until I knew the answers to these questions.

PSD: *When this experience occurred, where were you in terms of your life?*

MOA: At the time, I was a drug addict and a typical young African-American coming from a poor family. I had been in the military and served in Vietnam, and came back a drug addict and an alcoholic. I had never used drugs before then. My mother was a very Christian woman and I had grown up in a very Christian family. My father had left us. I remember only seeing my father once as a child, when I was four years old. He gave me a coin. My mother was amazed that I could even remember that one day. I didn't see my father again until I was 34 years old.

PSD: *So you embarked on a search for answers to these questions.*

MOA: Even with a Christian upbringing, I found that the church didn't have the answers to my questions. Something just didn't fit, so I knew I had to pursue it. It was overwhelming. Where do you go to find the answer to who you are? Which direction do you turn? Who do you go see? So I found myself just praying to the Creator.

One thing led to another, and I became involved in the Elijah Muhammad movement, which at that time was laboring under the label of Nation of Islam. Later on, I found out that there was a difference. But after five years with that movement, some good had come from it. I gave up alcohol, drugs, fornication, adultery, gambling, and stealing. But when I found out that the Elijah Muhammad movement wasn't what it was supposed to be, I left.

I discovered Islam by coming in contact with practicing Muslims. Seeing the difference in these people and listening to the things they said affected me. These people were praying to the Creator, to the Ultimate Being. I embraced Islam and was able to come up with the answers to my questions. Every man has to have these answers, but most people flee from the questions because they appear too complex. It is a complex course to travel, but it absolutely essential.

PSD: *About those questions. Who are you?*

MOA: I am a Muslim. Muslim means one who submits his will to the will of his Creator. Not only are human beings Muslims, but all of creation is Muslim in that it is the will of the Creator. Understanding that, I am a creation of the Creator. That is who I am. My responsibility is to submit my will to His and not to follow my own desires.

PSD: *Where are you going?*

MOA: My course is determined by my actions. If I do what pleases my Creator, then every day, every moment of the journey will be peaceful and positive. If I disobey my Creator, my journey will not be successful.

PSD: *Was the Vietnam experience difficult?*

MOA: When you look back on things after you have experienced them, naturally, they don't seem like they were that hard, because there are a lot of things you forget. You almost have to. If you didn't, you would have to be on medication or seeing a psychiatrist because of all the things you saw. You must be fortunate enough to put those things in the necessary files and place them in the file cabinet of your mind. But you never can forget, because the mind is the ultimate recorder.

There are times when you need to pull those files out and look at them, so you can remember, or draw strength from them, whatever the case may be. To answer your question, it was one hell of an experience, and I am still learning from it.

PSD: *You were raised without a father. Is the responsibility of raising a child and being a father very important to you?*
MOA: It is probably one of the most important things in my life. Being there for my son is essential, as it is for every young person. Children need their parents to be there for them. We need our parents, and not only in childhood. We are always our parents' children, even when we are 50 years old.

PSD: *How can one become a better parent?*
MOA: Make an effort to establish the best relationship you can with your Creator, and everything else will fall into place. I would tell a young person to recognize the fact that you have a Creator to whom you are responsible. Turn to Him and seek the proper relationship with Him if you truly want to be successful in this world.

PSD: *Are you still close to your mother?*
MOA: I draw closer to my mother as time goes by. As you get older, you mature, and in maturing you become more appreciative of things that you have previously taken for granted. Fortunately, my mother is still living and she has accepted Islam. Because of this, my mother and I have been able to acquire a better understanding of each other than we ever had.

PSD: *How would you define success?*
MOA: Success for me is recognizing what is right and what is wrong, and using the

strength I have been given to make the effort to carry out the right thing to do.

PSD: *What is the vibe on the street today?*
MOA: I don't like that word. There really is no 'vibe' out there. I would say that an atmosphere exists. If you go in the forest, there is an atmosphere. If you go into the jungle, there is an atmosphere. The same thing that is going on in Nashville is going on across the nation and around the globe. What I have found in my travels is that the key is respect. If you genuinely learn to respect creation, creation will respect you and respond to you in a positive way in return.

PSD: *What about the higher level of spiritual activity that I sense going on?*
MOA: I come into contact with a lot of different people over the course of a week or month, and I see what you're referring to. I am really fascinated by how spiritual the younger people are. I talk to dope dealers, politicians, lawyers, wealthy people, poor people, a lot of different folks. Young people's vision of what is going on and what needs to take place is so much clearer than the nation or the world could possibly comprehend at the moment.

PSD: *These children are the future of the world.*
MOA: They want to do something, but don't know what to do. A lot of them are selling drugs because this is the way they see to make money and lift themselves and their families out of the darkness to a more comfortable level of existence. A lot of them are becoming violent because they think that this is a means to a level of respect they feel they need. You have a lot of the youth doing some pretty negative things, but if you sit down and talk to them on a one to one basis and get to the human being there, cutting past all the other stuff, you will find that these young people express things that will blow you away.

PSD: *You have a connection to these kids.*
MOA: I love young people. They are the ones that I am excited about. A lot of the things they are doing, I did as a youth, and I have come out of it OK. Let us look at things in our own past that we have done. We are human beings who make mistakes that affect the lives of other people. We can't blame society for the problems that we have. We cannot judge.

PSD: *Are you optimistic about our collective future?*
MOA: There are some young people out there in the streets right now who are going to turn this whole thing in a positive direction based on the experiences they are having right now. Out of bad can come some of the best.

PSD: *Do you have a dream?*
MOA: Only to become my true self, a total and complete submission to the Creator. That is my major goal and also my biggest challenge.

PSD: *How would you like to be remembered?*
MOA: I would like to be remembered by those who knew me in a way that would influence them to do what is good. When they think about me, they would remember what I was about — the way I lived my life — and they would try to follow in that direction, too. That is the way I would like to be remembered.

PSD: *I sense that you embrace unity.*
MOA: This comes from embracing Islam. Before that, I had no consciousness. I was only for me and what would benefit me.

Now I understand that every human being is my brother and my sister. I must respect all human beings and respect the entire creation. I must try to be of benefit to my brothers and sisters regardless of their position in life. That is part of the struggle. Not to just try to bene- fit people you like, because that is easy to do, but to try to benefit someone you don't like.

PSD: *You see a brotherhood of man.*
MOA: Wherever I go, I see all people the same way. When I went to Manhattan, I was seeing people recognize something in me which is unusual in New York, and I would acknowledge that. It is my responsibility to acknowledge any person as my brother.

You never know when someone might be affected by your acknowledging and speaking to them, even though you may never see that person again. I remember times when I was feeling really down or depressed and some- body might have spoken to me and said, "Hey, son, how are you doing?" It affected me that this person spoke to me. There was a kindness, a concern, or some love in the voice. It put a little fuel on the flame and it kept me alive.

PSD: *Brotherhood is a most beautiful thing.*
MOA: To me, brotherhood is all about being able to feel and share the kinds of things that only brothers can feel and share, not just a word you throw about. Once each of us rec- ognizes that we need to try to do what is right, then at that point we begin to advance towards each other. You may be in India and I may be in Honolulu, but we are moving toward one another. Ultimately, we will all be gathered together in the end. But during the course of life, if we encounter one another in this world, we will automatically identify each other and say, "This is my brother."

Susan Hall

Teacher of the Year, Tulip Grove Elementary School

"I honestly care about each and every child that comes through that door. I want them to be healthy and to be safe. And to work at their potential. I care about every child that is here. So they know when they come here that I value them as a person and love them as a child."

PSD: *What made you become a teacher?*
SH: Way back when I was in school, there were not too many career choices for women. If you didn't go to school you could be a secretary, or you could go to technical school, or be a nurse. Teaching fit well into my family orientation. You could teach and still have summers to be home with your children. I wanted to be both a wife and mother, yet still have a career. The education field allowed me to do this.

PSD: *Did the desire to teach start when you were young?*
SH: I was one of those little kids who wanted to be a teacher. My mother had both a family and a career as a teacher, so I had a point of reference. I did not go into this blind.

PSD: *Where did you look for new ideas?*
SH: In 1984, I went back to teach physical education at Paragon Middle School. This is when I started thinking, 'I need to make this job better.' So I started looking for seminars, workshops, and conventions to help me learn. I guess I am a self-motivated type of person. Self-motivation, for me, is a lifestyle I grew up with. You didn't just go earn a salary, come home, and forget it. You always tried to do something better.

From those workshops, I found out that everything I learned in college was worthless. I needed to start over again, to change the way I was doing things. So in 1989, I came here to Tulip Grove already having been to enough workshops and conventions to know exactly where I was headed. I thought it would be a wonderful opportunity to come into a brand new school with some brand new ideas. But it took about six years for a new way to take hold.

PSD: *What is it you do with your kids?*
SH: I work on a process that is called Skills Themes Curriculum that was developed by a woman in Oak Ridge named Shirley Holt Hale with two other teachers. In a skill theme curriculum, you teach separate skills and concepts until the child is ready to play a certain sport. It used to be that they would teach the game first and hope the skill would develop as a result. We do the reverse. We teach movement concepts like force and flow, and relationships to objects and partners. You keep adding concepts until the child is on a comfortable level. We are teaching the accomplishment of short-term goals.

PSD: *Are kids these days more out of shape than they were in the past?*
SH: We are getting ready to measure height and weight in our school. It seems like the older the kids get, the more sedentary they become. I think kids in the United States are 10% to 20% overweight on average.

PSD: *Do you think television has contributed to this?*
SH: Of course. A lot of kids come from single parent homes where they get off the school bus, go into the house, and lock the door. So turning on the TV and having a snack is sometimes the best they can do. Plus these poor mothers work, so it may be a lot easier to stop at McDonalds on the way home than it is to cook a good meal. I wish we stressed nutrition more in our program, but mostly we stress an active lifestyle.

PSD: *Do you try to connect with these kids on a one-to-one basis?*
SH: There are 800 to 900 kids in this school, but I do have the same child from kindergarten through the sixth grade. So I connect more over the long term. One mother commented that the greatest thing she had seen was her children bringing home and applying the skills I had been teaching. Like when a child says, "Mom, let's jump rope and get your heart-rate up." So there is some transference.
PSD: *How would you define success?*

SH: For me, it is a career I enjoy and I continue to find ways to improve it. As long as I am continuing to better myself in order to improve the quality of education and learning I give to my students, then I consider myself successful. Basically, I am a life-long learner. If I ever level out and not continue learning, then I would not consider myself a success.

PSD: *Do you take that same philosophy into your home?*
SH: Yes, I do. I probably focus more on my students now that my daughter is gone. So over the last couple of years, the major thrust has been my career. I am a caretaker-type person who is not happy unless I am giving something of myself. Even if it is just an encouraging pat on the back. In teaching, you are constantly giving of yourself — whether it be about your subject matter or just helping children feel better about themselves. You cannot do this by just sitting behind a desk or a computer. You have to be there one-on-one in a lot of instances. If a child falls down, I'm there to pick him up.

PSD: *What is the hardest part of what you do?*
SH: It can be very demanding and draining. The first year I taught here, I came across some resistance to what I was trying to do. It took some time for me to sell my program. I eventually worked on a curriculum committee so that the whole school system could be on this program.

PSD: *Are you teaching confidence and socialization?*
SH: Confidence and socialization comes through the inner motivation of the student. I would like to believe they had confidence to go out and play the game, but I don't think I really teach and instill it. We do try to encourage the children to improve through practice.

PSD: *As teacher of the year, what do you feel is the most important thing you are trying to transmit to these children?*
SH: That I care about them, that I honestly care about each and every child that comes through that door. I want them to be healthy and to be safe. And to work at their potential. I care about every child that is here. So they know when they come here that I value them as a person and love them as a child.

I keep thinking that I am way too old to be doing this. I have a 21 year old daughter, but the children keep me young. Just their music alone. I would probably be back with the Beach Boys. (She laughs)

PSD: *Did you see the film* Mr. Holland's Opus?
SH: Oh yes. I told a friend, as the tears were rolling down my face, that the dream of every teacher was to be effective. No matter what you did when you had that student, they captured something from you — a skill, some knowledge, an attitude, or motivation — something that would make you be remembered. My mother used to say, "You never know what effect you have on children."

PSD: *What was it like to win the Teacher of the Year award?*
SH: I was dumbfounded! My teaching philosophy is that all children should be valued and loved. This was just something extra. I don't really believe in the concept of a Teacher of the Year. I think we should be working together, not competing. When I went to the reception for the award, though, I was very moved. I have been so humbled by the experience.

PSD: *Your class is very popular.*
SH: What kids like about my class is the boundaries and parameters that allow them to feel safe. Kids love discipline that is fair and secure. I feel like these are my kids. When I see them down at Wal-Mart, they light up and

say, "Miss Hall, Miss Hall." So I keep plugging away and hope that somewhere a light goes on. These kids will love anything or anybody that is nice to them.

PSD: *Your love for these kids really shows.*
SH: If they need me, I am there. Regardless.

PSD: *How can we make education better?*
SH: Money! If we could get class sizes down to about 15 kids per classroom, we would have enough educational materials and consumables. We need smaller class sizes. Children are coming to school with so much more baggage these days and there are physical problems, hyperactive children, kids whose mothers were addicted to crack cocaine.

Parenting is not a skill that is recognized as a viable part of life anymore. Children are not being raised, they are not being taught at home. Now I can't say that across the board. But children are being allowed to make decisions that they have absolutely no business making. They don't have the skills. I don't blame their parents, because they are struggling, too. Things like simple courtesy are missing, and as educators, we can't teach this. We can't teach table manners and etiquette on top of a full curriculum.

PSD: *Are you optimistic?*
SH: I guess I would have to say I am optimistic. Otherwise I would have to dig a hole some place and fall in. Where would I be if I didn't think that things could be better? I do get aggravated with politicians who want to believe that they have the bull by the horns but have never been inside a classroom. Children are our future and they are the ones who will be taking care of us. The government is spending our social security now, so if these children don't get educated and are unemployed in the future, what is going to happen? Where are we going to be?

PSD: *Why do you think the political process cannot get behind something that is obviously so vital and important?*
SH: I think the problem is ignorance. Many politicians remember what it was like when they were in school and have no idea what the current climate is like. When you start talking about funding for education, you have to look at the legislature's constituency. Elderly people don't want to be funding education, they want Social Security and Medicare. Kids don't really have a lobby of their own. Nobody wants to raise taxes. I wasn't opposed to the NFL coming to town, but I was opposed to the use of public funds. It is a shame that surplus funds from the water department could not have been used for better things. Unfortunately, you are not likely to see a lot of yard signs around town that say, 'Education YES!' I would like to see the NFL team coming here give a percentage to education.

PSD: *How would you like students to remember you?*
SH: "I remember her because she cared about me." That I cared whether they were healthy. I talked to a P.E. teacher one day who said he didn't like the little kids holding his hand and hanging on to him. I looked at him and said, 'You know, you might be the only person who hugged that kid today. If you miss that opportunity, that kid may go home without thinking that anyone cared about him!' In my book, kids walk out that gym door with a hug. If they want one, they got one!

179

Harry Bonnaire, MD

Physician

"You can basically look at human life as consisting of living, eating, working, and dying. But I think you need to transcend this, in terms of giving something back to the community, the world, and especially to the children."

PSD: *Tell me a little about your early life.*

HB: I grew up in a very nice town, in a very poor country, in a suburb of the capital of Haiti. I had a good family that taught me early on the importance of honesty and looking to get the best in life. My mother was a teacher, so I was also taught the value of getting an education. My father was a businessman who always worked very late. There wasn't much parent-child interaction, but lots of respect.

PSD: *Was it a supportive environment?*

HB: Yes. It was a real community where the neighbors looked after one another. It was a very easy place to grow up, compared to what I see now. There wasn't the opportunity to get in trouble. Basically, if you went to school, did your homework and studied, then you were free to play with your friends. This was a sane and healthy environment where parents knew where their children were.

PSD: *When did you first dream of a career in medicine?*

HB: My dream to be a doctor started when I was 8 years old. That summer, I spent a month at the house where my mother had grown up. One day, I heard this noise coming from a small shed behind the main house, but could not find where the sound was coming from. Finally, I realized that the noise was coming from a tiny egg. I hatched the egg myself, then put the tiny chick, which was very weak, under a heat lamp to keep it warm. So I went home from my vacation with this little pet. My family said that you have to be a doctor or scientist because of this. When I finished secondary school, I decided to go into medicine.

PSD: *Did you always have your sights set on coming to America?*

HB: I did not always dream of coming to the United States. Having grown up in a small country, my main goal was to just acquire more knowledge. Remember, Haiti is a French-speaking country, and I spoke absolutely no English. So I thought I would go to Europe. I was very poor and didn't think I could afford to come to America. I chose the United States mostly because of geography — it was a lot closer and easier for me to visit home.

PSD: *Why did you choose to leave Haiti?*

HB: Because of the political situation in Haiti at the time. When I asked myself the question, 'How do you see yourself five years from now?' I could not answer. I could not live in an environment of uncertainty, so I left and came to the United States.

PSD: *When did you first arrive?*

HB: I came to the United States in 1983 with $500 in my pocket. I could not speak any English at the time. I did not have a fear of failure, but was afraid of the unknown. In life, when something has to happen it will happen — it is bigger than you. Even though there was every indication that I would stay in my country, there was something else at every turn that told me I would leave — a gut feeling, an intuition, so to speak.

PSD: *Was it a struggle when you first arrived?*

HB: Not really. I started washing cars at first, then got a job working at a medical lab. I wrote more than 100 letters trying to find a hospital that would accept me in a training program. It was frustrating because there is a narrow window of time to get accepted. But I could not go home a failure.

PSD: *How do you define success?*

HB: Success is really happiness — how happy you feel about yourself and what you achieve in your life. It doesn't matter what kind of achievement it is — money, marriage, having a family, or something else. You must enjoy the process. For me, it's all the steps I take on the way to my goals and really feeling good about myself on the way there. It is not the destination, but the journey — that's the key.

PSD: *What ingredients are important for success?*

HB: Most important, you must have integrity. Never compromise yourself. Never compromise yourself and stay very focused.

PSD: *So in a sense you are successful?*

HB: I guess I am successful, because I'm happy and enjoy what I do. My only wish is that my parents, who have both passed away, could be here with me to share it all. I think they would be very proud, which for me would be another kind of success. I feel they are still with me in a spiritual sense, but I do miss their physical presence.

PSD: *Talk a bit about your patients.*

HB: Did you know that most of the people who come into my office are not really sick but just need to talk? They have a need to be heard, that someone cares about them. They need assurance. As a society, we live in too much isolation. People have very solitary lives. Maybe what I can do is to reach some of them, to make them feel a little better.

PSD: *Do you also teach medicine?*

HB: Yes, I have medical students following me everyday. My way is to not only educate them medically, but to also teach them about life. There is a lot to being a good physician. I teach them that life is always a challenge that you must be prepared to meet. I think what makes a physician great is how much he or she cares about people. This same fundamental principle would also make you a success in any field.

PSD: *What qualities have served you best?*

HB: I think it all comes down to integrity and never compromising yourself, because you may achieve a lot but not be very happy on the inside without integrity. You can basically look at human life as consisting of living, eating, working, and dying. But I think you need to transcend this, in terms of giving something back to the community, the world, and especially to the children. I think you have to give something back. It doesn't matter how, as long as you do it. Some people are artists, some are teachers. I think of my training young physicians as a way of giving something back to the community.

PSD: *What is difficult for you?*

HB: Right now, it is the daily challenge of life — not the big obstacles but the small day-to-day stuff ... getting my exercise, some time for myself, keeping my health in tact, and so on.

PSD: *Are the mind and body related in terms of physical health?*

HB: Yes, of course. In Latin, "mensana in corpore sano" means a good spirit is a healthy body. You cannot have one without the other. My advice on how to be healthy is make exercise a routine and eat well.

PSD: *Is love an important part of being healthy?*

HB: Oh, yes. You have your whole lifetime to learn, almost everything we do is learned. So I believe we must learn to love people. You can take things that happen to you and learn good lessons from them. Most things I learn come from talking to people — it's the best book you can have. Life and people.

PSD: *Any closing thoughts?*

HB: You must always be yourself!

Shankaracharya Swami

Preceptor, Sadhana Ashram

"If one has peace, if one has love, if one can live in dignity, if one can accept what life presents and bring awareness and love into every situation — then I would say that they were successful."

PSD: *How did you come to adopt an eastern way of life?*

SS: When I was younger, I was on a quest for greater knowledge. I worked in aerospace engineering and design at the time. I actually worked on a system for the Apollo moon flight and helped design it. Even though I was discovering more and more about mechanical things, I still felt somewhat dry in my own experience of life, of touching something that would really give me fulfillment. I wanted to know why people did things, what their motivations were, and to get more into the human heart — to understand at a deeper level.

PSD: *Was this during the 1960s?*

SS: This was a time in the mid-'60s when the psychedelic movement was flourishing. People were looking for answers, for something more. The next logical step was to look for masters, or people that had found a way to be able to stay in steady states of awareness. Through their spiritual practices, they were able to attain something deeper within themselves. The psychedelic period showed other possibilities in consciousness, but it was difficult to find anyone who was really able to have a positive transformation through the experience. I was looking for people whose lives reflected a deep state of spiritual experience, regardless of their religious context or spiritual approach.

PSD: *Did you undertake a spiritual quest?*

SS: I started wandering the world looking for people that had found some kind of spiritual fulfillment. Generally, I was looking for saints in different traditions and different places. I just wanted to spend time with them and see what kind of effect it would have on me, hoping that it would counter the dryness I felt inside.

PSD: *You went from an external model of fulfillment to an internal model.*

SS: Originally, I was looking for fulfillment through my career or trying to climb the ladder into a good position. But the ideas of 'Who am I?', of divine love, or of feeling a oneness with everyone else were still within me. I wasn't able to attain those things through my career. I wandered through Africa, Europe, and the Middle East. Eventually, I wound up in India.

In India, the basic context is that divinity dwells within all beings. The culture is based on the belief of honoring the God within you and the other. The idea of the spiritual path is to remove whatever it is within you that obscures that divinity within, so that you can realize it or become one with it. It's just like where the Bible says, "The kingdom of heaven dwells within."

PSD: *Did you find common traits among the varied traditions?*

SS: Even though I spent time with a number of saints from a number of traditions, I started to notice that they all possessed the same characteristics. Even though they had different approaches, there still was a spiritual energy that could be felt there, there was still love and compassion, and they had come into some experience of love. This was a love that embraced the whole world and all situations. So by spending time with these saints and patterning after them, I was able to tap into things that I wasn't able to tap into merely by reading books. They all taught universal principles, even if they did so within different frameworks.

PSD: *What are these universal principles?*

SS: The first principle is that love is inherent within all beings. People are always looking outside of themselves to find love. They may find it for awhile, but the situation may change and then there is sorrow. Actually, the situation outside is only an occasion for love to flash forward from within a person. Most people don't realize that love is their own inner treasure. If they can find it within themselves, then love can radiate outward into everything they do, and isn't dependent on the external situation or a relationship.

The other principle is unity. We are not really separate. Eastern belief is that the supreme consciousness manifests in different guises. In some it is more revealed, and in others, more concealed. Everything in the universe is connected. If we find love in our selves and also realize that this is one sea of consciousness with different individual manifestations in it, we can create a whole different way in which we look at the world and other people.

Actually, the great saints and masters like Jesus or Buddha are people who realized divine love and experienced it within themselves, thus manifesting it in the world. They became examples for others to pattern on to come into that same experience.

PSD: *These great beings were completely self-actualized.*
SS: Jesus was someone who experienced that divinity within and manifested it forth into the world. But it doesn't mean that a Muslim or a Jew doesn't have divinity or awareness within him. A Christian can pattern on Jesus, and because of his state of being, can hopefully bring forth the same qualities. These great beings and religions are not here to divide people. If you start out with the idea that divinity dwells within all people and can be honored, then the potential for self-actualization is there for all people regardless of their religious belief.

PSD: *The key is to believe you are not separate from the Divine?*
SS: Instead of thinking divinity is out there somewhere in God or a God-like being, bring it to where it is part of one's own self. If we could do this, it would break down the friction between a lot of people. Even if we did not agree with the way they were trying to manifest divinity, we could still honor it.

PSD: *Isn't one's ultimate experience with the Divine unique, and also especially difficult to communicate?*
SS: The experience of Divine love and unity manifests through one's own field of karma or one's nature in it's own unique way. But it is the same love and the same inner self. If light passes through different glasses it has different colors, but is still the same light. The universal love and principles that we come into communion with express themselves through our nature in a way that appears to be unique because of the display. But the love is still the same.

PSD: *In it's infinite manifestations, it is still the same light.*
SS: That's right. In certain ways, you have to look at life as a school that we are all looking to learn something from. We are looking for peace, happiness, and understanding, and going to a great school. There are a lot of experiences that can be difficult, like suffering and pain, but they can be vehicles for one to learn greater tolerance and compassion. It is not the situation, but how one looks at the situation, and how one deals with and is affected by the situation.

PSD: *It is a matter of what we choose to embrace.*
SS: There can be certain thoughts that enter the mind. The thoughts themselves can't really do anything to the person. It is how one looks at the thoughts, and how one judges the thoughts. Which thoughts does one choose to empower? What we are doing here is trying to help one use life situations to help bring spiritual transformation and growth. We also try to help one make friends with the mind and not to have identifications that would detract from their own innate radiance that dwells within them, which is joy and bliss.

PSD: *Joy and bliss is our natural state?*

SS: The source of all things is within your own being. If one can contact that loving place within themselves, it will radiate into all their situations. If they have love within themselves, they can see love in others. So one good way to help the world is to find joy and love within one's self and bring that into the world.

PSD: *The influence of one vital person can be tremendous.*
SS: That's right. The sense is of awe and wonder, not one of power.

PSD: *So it is not an ego-oriented experience.*
SS: No. We are all manifestations of the One, if we realize that the ego has a different connotation. Because everywhere we look is a display of the One. So we don't have the sense of individual separateness that divides us and puts us in competition with other people. Or even seeing other people as 'other'. That is different from the ego that sees itself as separate. How will you treat someone you see as part of your own divinity? It is a whole different consciousness. The way to bring about harmony and peace in the world is for the divinity to be revealed rather than concealed. God dwells in all beings.

PSD: *How do we find inner divinity while we are in this human form?*
SS: The way to find it does not come from a set of rules or a set of techniques. The first thing to recognize is simply that it is there, that the love dwells within.

PSD: *What if I am skeptical, but searching anyway?*
SS: Use the rational mind. For example, say you love your girlfriend. Five minutes later, you find out she slept with your friend. All of a sudden, you don't feel the same love. But your girlfriend is exactly the same as five minutes ago, only the way you looked at her has changed. So the love didn't come from the girlfriend, she was an occasion where love flashed forward from within yourself. It is logical. Love dwells within and everyone has had experiences of that love. What the mystic is trying to do is tap the love within and radiate that into all experience.

There are many religions, spiritual techniques, paths, and approaches to doing this. However, the fundamental task is to first recognize that 'It' is indeed there. The second is to want to come into the experience of it. Because if there is a want and there is a will, then there is a way. If the intent is there, and the recognition is there, then the way opens for that to happen.

PSD: *Will consciousness find us if we seek it?*
SS: Yes, because it is the One who appears as the yearning and the One who fulfills the yearning.

PSD: *It is all just consciousness at play?*
SS: Yes. That's the whole deal. Have an honest yearning and the recognition that love dwells within you. Be aware of the air that literally connects you to another. One has to court unity and court love.

PSD: *God is a mask or metaphor for the Oneness of all creation?*
SS: It could be looked at that way. You can embrace the world, but you have to be careful not to lose your connection to divinity. To embrace means that you are not detached from the world around you. The key is to practice both detachment and embrace simultaneously.

PSD: *Why did you want to have an ashram?*
SS: We are basically looking to present an environment that people will come into, that will help things to come forth from within one's self. I am not necessarily telling anyone how it all is. I don't even pretend to know how it all is. To consider some of these possibilities opens a person to more flexibility and tolerance.

PSD: *How would you define success?*

SS: Real success has to do with divine love and unity, with finding something within yourself to bring into your life that helps make the world a better place. To help bring about a feeling of love, compassion, and deeper understanding. One could be a successful carry-out boy at Kroger. People could have their groceries carried out and by just coming into contact with this boy, there could be some light brought into their lives because of his attitude. They might say, "Look at that guy carrying the groceries. He seems to be more happy and have more joy than I do, and I am a millionaire."

PSD: *Yet I don't hear you diminishing achievement.*

SS: There is something great about reaching a lofty position or going to the top in one's chosen endeavor that is not to be diminished. It is an accomplishment. At the same time, it is really important that one does not sacrifice the roots of one's being.

If deeper understanding and compassion can come forth in one's life, then I would think that to be a great success, regardless of the person's status — whether they have cancer or AIDS, work as a carry-out man, or they are the President. If one has peace, if one has love, if one can live in dignity, if one can accept what life presents and bring awareness and love into every situation — then I would say that they were successful.

PSD: *In our culture, we have achieved a great deal on the material plane.*

SS: It is a double-edged sword. Material wealth and all that goes with it has its beauty. At the same time, there are all kinds of problems and sufferings. I see that everywhere and in the people who come here every day. The material things are nice, but you have to find the thread within yourself to give your life resonance. You can get so caught up in the rat race, you fail to see all the beauty that is around you.

PSD: *I know you don't identify with your form, but how would you like people to remember the experience of your physical manifestation?*

SS: I am just part of a process. Being a spiritual teacher, what I teach is that the spiritual teacher dwells within all people as their higher intuition. I am here to help turn people inward so they can realize that within themselves.

PSD: *You are a spiritual facilitator?*

SS: For me, it is just being part of a process to help someone discover more of what is within themselves. If I can help with that, if that is what is happening, it is a great thing. I don't take any credit for it. It is just happening.

PSD: *Yet it is nice to be part of it.*

SS: It is nice to add my life to the current of unity and love. Life is a beautiful thing. There is a lot of suffering, but within this dance there is a divinity. To be able to dance in a beautiful way through whatever situations might occur, and bring awareness into them, with poise, is a great thing. Hopefully, that is what is happening here.

John Seigenthaler

President, First Amendment Center and Chairman Emeritus, *The Tennessean*

"I would like to be known as a journalist who made a difference, but also as a father who made a difference. I would also like to be remembered as someone who made a small difference in the field of civil rights and worked in other ways to right civil wrongs."

PSD: *When did you first fall in love with words?*

JS: Pretty early on, in the sixth, seventh, and eighth grades. I had the same wonderful teacher all three years, a nun, who told me I could write poetry, essays, and short stories. I loved words and continued to through high school. My mother and father both read to me from the first days that I can remember. I remember getting a record of Sir Lawrence Olivier doing *Hamlet* and *Henry V*; I memorized every word. I could probably still recite a soliloquy or two.

PSD: *What drew you into the newspaper business?*

JS: I really wanted to be a teacher. Thinking I would have been good at it. But my uncle got me a job at *The Tennessean*, and I got hooked as a reporter. It was clearly the right thing for me. I never thought about doing anything else after I had been there a short time. Ironically, the first lead paragraph I ever wrote didn't even have a verb in it. (He laughs.)

PSD: *What is the First Amendment Center about?*

JS: The First Amendment, those 45 words the founders gave us. Talk about eloquence! We are about raising the level of debate, dialogue, and discussion, thereby raising the appreciation and understanding for freedom of religion, speech, press, assembly, and redress. All of our programs are dedicated to raising that level of discussion with hopes that people will realize there is more to the First Amendment that touches their lives than they ever understood. Many people think of that amendment in a negative way, like an intrusive or abusive press or pornography. People are very cynical about the First Amendment.

PSD: *This amendment is really the cornerstone of our country?*

JS: Absolutely. It was actually the third

amendment the Third Congress proposed. Polls show that people today would probably not ratify the Bill Of Rights or the First Amendment. Then you get into something like a Flag-Burning Amendment. The Supreme Court said that flag-burning is protected under the First Amendment, although when I see someone burning a flag it pisses me off.

PSD: *But you still have to protect the right to do that.*

JS: You're right. If I had been born a Native-American, been screwed out of my land, been put on a reservation, denied an education, and the only way I can make any money is to work in a bingo parlor, I damned-well sure might want to burn one. If my skin had been black, and I had been treated in the horrendous way African-Americans have been treated, I might want to burn one. If I were a pacifist and wanted to protest my country's involvement in Vietnam, with the wanton bombing of cities where women and children were killed, I might want to burn a flag.

PSD: *The foresight and genius of our founding fathers in creating the First Amendment astounds me.*

JS: A legitimate question to ask is, "Why the hell did they do it?" The reason was that they didn't trust themselves with power. They had seen what the British had done with power. The founders basically said it was better to leave the power in the press to be wrong than for us to exercise the power to be wrong. I think it was the ultimate act of conscience and unselfishness to give up that power.

PSD: *Are you distressed by the abundance of tabloid press and its focus on what seems to be the lowest common denominator?*

JS: I have seen some of it that I deplore, but I have never seen any of it that I would censor. I have seen some I would censure, some I would criticize, but none I would censor.

PSD: *What's your view about the media actually creating violence as opposed to just being a reflection of the culture?*

JS: If you took every violent show off the air, I don't feel like you would decrease violence one bit. I just don't believe that. The larger question is whether the media should show some restraint in deference to people who believe differently about that than I do. And the answer to that question, in my opinion, is "Yes, they should." I think there is excessive violence and sex on television that is gratuitous. I don't think society needs it, and there may be some minimal hurt that accrues from it.

PSD: *This form of media tends to trivialize life.*

JS: There are a few people in society who may be triggered by something they see in the media. I have thought about this a great deal because it doesn't help my cause with the First Amendment. More self-restraint would be helpful.

PSD: *Are you disturbed by these major corporations buying media networks and controlling the news departments?*

JS: We are headed in a direction now, where in a relatively short time, we will have five or six major media giants. We need to start worrying about that now. I think they will also be heavily regulated. So I am concerned about it.

PSD: *How do you define success?*

JS: That is a very tough question for me. I know that I would have to be described as a person who has been successful. The only goal I have ever had was to be a great journalist. My only ambition was to make whatever I was working on at the moment the best it could be. I have done the things I have in my

life because they felt right in my stomach. There are reporters and editors I have touched and influenced all over the country. The Vice-President of the United States is a reporter I recruited. I see some success of my own in their success, and maybe that is vanity. But from my perspective, that is success. I am extremely proud of the fact that my son is a journalist.

PSD: *What has worked for you?*

JS: There are two things that I have always been able to do that have helped guide me. One is that I have been able, at times, to go somewhere for an hour or two and just think through problems. That has been a wonderful advantage for me. The second is that I have always had somebody around me who could privately come to me and say, "Bull_ _ _ _." Years ago, I decided you always had to have somebody to challenge your deepest-held convictions. I guess I am an intuition guy based on experience.

PSD: *With all of your drive and passion as a newspaper man, was it hard to strike a balance as a family man?*

JS: I'd say so. I am willing to accept traditional definitions of success in terms of high achievement, but high achievers are not always successful. Remember, it is very difficult to be successful in every area of human existence. It is very tough to be successful in business and be successful as a father or community leader. I guess if one area was shortchanged in my life, maybe it was the community. I thought my position as editor precluded my involvement in the community. I was a member of the Rotary club for a short period of time, until one day they refused to allow black members admittance. So I resigned that day.

PSD: *Were you a difficult man to work for?*

JS: The most important lesson I learned in my whole career was that power over subordinates is a monstrous weapon. If you are going to encourage subordinates towards high performance, you really have to be willing to understand how that power can punish. Then you have to understand that the people you have to work with on a daily basis have to be encouraged. They can't be intimidated and bullied.

PSD: *What made you a journalistic blood-hound?*

JS: A lot of it is upbringing. I was raised a very devout Roman Catholic, and was brought up to believe strongly in right and wrong, good and evil, justice and injustice. I was raised by parents who were very loving. I think I had a clear sense, pretty early on, of what it meant to be moral and ethical.

PSD: *What brings you the most pleasure these days?*

JS: I am really happiest when my wife and I are doing something together, particularly if my son and daughter-in-law are part of it. We have been married almost forty-two years. My wife was a professional pop singer who came here from Rome, Georgia. I met her when she was singing at a concert sponsored by *The Tennessean* at Centennial Park. She was singing there on Father's Day. I covered the event, and that is where I met her.

PSD: *Were you quite smitten?*

JS: I was, but she wasn't. (He laughs) The first five years we were married she made five times more money than me. She sang with Arthur Godfrey and his band, and was very successful. She sacrificed a lot for my career, and after I became Editor, she rarely sang for money.

PSD: *Do you thrive on competition?*

JS: I am very competitive, and hate to lose. I played tennis every day for years and won a lot of club tournaments and trophies. I think competition is part of what has driven me all

these years. The other thing was luck. My gene pool had some talent in it. My mother and father gave me some gifts that I was blessed to have.

PSD: *You fought against institutionalized power blocking the rights of human beings.*

JS: Yes, because that pisses me off. Like when they tried to turn the lights off at Fisk University because the school hadn't paid its gas bill. I fought like hell, and eventually we raised the money to get them back on.

PSD: *You lost a brother recently.*

JS: I was the oldest, and the brother who was right after me — a bloody saint, a social worker — died last year. He was terrific. It was hard to lose him. Shortly after he got his Master's degree, he started a place called Richland Village, which was a home for children. I remember one night shortly after becoming Editor I was on my way home, down some side street, when I came upon my brother walking along the gutter. I said, 'What the hell are you doing walking along this street?' He said, "A couple of the kids have run away from the home and I was walking over to their house." I said, 'You are out of your skull. Go home, call the police, and have them bring them back. You go home and go to sleep.' He gave me quite a piece of his mind. I didn't understand that he had to be there for these kids. He loved those kids.

PSD: *It sounds like he was successful in a different way.*

JS: I can talk about winning prizes and awards. But what makes a difference in life is a guy like this, who is a success, who gives of himself enough to make a difference in some kids' lives. All of us consider him the most successful amongst us. My achievements mean nothing compared to him. This man truly defines success.

PSD: *Are you a spiritual man?*
JS: I was born a Roman Catholic and I am still one. That's not to say I am comfortable within the religious dogma of any religion.

PSD: *How would you like to be remembered?*
JS: I don't want to be phony about it, but I would like to be remembered. I would like to be known as a journalist who made a difference, but also as a father who made a difference. I would also like to be remembered as someone who made a small difference in the field of civil rights and worked in other ways to right civil wrongs. I relate to people who are in trouble.

PSD: *Do you ever think of the miraculous wonder of being?*
JS: Let me put it this way. My favorite poem is by Walt Whitman, and is in his book *Leaves of Grass*. It is called *Miracles*. It says, "Who makes much of miracles, as for me I see of nothing else." Then he recites a litany of the miracles that are around him. I identify with 'miracles' as Whitman, who was an agnostic, saw them. I have told my wife that whatever else happens at my funeral, I would like my favorite poem read. Whitman sees miracles everywhere — riding in a car, walking along the water, in the fishes in the sea. I relate to that poem in a very meaningful way.

MIRACLES

WHY! Who makes much of a miracle?
As to me, I know of nothing else but mira-
cles,
Whether I walk the streets of Manhattan,
Or dart my sight over the roofs of houses
toward the sky,
Or wade with naked feet along the beach, just
in the edge of the water,
Or stand under trees in the woods,
Or talk by day with any one I love—or sleep
in the bed at night with any one I love,
Or sit at table at dinner with my mother,
Or look at strangers opposite me riding in the
car,
Or watch honey-bees busy around the hive,
of a summer forenoon,
Or animals feeding in the fields,
Or birds—or the wonderfulness of insects in
the air,
Or the wonderfulness of the sun-down—or of
stars shining so quiet and bright,
Or the exquisite, delicate, thin curve of the
new moon in spring;
Or whether I go among those I like best, and
that like me best—mechanics, boatmen, farm-
ers,
Or among the savants—or to the soiree—or to
the opera,
Or stand a long while looking at the move-
ments of machinery,
Or behold children at their sports,
Or the admirable sight of the perfect old man,
or the perfect old woman,
Or the sick in hospitals, or the dead carried to
burial,
Or my own eyes and figure in the glass;
These, with the rest, one and all, are to me
miracles,
The whole referring—yet each distinct, and in
its place.

To me, every hour of the light and dark is a
miracle,
Every cubic inch of space is a miracle,

Every square yard of the surface of the earth
is spread with the same,
Every foot of the interior swarms with the
same;
Every spear of grass—the frames, limbs,
organs, of men and women, and all that concerns them,
All these to me are unspeakably perfect miracles.

To me the sea is a continual miracle;
The fishes that swim—the rocks—the motion
of the waves—the ships, with men
in them,
What stranger miracles are there?

Whitman, Walt. 1900. *Leaves of Grass.*

Joe Rodgers

Venture Capitalist, Former Ambassador to France

"It is nice to be able to do something that helps other people. Then you really feel good. Education is terribly important, but so is that desire. You don't have to make a lot of money to be successful. Just look at all the people who run YMCAs. My God, they are successful."

PSD: *Who was the biggest influence in your life?*

JR: My parents, though it is hard to pinpoint what I got from my mother and what I got from my father. My father stressed integrity in every way. The times I got in trouble with him were the times I wasn't honest. This seems to be a trait with kids. They don't want to get in trouble, so they tell a little white lie, not a dark, black one. I would get in trouble with my father for that. My mother was always there, she loved me. When I felt bad, she rubbed my head. They gave me a feeling of self-esteem, a feeling of being loved, integrity, and the meaning of a day's pay for a day's work.

PSD: *Do you remember your first job?*

JR: The first job I ever had really working for a paycheck was with a pipeline contractor. On the first day, I brought my sack lunch. Everyone in the crew was black except me. My job was to cover up the cement joints with dirt so they wouldn't wash out. I worked without my shirt on like the rest of the crew. Then I went to get my lunch and found it covered with ants because I had set it on the ground. When I got home that afternoon, I was burned to a crisp like a piece of bacon. (He laughs.) The next morning, I said I was sick and couldn't go to work, but my Daddy got me up and sent me back to work. So my parents were a good influence. I worked from six in the morning to six at night, six days a week.

PSD: *Where did you grow up?*

JR: In a little town of about 1,800 people down in Alabama. My Daddy was the county engineer, the guy who repaired and repaved the roads. Later on, he became the highway commissioner, so we moved to Montgomery.

PSD: *How did you get involved in contracting?*

JR: I went to the University of Alabama civil engineering school. Then I was in an engineering group in the military before moving up to Nashville in 1961 to work for the Dixie Pipe Company. I worked for them about four years before I started my own company. I later sold that company in 1979 to Centex for about ten times what it is worth. Over the course of 12 years, I built over 200 hospitals for Hospital Corporation of America — that was over $1.5 billion worth of business from just that one client! Doctor Thomas Frist Sr. and his son Tommy really gave me a once in a lifetime opportunity.

PSD: *How did you come upon Dr. Frist and the HCA business?*

JR: I had started my company in 1966 and they had started theirs two years later. I met Dr. Frist at the Master's Golf Tournament through Sam Fleming, who was with Third National Bank. We were put in the same cottage together and Dr. Frist said that he was starting a chain of hospitals. I giggled to myself and thought, 'Yeah, sure.' Then two weeks later he called me up and said, "Do you want to build a hospital?" And I said 'Yes, sir!' To my recollection, we built the first five hospitals on a handshake without a contract. They are unusual in their loyalty.

PSD: *What is your definition of success?*

JR: I have a different twist on success. So many people feel that success is to make a lot of money or to own a company. That might be success when it comes to a career, but success in life is a lot more. I try to be successful as a father, as a husband, as a community leader — and I'm not, in all of these. I try hard to be a good fund-raiser for charitable and civic organizations. I feel obligated to be involved with the Salvation Army or working with Junior Achievement and the Boy Scouts. I feel that making a lot of money so that you can give that money back to worthy causes in the community and people who are less fortunate is a part of being successful in life along with being successful in a career.

I feel very strongly that you should have a relationship with your Lord. You should spend time making certain that you understand Christianity. You don't have to accept it. If the Bible is 10% correct and there is a heaven and there is a hell, and you are going to spend eternity in one or the other, it makes sense that you should understand it. Hopefully, you can come to the point where you can say, "I'm going to ask Jesus Christ to come into my life." Or maybe that is not for you. It is your decision. But I don't think you can be totally successful in life without having a relationship with your Lord.

PSD: *Have you always had such a relationship?*

JR: No, no, no, no. (He laughs.)

PSD: *What was your catalyst?*

JR: A bible study when I was about 32 years old. I had all the money in the world. My headquarters was that big gold building at the airport. I had a Lear jet and a King Air, two vacation homes, a Mercedes, the fastest car there was. I had everything that money could buy, but I was still totally empty. I was miserable. I spent money on foolish things trying to make myself happy. It was a God-shaped hole and nothing can fill it but God. I never tried to fill that hole with drugs, but I did a lot of other things.

My wife had accepted the Lord a couple of years before me and I saw a real change in her life. She was happier and more content. She mentioned a bible study to me and the only reason I went was that I knew the five other people who were also going were as bad off as I was. (He laughs.) Isn't that a shame? I would not have gone to a bible study with a bunch of goody-goodies for anything in the world. But these were guys I knew that had been bad. So we read the bible and prayed out loud, something I had never done before. We told each other about our problems. I had never told anybody about

my problems before. I was 'too strong, I did not need anybody.' But I always felt better going home from that bible study than I did going to it. I asked Jesus to come into my life during that bible study and my life did change.

PSD: *You noticed a difference.*

JR: Construction is a rough business. There's a lot of drinking and cussing. There are some good people, but it's a very hard business. I just found my life changed. I found myself being nicer to people, being nicer to my family. I was happier and more content. I felt more successful. I have never known a person who was truly successful who wasn't happy at home. Nobody can come to work and do their best if they feel like they have failed as a father or as a husband. To be totally successful in all of life, you have to feel like you have accomplished something at work and also done some good at home.

PSD: *That's tough to balance.*

JR: If you are really trying to be successful in all of life, you try hard in all of those areas. I don't believe that people can make a lot of money, and not give any of it away, and still feel good. Being able to give money away is the best feeling in the world.

PSD: *You are in love with the free enterprise system.*

JR: It has given me everything. I came from a great family who sent five kids to college. I didn't have a nickel. I started the Joe M. Rodgers Corporation with $1,000, of which I put up $250.

PSD: *If he should ask, what advice would you give your own grandson before he went out into the world?*

JR: Just by asking that question, he would show me that he has the desire. If you come across honestly and with integrity, and show that you really want to do something, there are so many people that will help you. There are loads of people who would be more than willing to help those who want to really help themselves.

So the first thing is that you really have to have the desire to do something. You have to believe. It is nice to be able to do something that helps other people. Then you really feel good. Education is terribly important, but so is that desire. I read that 36% of Davidson County high school students drop out. How would you like to have a business that lost 36% a year? You don't have to make a lot of money to be successful. Just look at all the people who run YMCAs. My God, they are successful.

PSD: *It is interesting that such a successful venture capitalist would say, "Money isn't everything."*

JR: People say, "Well, that's easy for you to say because you have got a bunch of it." That is a fact I worry about sometimes. Would I be as outspoken as I am about success being a lot more than money if I didn't have a lot of it?

Another piece of advice for success — networking is very important. Like the Junior Chamber of Commerce. Get involved with things, it will make you feel better. Everyone should be involved in non-profit causes. Also, I tell my son to get to work 15 minutes early and leave 15 minutes late. People will notice you and you will get more done.

PSD: *What was your philosophy and experience as a parent?*

JR: That is probably my one regret, though my children turned out great. I have a great family and we love each other, but I spent very little time with them since I was always working. Success to me was about making a lot of money, so my wife raised our children. If I had one thing to do over again, I would spend more time with them.

Children grow up so fast, and then they are gone. I am spending more time with my grandchildren. My wife was a listener and I was a talker. All I wanted to do, since I spent so little time with them, was tell them how they should do everything. My wife listened to their concerns. To be a successful parent, you have to be a good listener. I wasn't.

PSD: *Were you raised with the model that parents had to be tough?*

JR: I don't think so, but that's the way it was back then when I was a father. You didn't love and hug and kiss your son, but I kiss him now and he's 31.

PSD: *Have you become more compassionate over time?*

JR: Some of my real conservative friends say I am a moderate now. (He laughs.) Actually, I'm ultra-conservative.

PSD: *It's funny you used that term. I think that all these labels we use to identify ourselves and others tend to divide us. I could talk with you for months and never come up with a label or definition to capture all that makes up Joe Rodgers.*

JR: Everybody has different definitions. To some, an ultra-conservative could be a real nut.

PSD: *Is building self-esteem a key to personal success?*

JR: We have to give people hope that there is a better way than what they have, if they would just make the effort. We have to somehow make people believe that.

PSD: *Do you think love is the key ingredient?*

JR: I think so. Christianity has changed my life. I believe that people who don't accept Jesus Christ as their Lord and Savior will live an eternity in hell. And that is so bad it makes me cry.

PSD: *What do you think was the message of Jesus?*
JR: Forgiveness.

PSD: *Where does Christ's forgiveness come into play?*
JR: He will forgive you while you are on this earth if you ask Him. That is one reason the death penalty worries me, because sometimes men find salvation while in prison.

PSD: *What keeps you going?*
JR: I enjoy doing deals and building things. I could quit and go sit out on my farm, but idle hands and idle minds get you in trouble. The times I've been in trouble when I was young were the times I was hanging around with nothing to do. I like to keep busy.

PSD: *What are your current goals?*
JR: Watching my grandchildren grow is very important to me. I hope I live long enough to know all of them. A lot of causes that I am involved with are struggling for money. I'd like to continue to help them, not only by giving money, but also by fund-raising.

PSD: *What was your experience as an ambassador like?*
JR: It was a great experience but I burned out. I served three years and six months. It was a very hard job. It was like running a business with 1,200 employees.

PSD: *What was your impression of Ronald Reagan?*
JR: Great guy. Frankly, I don't know if he would be able to run a business unless he surrounded himself with good people. He was a great motivator of people, like Dr. Frist was.

PSD: *What makes a good leader?*
JR: Caring. That doesn't mean being easy on people. Caring for them means feeling and knowing they are human beings, not robots. They can't do everything. Figure out what they do best and motivate them. You have to care about them as human beings.

PSD: *Is integrity the cornerstone for success?*
JR: Absolutely. I can take somebody's poor, sloppy workmanship as long as they are honest. Who suffers the most is the person who is cheating.

PSD: *How would you like to be remembered?*
JR: I probably won't be remembered as a nice person. Well, maybe I will. I would like to be remembered as a good family man who was also successful in business. Someone who was successful in the community. Actually, someone who was successful in all of life — family, community, and business.

Ken Kanter

Rabbi, Congregation Micah

"The whole issue of recognizing both the fragility and preciousness of life inspires me and keeps me going everyday."

PSD: *What is your congregation about?*
KK: A 15-year-old here summed it up quite beautifully when he said, "Micah is a place for people who have no other place."

PSD: *It is a family, isn't it?*
KK: Right, but it is the family of the world, not just the Jewish family. The other aspect of what I do is I am the first Chairman of the Metro Human Relations Commission, meaning the civil rights commission. That means working with 17 men and women, African-American, white, professionals, ministers, volunteers, every member of the community. I recognize that though I am a clergy person of a minority religion, and a very small minority in Nashville, that my responsibility is to reach out to all segments of society — Hispanic, Asian, African-American, Christian, Jewish, Moslem, whatever.

PSD: *A brotherhood of man.*
KK: That is why the choice for the name of this congregation is so appropriate. The prophet Micah poses the question, "What is it the Lord requires of you? To do justly, to love mercy, and to walk humbly with God." That very much ties in with my philosophy and keeps me going.

PSD: *Rabbi means teacher.*
KK: Yes. It is also more than that. It means friend, parent — it is all of those things.

PSD: *Did you feel called to be in the rabbinate?*
KK: I don't think I ever had a moment when God said, "You will be a Rabbi!" Maybe there are colleagues in the rabbinate or the ministry who feel that way. Maybe it is a calling, but I don't see it that way. The rabbinate is one of those occupations — one of those privileges — where you impact someone's life every day. You are there for people — when they get married, when they are sick, when they have lost a loved one. With everyone who is in the congregation, you are

a part of their family in some way. It is an extraordinary opportunity to love people and be loved by them in return, and to be part of their lives. At the same time, I represent something that is very important to me — Judaism, the Jewish people, Jewish traditions and religion. It is a wonderful opportunity. I would have never met you, as an example. I would have never done countless other things that are wonderful.

PSD: *When did the desire to be a rabbi first surface?*
KK: When I was twelve. I was fortunate to be blessed with wonderful rabbis growing up — men who represented really important things. For example, my first rabbi was very involved with the labor movement. This rabbi, whose name was Jacob Weinstein, was one of the great civil rights rabbis of the '50s and '60s. He was a labor champion and a great liberal. This was a man who was a rabbi when I was in those formative years looking at what a rabbi ought to be.

When we moved to Cleveland from Chicago, we went to another rabbi, who was the opposite of Weinstein. But this man was one of the great intellects and a voracious reader. Often, he would weave the books he was reading into his sermons, so that we sat there and learned. He was a great scholar and lover of learning.

Then we moved to Coral Gables, Florida, where the rabbi was a real builder. He took a tiny, little temple and built it into a 2,000 family place — a massive campus with classrooms. One day, someone drove by and sprayed the temple with machine gun fire right where the rabbi should have been standing. Luckily, the service had ended or the rabbi would have been killed. We later found out that the rabbi had been very quietly working on civil rights issues behind the scenes. The Ku Klux Klan had taken exception, and even took credit for the shooting.

PSD: *You studied at Harvard University back in the early 1970s.*

KK: Yes, I started at Harvard in September of 1970, in the midst of the Cambodian riots in Boston. In fact, I was directing a play at the time. It was in the spring of that year that they trashed Harvard Yard to protest the United States invasion of Cambodia.

When I came to Nashville the first time in the early '80s, Harvard was in the midst of their first billion dollar fund drive. I was the head of one division, and then-Congressman Al Gore was the head of another, so we got to be friendly. I am now the chairman of the Nashville Schools and Scholarship Committee, so I have the joy and privilege of setting up all the interviews for kids who want to go to Harvard.

PSD: *Harvard is a hard place to gain acceptance to.*

KK: It is hard to get in, and it is expensive to get in. The great tragedy of the system is these kids look at acceptance or rejection as if it is an acceptance or rejection of themselves. There is a system that is wrong here, when it is so hurtful to kids.

PSD: *You also do a musical review show.*

KK: I have been touring all around the world for almost 20 years doing musical review shows, which are tributes to the Jews of American popular music. I was on the "rubber chicken circuit" for a few years, which actually helped pay my tuition to rabbinical school. I would go to these little towns as the visiting rabbi or student and do these shows. I have been all around the world — Australia, Europe, and Israel — and the United States; I still do them. I have also written three books, the first of which is called *The Jews of Tin Pan Alley*. So I have taken my love of music and love of Judaism and put them together into what has become a really wonderful avocation, which is writing, lecturing, and doing concerts.

PSD: *Do you ever wish you had gone on to a career on the Broadway stage?*

KK: No, not a bit. I love going to shows and seeing my friends in them, but I don't think I had the fire in the gut to do it. I didn't have the strength of inspiration, and as a director, I was never clever enough.

PSD: *How did someone so in love with the world of theater become a rabbi?*

KK: That is a good question. I had a very interesting experience with theater at Harvard in that I was the first freshman to direct a main-stage production. The show was fabulously reviewed, and from there, I founded another theater company. But all of this time I was involved with the Jewish community. I always had it in the back of my head that the theater was fun, but where I really belonged was in the rabbinate.

PSD: *As a rabbi, you take part in many magical moments.*

KK: You're right, there are many special moments. For example, a number of years ago I was dealing with this elderly woman who was dying. She said to me, "Rabbi, my children will not let me die and I want to die. You must help them let me go." She was in her 90s and her children were in their 60s. I went to each of her four daughters and their four husbands, talking with each one individually. I said, 'Your mother is ready to go and you have to let her go. Now go in and talk to her, make peace, and give her closure.' And, to their credit, each of them did. When the last one was done, and the mother had blessed each one, the old woman just went to sleep. That was my chance to make her journey from this world to the next as comfortable as possible.

PSD: *What is it that makes you want to serve others?*

KK: I don't know that there is a sense of having to do something. The whole issue of recognizing both the fragility and preciousness of life inspires me and keeps me going everyday — no matter how much bull____ there is, how much annoyance, and how much frustration. There is still the moment when that phonecall comes and the voice says, "We need you right away. You are the only person who can give us strength and courage or love." Just by being there. You may not have to do or say anything but just stand there.

PSD: *You are married to a wonderful woman.*

KK: I happen to be blessed to find a woman who is equally committed to Judaism and is a great source of inspiration — even though I was pretty old when I got married at 39. I can be cynical about a lot of stuff, and get frustrated and pissed off like everybody else. Then I come home to Wendy, who sees the best in the world, not the worst. She sees the good in people. She is a wonderful source of that kind of spirit. Sometimes it even gets in the way, when I come home and say, 'Enough already. I don't always want to hear the nice side about everybody, let me deal with this.' But she is always right. She has faced her own challenges with her health and overcome them. That is why she turned to the field she is in, massage therapy, trying to make people feel better.

PSD: *How would you define success?*

KK: I obviously made a decision that success was going to be based on my ability to help and impact the lives of other human beings. Ever since I was a little kid, if there ever was a choice between doing what was expedient for you or doing what was best for someone else, I would always do what was best for the other. I always answered the call of a friend. People have always been my first priority.

So success, on that level, is making a difference in the lives of the people you care about and even the people you don't know. It is not a question of high visibility. I don't need to be on center stage or the top of the pyramid, but when I see kids thank me for having given them so much time that they feel confident and good about themselves or what they are doing, then I know I made a difference in that child's life. And that is a pretty important thing. When you walk in on Sunday morning at religious school and 25 six-year-olds want to give you a hug, and say they love you, then you know you have made a difference in someone's life.

PSD: *What is the hardest part of your job?*

KK: The hospital visits to really, really sick people. The hardest thing is when they say, "Why does God do this? Why am I suffering? Why am I in such pain?"

PSD: *What do you say to those questions?*

KK: There is no answer. Often times, they don't even want an answer. They just wanted to say it. I don't give them an answer because I don't believe there is one. Seeing people you love having to suffer is terribly difficult, and I do this all the time. I have had two or three very close friends die of AIDS, and watching that happen was the worst. It is terribly slow and terribly painful.

PSD: *What do you tell young people who come to you for words of wisdom?*

KK: Six years ago, when I was in Chattanooga, I was abducted at gunpoint and stuffed into the trunk of my car. While I was in the trunk, my first minutes were panic-filled, but then I started to go through the names of all my friends. I kept repeating their names over and over again. And I thought, 'If I die today — if he shoots me today — these are the people who will miss me. And if I don't die today, the first thing I am going to do is let these people know how much they really mean to me. Secondly, I am going to let other people know it when they mean something to me.' I am going to use as my message, 'Tell people how much they mean to you and how much you love them.'

PSD: *Today?*

KK: Today. Do it now, because you never know when you will lose the chance. So I have said that often. When I talk to young people about success, I say to them that success is not just the degree, the car, the ring, or the clothing. Success is the family you are fortunate to have. It is the life you are able to build for yourself with people. To me, success is built on relationships, not built on acquisition. These are the values that I talk about with kids.

PSD: *How would an 18-year-old cultivate these values?*

KK: Look at where you have been blessed. If you have a good friend, you have been blessed. If you have a parent who loves you, you have been blessed. If you have a skill, an ability, or a talent, you have been blessed.

Look at where you have made a difference in someone's life. If you feel you haven't done much of that, then get on it. Help someone, do something, put yourself out. Invest in the bank of life, so to speak, by helping other people. Don't just take what is good for you. Whether you have $300 Michael Jordan tennis shoes or $6.99 shoes from K-Mart isn't as important as investing in the lives of other people. Things are less important than people.

Success is also based on how you have improved yourself emotionally, physically, and spiritually. Get out there and read some books. Broaden yourself in art or in music. Every year, I give kids a homework assignment at the end of the year. Take a long walk, read a good book, and make a new friend. Why those three? Because biblical teaching tells us that the world stands on three things; on learning, on worship, and on doing good things.

PSD: *Are you optimistic?*

KK: Very much so. I see kids every day who are incredibly special. I have been a rabbi for 17 years now, and when a kid of any age says, "He is my Rabbi," there is a beautiful, meaningful, and rich mosaic of connection, woven within that phrase. It is the greatest gift that anyone can be given.

PSD: *How would you like to be remembered?*

KK: If they can say, "He was my Rabbi." That's it. Or "He was there whenever I needed him." In a way it is like teaching college, because you teach this kid for four years and then he is gone. It breaks your heart to have such a wonderful connection with this kid, and then he is gone. But they are not gone too far. I have had various kids call me 8 years later when they are getting married and they want me to do the service.

PSD: *You have put a lot of love into your life and work.*

KK: Yes. Markham has this wonderful poem we used to recite at camp that I really love. It goes like this: "There is a destiny that guides us, none goes his way alone. What you put into the life of others comes back into our own." Those words are very important to me.

Adolpho Birch, Jr.

Chief Justice of the Supreme Court, State of Tennessee

"To positively affect people is a good feeling, to realize that there are some people who may look at you and what you have done and what you stand for and say, 'There is a chance for me, too.'"

PSD: *Did you know as a young man that you wanted to head into the world of law and justice?*

AB: Yes, I did. I can't tell you the exact basis, but I believe some of it had to do with a lawyer who lived across the street from me. I used to always peer into his office; he had these big French doors on a big house with a lot of books. I just can't ever remember having wanted to be anything other than a lawyer. I may have wanted to be a cowboy, an indian, or a fireman, but I only recall wanting to be a lawyer.

PSD: *What appeals to you about this work?*

AB: It has provided me with a sense of inner reward and inner satisfaction. I know my job is difficult, and hope that I do an acceptable job with it. At this point of my life, to be able to make a difference in the lives of others provides a sense of satisfaction. Whether it is five others, ten others, or hundreds or thousands, one will never really know. To positively affect people is a good feeling, to realize that there are some people who may look at you and what you have done and what you stand for and say, "There is a chance for me, too." I think that is a wonderful thing.

PSD: *So, in a beautiful way, you are meeting your highest need and also serving others in the process?*

AB: I hope so.

PSD: *Who influenced you in terms of your paradigm of service?*

AB: Well, the closest I had was my father. He was a public servant in a sense, not a government servant. I guess he was the Lord's servant, to be honest with you. He was quite devout and faithful to his calling and I guess some of it rubbed off. I hope that it did.

PSD: *Do you find yourself a spiritual man?*

AB: What do you mean by spiritual?

PSD: *I would try to define it as 'someone who is in awe and reverence of the mystery of being.'*

AB: Sure.

PSD: *Do you take time for inner connection?*

AB: I have no ritual. There are occasions which cause me to reflect in a spiritual way beyond the ordinary reflection that one makes time for anyway. They are not for the most part programmed or planned.

PSD: *How would you define success?*

AB: Success, I would think in a very simple way, is being able to make a difference — a positive difference in the world or the environment in which you operate. There are a lot of ways to make a difference.

PSD: *What would you tell young people looking for some guidance in their quest for success?*

AB: Simply that, regardless of what attracts you, regardless of whatever characteristics or traits you see in others that you like, at the base of it all there has got to be determination, deep integrity, and an intense focus. To the extent that you maintain those as a basis, I don't think it makes much of a difference whether you decide if you want a big house or little house, a big car or a small car, fancy clothes or not. I simply think that is all a matter of your preference, as long as that basis of integrity, responsibility, devotion, and focus is there.

You know, I have so often heard people in my generation tell young folks, "You can make it if you try." There are times when I question that myself sometimes. How do you convince a young man or woman that they can make it if they try? Maybe they have been trying for a month to get a job. At what point does the young person say to me, "What you told me doesn't work." It is the loss of hope that I think is the tragedy. I said when I was in law school, 'I am not brilliant. I am not a great scholar. But I want to get through this law school and I am willing to do anything legitimate to do that.' It means I will do anything that is required. If it means I have to spend 10 to 14 hours a day working because of my ability, then I will do it.

Now I don't fault young folks and I don't criticize them. They live in a world that we created and we have not made it ideal. We all know what the problems are and I don't need to go into them here. What caused them? What the cure is? I don't know. I think that the big thing is just making a positive difference. Anybody and everybody can do that — the unemployed, the handicapped, even the person who has nothing can make a difference in somebody's life. That is where I am.

PSD: *So it boils down to one person at a time doing the best they can do.*
AB: Your moral obligation may include many, many others. But I think you are personally responsible, in a sense, for what you can do and how it affects others.

PSD: *Are you distressed by the lack of hope in society?*
AB: Am I distressed? Sure, because I consider myself part of a greater society. To an extent, what distresses society distresses me. Leadership is a fragile term that has no fixed meaning. I don't consider myself a leader.

PSD: *Are you a role model?*
AB: I have come to grapple with that term, not in terms of whether I am or not, because I don't think that is up to me. That seems to be up to others. I have often wondered why talk shows and television and such, especially white people, always want to point young black people toward those they consider role models. The word has come into such common usage that it has no meaning. Every time a black person achieves something, whatever that may be, white people are quick to say he

is a good role model. But why is he a good role model? Where are the white role models? I never hear anybody talk about white role models. Why is that? Because you don't need any paradigm, you don't need any model.

PSD: *I actually think I do.*
AB: Well, I don't mean you personally.

PSD: *Why do you think this is?*
AB: You (white people) already know, and it is us 'backward' folk that don't know and need somebody to show us.

PSD: *Do you think that is what is inferred?*
AB: I don't really know. It depends on the motivation of the people who have perpetuated this. When you talk about role models, I think about parents or the ordinary man who lives next door who goes to work every day and keeps his yard mowed. That to me is a role model. I don't see why you have to be a celebrity or have achieved something to be a role model.

PSD: *You can't ignore the fact that you have achieved something that crosses race lines.*
AB: Why, then, am I not a role model for white kids?

PSD: *I would say you definitely are.*
AB: That is you personally. Why was not the Chief Justice before considered a role model for white kids?

PSD: *I would have assumed he was considered a role model.*
AB: I never heard him talked about in that manner. Why is the Governor not a role model for somebody?

PSD: *Maybe because it is not only a difficult task to become Chief Justice, but you went against the inertia of history and broke through the invisible wall of racism to become*

Chief Justice. Perhaps you accomplished more than others before you by doing this. You may have ended up in the same place as the previous Chief Justice, but you came much further in your quest. In so doing, one would assume it is a reflection of your superior character.

AB: So the whole thing depends on how much effort one puts into getting there.

PSD: *Perhaps. To me, Phil Bredesen is an excellent role model.*

AB: Well, that's right, but you are talking personally and I am talking generally. Why is it every time I pick up the paper and read about a black person who has achieved something, and that he or she is a good role model? Now that may be. But why are white people so anxious to point out role models to me or other black people? It seems to me to be a veiled message, "That's how I want you to act. I want you to do what he or she did." Where are the white role models? This is just food for thought.

PSD: *What is the hardest part of your job as Chief Justice?*

AB: Finding enough time to get it done properly. There are so many demands, and each demands it's own time, space, and attention.

PSD: *Is this job a hard one to leave behind at the office?*

AB: Well, in literal and figurative terms, I take it home. I take work home with me. Even when I am driving I may think about some problem or a solution to something that may have been bothering me. Seldom does the work leave resonance at the top of your mind. It resides there like a program resides in a computer.

PSD: *Is there any thought or dream of what you might do when you are finished with this position?*

AB: I hadn't much thought about it. I would like to be active in some worthwhile endeavor or pursuit, whatever that may be, for as long as I am able — to keep moving in a worthwhile direction.

PSD: *Is that determined by your heart?*

AB: I don't know what determines it. I guess the compass is in your head. Morals are thoughts. You are not born with them, are you?

PSD: *No, but I have heard people say they go on their gut feeling.*

AB: I guess there is some of that and some of the other — a comfortable blend of emotions and thoughts.

PSD: *Who do you admire?*

AB: Many, many, many people. I admire those who laid the paths and foundations, who struggled in years past, so that I and others can enjoy things right now. People who gave their lives to vote for one thing. People who sacrificed economically to protest the conditions under which they were living and died for their sacrifice. Those are the people I admire. I am talking as far back as pre-slavery. People who died or sacrificed substantially for a just cause, and so many of them are nameless to me. These are people whose struggles and protests you never know about. Their sacrifices have been as great or greater than those we have read about. But the ones we don't know about are the people whom I admire.

PSD: *What was it like for you in the 1960s with the climate the way it was?*

AB: It was very difficult in the '60s. There was a wave of change in the air that gave courage and hope to those of us who were discriminated against. You could feel a fresh wind blowing. And while it was difficult then — while the struggle was still very much in bloom — you sort of sensed that it wouldn't be long before state and federally imposed barriers would fall. In that regard, it was a very welcome time. I guess the part that was worse was the awful treatment protesters received in the '50s. Otherwise, it just kept getting better. There was an abundance of emotion. You took courage from small acts of kindness or from small protests. Or the words from unheralded spokesmen who said, "This is wrong and I want to be on the side of those who are fixing it or changing it."

PSD: *Are things better today in that regard?*
AB: I don't know, I really don't know. It would seem that it is better. But one has to be careful. What is better? The real question is, 'how much better'? Better is a term of degree, quantity, quality.

PSD: *We still have a long way to go.*
AB: Absolutely.

PSD: *What was it like to deal with prejudice?*
AB: Very difficult, especially when the circumstances involved an encounter with a person who had what you needed or held some degree of power over whether you got what you were after or not. Like a clerk with whom you had to apply for a license plate. If that person insults you, what could you do? You could blow up and complain, but you may not get what you needed. Things of that nature, you just have to grit your teeth.

Or a judge who exhibited prejudice on the bench. You know you are getting less than you deserve in terms of treatment, but what can you do? You feel so powerless about it because it is the person who is in the superior position who is giving you the grief. So, often times you have to bite your tongue. Then there are those times that you unload it, as if to resolve all of those times in which you had to hold back.

PSD: *Has it left you at all bitter or angry?*
AB: It has been a long time ago. I think bitterness and anger fade with time. Time reconciles and heals. I don't feel bitter now, I don't feel angry now. I have learned that bitterness and anger don't do anything to the people to whom it is directed, but it eats you up instead. I don't know if you rise above it or simply decide that it is unhealthy.

PSD: *What brings you the most pleasure these days?*
AB: I would say my children and grandchildren. I have three children and three grandchildren.

PSD: *What was your philosophy as a parent while they were growing up?*
AB: I tried to be the very best parent I could. I had one basic belief — well, actually several beliefs — but among those, one of the most fundamental was that I should provide for my children the very best education that I could afford. There was not a single day in our house that our children didn't know they were going to college. There was never any discussion to the contrary. It was just expected of them and it became their expectation for themselves. I don't ever remember saying, 'You have to go to college.' It just sort of evolved without discussion.

PSD: *How would you like to be remembered?*
AB: As someone who made a difference, that's all.

Patricia Reiter

Minister, Unity Center for Positive Living

"Inner knowing for me is a body feeling when you are in the moment of choice, listening to your spirit rather than your ego. You are weighing decisions back and forth, and there will be a moment of 'Ahhh'."

PSD: *You became a minister rather late in life.*

PR: I spent 40 years of my life in the secular world, which culminated in a very disastrous second marriage back in 1984. I lost everything — most of all, my self-esteem. I continued to go down-hill until 1986 when I went with a coworker to hear a wonderful lady named Carol Ann Brown. Carol Ann was talking about spirit and soul, which really resonated in my soul for the first time. I was pretty resistant because I was really feeling like a victim. I then started attending a Unity Church featuring a class on *A Course In Miracles.*

PSD: *Did you ever have a metaphysical experience in terms of becoming a minister?*

PR: I had a spiritual experience in church on Valentine's Day in 1988. I was in a meditation, praying about this new dream job I had just been offered making over $100,000 a year. For some reason, I just couldn't say 'yes' to the offer. In the meditation, I heard a very loud voice say, "You don't want that job because you are going to become a Unity minister! The time is now, you are going to make an appointment with the minister tomorrow." The instructions couldn't have been more specific.

I believe I was called to serve the church. This is what I came to do in this lifetime. I just needed to wander around in the wilderness first to give me enough life experience, and help me become more compassionate as a minister.

PSD: *Compassion is so important.*

PR: We are all wounded healers. We bring the learning from our own wounds into the process of healing others. This is part of our own healing.

PSD: *Are you very intuitive about making choices?*

PR: Inner knowing for me is a body feeling when you are in the moment of choice, listening to your spirit rather than your ego. You are weighing decisions back and forth, and there will be a moment of 'Ahhh'. Sometimes it can be fleeting because the world's energy is so strong. It is just a moment of knowing, a little bit of peace where a stillness comes over the mind. Tuning into our inner knowing that has been closed off by the world's conditioning is work for all of us. We have lost our instinctual responses.

PSD: *What is your new church about?*

PR: Our church is about empowering humankind to awaken to their true nature. To wake up to that knowing place and remember that we are all divine beings. You can offer tools and opportunities for that inner knowing to get stronger.

PSD: *I know you also do some work as a hands-on healer.*

PR: I feel like I'm really an instrument for healing to happen. A lot of it for me happens intuitively. I know that the body is just a massive energy field. We all have the opportunity to work with universal energies that are present everywhere to restore the body to health and to help the body release old cellular memory blocks. I work on the mental, spiritual, emotional, and physical level. I know that there are people on the planet who have the ability to touch someone and heal them physically. I also know that if you don't get in touch with what caused the illness on the soul level, then the healing will not be lasting. I don't believe that illness happens to us, but happens through us, from the inside out.

PSD: *How would you define success?*

PR: Success is doing what you love to do, feeling joyous about getting up in the morning to do what you love, and getting financially rewarded for doing it. It doesn't have to do with the monetary amounts you are paid, but having the opportunity to choose the life you want to be living and having and the freedom to do that. Freedom to do it personally, on a soul level, the way you want to have it done — not according to anyone else's standards. This to me is success.

PSD: *So it is not only choosing the profession, but the way you perform or are permitted to perform in that capacity?*

PR: If I am not able to minister to people in a way that feeds my soul, then I would not be successful. I have to be able to interact with people on deeply personal levels. I'm a hands-on person all the way through. I need to be able to do this without being restricted by someone else's agenda. To take it one step further, if in doing what you love to do, you are able to change one life, that is success for me.

PSD: *What do you love about what you do?*

PR: I love to see people healing and changing their lives. Counseling is one of the things I love to do as a minister because I can see transformation happening right before my eyes. There is no delayed gratification in that. You see that moment of "Ahhh" in their eyes and nothing is ever the same for them. I love to be a part of that.

But I know that it is God working through me. It comes from a very deep place far beyond my intellectual understanding or my learning. I open to the best of my ability to let it come through.

PSD: *Standing on the pulpit carries a lot of responsibility.*

PR: It is an enormous responsibility to be a minister. You must be ever mindful of the ego and it's power to self-destruct. You must be so mindful of what you do or say and how you act because you are seen as an example. People take it to heart and are easily wounded by ministers. You have to be very mindful and vigilant about the ego and it's desire to control. For me it is the most humbling experience to see how God works through me. I

stand in awe and humility. I am still like a little child in awe of the power God expresses through all of us.

PSD: *What are you working on in terms of personal growth?*

PR: My greatest challenge is to not get so caught up in the details of running the business of a church that I forget to do what I do best and what spiritually feeds me. I want to stay in the excitement of the creation of this church. My greatest challenge is to give up my control issues. I have some real strong perfectionism issues.

PSD: *Are you optimistic in terms of the world becoming a more loving place?*

PR: I believe, if the world is going to transform, that we have to take the spiritual and bring it into the practical. We must take the spiritual element and bring it into the management of a church, or the management of an IBM — into the management of our personal lives.

When we can integrate instead of separate this is when we come into the fullness of God as humankind. There are people who can sit on a mountain top and be fully tuned in to God. But I believe God put us in these human bodies for the purpose of staying fully tuned in while living in the body, while living in the world. This is the challenge for every one of us.

PSD: *This church feels like a very loving little community. It really takes a team to make something like this work.*

PR: What we are doing here at this church is to help people realize that every task is of equal value. The person making the coffee is equal to the person giving the sermon.

PSD: *What gives life meaning?*

PR: I think life is about loving, open-hearted service. Serving God through everything you do.

216

PSD: *How about your life?*

PR: I want my life to be about empowering people so they know they are loved and important. I love people. It's about giving.

Phil Hickey

Co-founder, The Cooker and Green Hills Grille restaurants

"I believe success begins with your purpose on earth. What are you all about? I think the real challenge is finding and having a purpose, a kind of higher purpose. I define success as footprints—not the numerical stuff, but the lives I've touched."

PSD: *What is Phil Hickey about? Do you have a personal mission statement?*
PH: Yes. My personal mission statement is "to use the gifts that I've been given to enhance the quality of life and peacefulness of those I encounter."

PSD: *Who influenced you early on?*
PH: I had some great mentors like Gil Robinson, the founder of the parent company who owned the restaurant I worked in. Also, Joe Gilbert, who had been successful for 50 years. Here I was, fresh out of school with all this theory, going to save the world by applying it. They taught me a lot about principles, which became the founding principles of the Cooker, the Green Hills Grille, and now the Rio Bravo chain.

PSD: *What are some of the elements of your business philosophy?*
PH: Respect. A humanistic approach — respect for the individual, heavily laced with optimism. Also trust. Joe taught me a lot about trust. When I begin a relationship with an individual, whether it be a guest or co-worker, I walk in and hand over a glass full of trust. You have to spill it in order for me to trust you less. If you establish that route with trust, respect, and truthfulness, on every level, the world will gravitate to it. It's magnetic.

PSD: *Are you still in the restaurant trenches?*
PH: To some degree. I was at the Green Hills Grille today, one little restaurant that has been a phenomenal success just by finding people with the same level of trustworthiness and integrity. The actual skill set of restaurant employees is about 5 or 6 on a scale of 10. I look at the peak performers in our company and see a love for life, a respect for the individual.

PSD: *I know the Green Hills Grille is booming. How is the Rio Bravo chain performing?*
PH: We are fortunate to do the highest volume, by a considerable margin, in the Tex/Mex business versus our publicly-owned competitors. Neither the land, the brick, nor the layouts are all that different. For us, the difference is the attitude — how we treat our crew.

PSD: *Are you fascinated by success?*
PH: The same thing that you are trying to manifest through a book is the thing that I try to do all the time — which is to study success. I study success in politics, art, music, sports, and business. There are incredible similarities across the board. Common themes, so to speak. I have friends all across those different occupations and walks of life that I learn from. If you study who you would recognize as achievers, there are a lot of similarities.

PSD: *How would you define success?*
PH: I believe success begins with your purpose on earth. What are you all about? I think the real challenge is finding and having a purpose, a kind of higher purpose. Once you align with that, then it's really a matter of defining how you want to get there, and what your methodology will be. There is magic in defining and having goals.

PSD: *Visualization?*
PH: The mental picture is the single biggest driver in getting there.

PSD: *How does one get started on a path toward success?*
PH: It all starts with a having a mission.

PSD: *Is the setting of goals important?*
PH: I write goals down relentlessly. Company and personal goals.

PSD: *What surprises you these days?*
PH: It amazes me how many people don't have a purpose or even a plan. Their thinking is really short-term. They just want to buy a car, buy a house, make some money, get out of debt.

PSD: *Have you always been driven?*
PH: I wasn't one of those people who had 'it' when I was 12. I floundered for a long time. I went to school at Michigan State, came out and tried the restaurant business as a means to an end — the end being a real job.

PSD: *Do you have an actual success paradigm?*
PH: We have something we use called the Hickey Success Pyramid. It is my version of Maslow's hierarchy of needs.

This is where the magic happens. It's not a one-dimensional aspect, because this is where the enrichment starts.

PSD: *How important is communication in terms of success?*
PH: Ichak Adizes has done a lot of studies on organizations, but his work on the human relationship organism is really beautiful stuff. He is able to predict the probable longevity of a relationship within 30 minutes. There's a great adage, "It's how conflict is resolved that determines the nature of the relationship. There is always stress. Life is change, change brings conflict, lots of change brings lots of conflict. There is a filter or box that you exist in within a relationship and there must be truthfulness, trust, and respect."

PSD: *Have you read a lot of his work?*
PH: Adizes has had a profound influence on me. He also said, "There are small and large companies and companies that act young and old. Now most people think that when you're small you act young, and when you are big you act old." He said there's not a correlation.

PSD: *Is it hard to get to the top and even harder to stay there?*
PH: A lot of companies will go through a birth, boom, and death because they are not relentless. They are not constantly trying to improve. Anthony Robbins, the motivational author, calls it CANI: Constant And Never-ending Improvement.

PSD: *Do you read a lot of material?*
PH: On my master bathroom bookshelf I have *Jesus CEO, Flight of the Buffalo*, a Sam Walton biography, and Robert E. Lee's biography. You know, it never fails — I read Walton one night and Lee the next and inevitably see a lot of correlations. Similarities about focus and decentralized power. Studying success and successful people, I also realized these icons were regular folks who made a lot of mistakes.

PSD: *What about the personal side? Do you bring the same intensity to your role as husband and father?*
PH: I try to with my wife and children. We also foster-parent newborns, so every couple of months we have a day-old baby in our house crying and screaming.

PSD: *What tends to be illusive for you?*
PH: One thing I am always in search of is balance, every day of every week. It is a swinging pendulum, so I have never had the sensation that I am absolutely in balance. What has suffered lately is my exercise, as you can tell by looking at me. (He laughs.)

PSD: *Did you always want to be a leader?*
PH: My desire is not to lead large legions of people. We have 2,200 people in our company. If that were 200,000 or 2 million it would still basically be about touching lives. It may sound hokey, but if you look at our mission statement, what we are really trying to do is make lives better. If we can do that at work, make our people feel like they are part of something, hopefully they will go back and treat their families better.
PSD: *You sound very spiritual. Is that also part of the company ethic?*
PH: A lot of the Unity principles about values are interfaced. Like the theory of abun-

220

dance. We expect prosperity and abundance. It's not 'if', but 'how'. We expect success and a level of dignity. You have to have quality individuals, but it's all about relationships. If you want to build a structure tall and strong, start with your relationships.

PSD: *How important is integrity?*
PH: I think it is possible to have success without integrity but not long-term success. The way the world is working now, you have to have a humanistic approach.

PSD: *Do you feel like you are a success?*
PH: Moderately. I define success as footprints — not the numerical stuff, but the lives I've touched. Helping people to achieve their goals. Kind of a cosmic domino effect. The success of having children that are gentle people. Or as the Yiddish word suggests, a 'mensch'.

PSD: *Which means that it is important for you to give something back?*
PH: I'm trying really hard to model the theory of giving back to the world — to follow the biblical adage, "Much has been given, much is expected." I think we are all really so blessed. It is amazing to me how the people who seem to achieve the most are constantly focusing on trying to help others achieve their dreams, and achieved their own success as an outcome.

PSD: *So in that sense you are a success?*
PH: As of right now, I have had some success. I'm happy. Wayne Dyer says, "Success is not the goal, it's the way." Once I grabbed onto that theory, I realized that it's the process, not the end. If I'm not having fun along the journey, it's time to change the journey.

PSD: *Do you have any advice for those trying to find themselves or their purpose?*
PH: Get in touch with what you really want to do and connect with that. Is it lifestyle,

money, geography? You need to have some kind of vision of where you want to go. Figure out a plan on how you will get there.

PSD: *What is your biggest challenge at the moment?*
PH: My biggest challenge right now is achieving and finding balance. I was on the board of directors at our church and for 52 consecutive weeks we had a prayer meeting. This was my prayer — balance.

PSD: *Do you feel that spirituality is an important part of your happiness?*
PH: For me, I need a higher power as part of my success. Many don't have it and that's OK. But I find those who have the most enriched lives have some sort of higher power or spirituality. There are people who have achieved some modicum of success in their businesses, but there would be an emptiness without the spiritual side. I try to encourage a spiritual side, although I have no say on what is the right or wrong way.

PSD: *Service?*
PH: It's really about service. There is a prayer I say everyday in a my spiritual time. I say, 'God, I am your vessel. Use me as you will, make me your hands, your lips, and your eyes. Let me live my mission statement, but I am your vessel.' Sometimes I might say it through clenched teeth, but I still surrender.

PSD: *What type of impression do you want to leave behind?*
PH: I would like for people to say that, "Even though I knew him for a couple of days or 20 years, he touched my life. He was giving, he was trying to make my life better." It's not about founding two companies. I would like my children to say there was a soul connection and they modeled how to live their lives after me. That is really the measure — the lives we've touched and the relationships we set in motion.

Dr. Bill Sherman

Pastor, Woodmont Baptist Church

"To fight racism and to build bridges is kind of like shaving– you have to do it everyday. It is an ongoing proposition, a process, not an end result."

PSD: *How do you see success being measured in today's culture?*

BS: On today's wavelength, the movers and shakers are the ones who have the money, the power, and the position. But I believe that no person is a success — no matter how much wealth you have or how high a position — if you fail in your family.

PSD: *Who has the influence?*

BS: If you are talking about values, the influential ones are the people who love people, who care about people, who believe in people, and who have invested their time and sweat. These are the people who make a difference in this world.

PSD: *What is your main criteria for defining success?*

BS: Is the person a decent human being? Have they done a good job in their marriage, and in the love and care for their children? My test is if sons and daughters speak well of their parents, and they are devoted as a family, I would hope they would make a contribution to society and the kingdom of God.

PSD: *So success for you is about service and selflessness.*

BS: I'm hard-pressed to name anyone who lived in the 12th century who was a successful merchant, a millionaire, a political leader, a conqueror, or a mover and a shaker. But when I mention St. Francis of Assissi, it rings some chimes in your head. Everybody remembers St. Francis. Why do we remember him? He found out where our real values are. I think success is related to values and personal integrity.

PSD: *Success is giving something to the greater community?*

BS: There are civil responsibilities, we are called upon to make a contribution. I am very angry about *Fortune 500* companies making record profits while laying off 15,000 people — the very people upon whose backs they rode to success. These people with a so-called "Contract with America" want to then come and tell these poor people they can't have their $145 a month. I'm not for loafing and goofing off, but I'm more leery of corporate welfare in the form of big tax breaks.

PSD: *Money is often related to success, but the two are not always connected, are they?*

BS: One Christmas day, I received a call from a gentleman who lived on Belle Meade Boulevard who said he was seriously thinking of taking his own life. He had been drinking but he wasn't drunk. He had been thrown out by his family. I went out there and spent about two hours with this guy. He sat there and told me all his troubles and then said the most perceptive thing, "You know, I have everything and I have nothing." Afterwards, I went home to my family and thought, 'I am one of the richest people in the world.'

PSD: *What was your background? Were your parents very religious or in the clergy?*

BS: I grew up in a Christian home. My father and mother were active in the church and together put in over 100 years of service. This was my heritage. I was the baby of the family, born in 1932, and I have an older brother who is a preacher. We had three things in our lives that were important: family, church, and school. I still think those are the stag poles of society. When I was about 13, I felt God's impression in a church service, and that He wanted me to preach. At the time, I thought it was going to be missionary work.

PSD: *You felt called to the ministry?*

BS: Not in a voice, so to speak. For me, God works impressionistically.

PSD: *What is the most difficult aspect about being a minister?*

BS: Two things are hard about my job. The

first is that you are never through. When I lay down at night, I can always think of someone I could have called or gotten in touch with. The second thing is that you can't always see the end product. I like to mow my grass because I can start, I can work, and I can finish. I can see the end product. In ministry, you can't always see the finished product. Though, when you are here for 29 years like I have been, you do get to see the whole process at times and it is beautiful.

PSD: *You have had some monumental personal struggles. Do you mind sharing some of them?*
BS: My oldest boy had a terrible case of melanoma in the summer of 1988. Ninety-four percent of people who get it die within 15 months. It is a miracle by the Grace of God that he is alive today. He has a four-year-old daughter and is doing well. I recently had a melanoma removed from my own leg.

PSD: *Did you ever question the will of God or become angry as a result of your suffering?*
BS: I have never questioned the Lord or got mad at God, but I did get angry at the human predicament. We live in a human body and we get sick and die, we live in mortal bodies. The human predicament makes me angry at times — just look at Cambodia, Sarajevo, Beirut, Bosnia. People say, "Why does God allow this to go on?" But God never created an army. God has created us to be free, and when He did so, He ran the risk that we will use our freedom wrongly. Now God could either take our freedom away, or try to work within the system as it is. And I believe that the latter is what He does.

PSD: *The death of children causes such great suffering.*
BS: Twice I've had to bury children who were two years old or younger. I could never tell their parents it was the will of God. A drunk driver ran over a toddler who was

playing in the yard. The irresponsibility of one person cost the other person. We are all in this together. I don't think God is unfair, but I do believe that life can be unfair. The Christian promise is "Come to Christ and He will give you the coping powers to deal with life's sufferings."

PSD: *When you assume the responsibility of the pulpit, you really open yourself to criticism.*
BS: The ministry is an enormous responsibility. Any time you get up and preach, there are 360 degrees around you and if you are going to take a stand, sometimes someone won't agree with you. But you have to do what you believe in.

PSD: *Someone who did what he believed was right?*
BS: Yes. When the race issue was hot in this town, we tried to do the right thing. I gave a sermon that said Christians are bridge-builders between races. We don't stand against each other. We had joint services with the 15th Avenue Baptist Church starting in 1970 and have had about 23 since then. Back in 1970, we had bomb threats on the church and nasty calls to our house, all because of the racial issue. But we had to do the right thing.

PSD: *There have been a number of churches burned recently, most of them in the African-American community. What are you doing in response to this?*
BS: We are trying to pull together the Nashville religious community — Jewish, Roman Catholic, Church of Christ, Baptist, all the churches — and we want to break the silence. Church-burnings have been going on for years, and nobody has been preaching against it. It has been in the news recently, but there was a long dry spell where you heard nothing about it. So we have clustered together under the name "Project Goodwill." We are trying to do four things: break the

silence by condemning the acts, work on restoration and reconciliation between the races, collect money for rebuilding and resources, and enlist the muscle of people to actually put up these structures, like Habitat for Humanity. We are going to focus primarily on eight African-American churches in Tennessee. We are trying to figure out just how much their insurance will cover. There is another entity that has promised to cover any short-fall we may have.

PSD: *Is this an anonymous donor?*
BS: Though they don't want any credit, the organization called Promise Keepers has a million dollars they are going to underwrite.

PSD: *During the civil rights movement, many Southern churches sat on the sidelines and chose not to get involved. This is quite a different response.*
BS: Some of our churches have said the same thing. Reverend Shelly said that, "We were silent in the Church of Christ for years and we should have been vocal." But there were also plenty of Baptists that were just as guilty, so no one is really singled out.

PSD: *Do you feel that we might have learned something from the past this time around?*
BS: I hope so, but knowing human nature the way I do, we always have to do battle with the same stuff, whether it is now or 2,000 years ago in the time of Julius Caesar. To fight racism and to build bridges is kind of like shaving — you have to do it everyday. It is an ongoing proposition, a process, not an end result. And I think we will be in this process for as long as we live because human nature is the way it is. A lot of people are insecure, arrogant and self-centered, no matter what the color of their skin.

PSD: *There is no way for you to stay on the sidelines when it comes to something like this.*
BS: I really can't. Once they burned that

church up in Richmond, I talked about it in a sermon and in a Bible study group. A lot of people came up to me saying that we had to do something about this. In fact, one gentleman handed me a check for $1000. Victor Hugo said, "Nothing is more powerful than an idea whose time has come." And in terms of this idea, its time has come. I know that a lot of organizations and the government are kicking in money, but it won't be enough. There will always be a little short-fall, but money is not the only issue here. I think the building of relationships is very important.

PSD: *It's ironic that a negative act might serve a positive purpose by bringing people together.*
BS: I think that God can take a bad situation and make good of it, and that is what we are saying.

PSD: *Do you ever think about how you would like to be remembered?*
BS: I would like to be remembered as someone who had a sense of integrity. "Even if I didn't agree with him all the time, I respected his conviction. He had faithfulness, he was faithful. He was right in the areas that mattered: family, integrity, and contribution."

PSD: *Any last thoughts?*
BS: When it all comes down to it, love gives people a sense of value and a sense a belonging. Love gives you self-esteem and a sense of worth. It all comes down to love.

Thelma Kidd

Co-owner, Davis-Kidd Bookstores

"There is this part of me that struggles between self-exploration and being self-indulgent. I don't want to be self-indulgent, but I do want to be self-respecting. To allow whatever is happening to happen, and to nurture whoever I am on the core level."

PSD: *How did you get into the book business?*
TK: Karen Davis, my partner, and I have been friends for years and years. We met in Texas when I was finishing school and she was working a job there. We ended up sharing a place to live and starting a friendship. Over the next 10 years we lived in different places and were exploring different things. I ended up marrying and living in Ann Arbor, Michigan. While there, I got my Masters Degree in Social Work. I also became familiar with Borders Bookstore in Ann Arbor, which at the time was privately owned.

Karen and I had always thought about doing something together, whether it was traveling or starting a small business. We had even thought about an antique shop, but a bookstore really felt like the most viable option. This was also something Nashville didn't have at the time — a place with a large inventory and a place to sit, with atmosphere.

PSD: *Did you ever actually work as a social worker?*
TK: I was a practicing social worker for a couple of years and I had various ideas throughout my life that were great. All it took was money and time to make them work. But the money part was always a drawback. You always had to go out and find somebody to give you some money if you wanted to do anything. For a while, I worked in a Vista-type program in New Jersey where we had to raise our own money. It was a missionary-style program for kids in the inner city. But you always had to raise money.

The idea with this bookstore was, 'We will just generate our own money.'   We will sell a product that will enable us to do all kinds of things within the context of the bookstore.

PSD: *The bookstore is a real watering-hole of divergent interests and people.*
TK: I have thought about it recently, why I did this and what really appeals to me about

being a middle-man, sort of a matchmaker. About having a resource — something good — and providing it to people. About ferreting out a way to bring people together with books, a children's program, or an author coming in. Or it could be the space that people will come and participate in that is dynamic, because that is who we are. Part of the reason you like Davis-Kidd is the people who are shopping next to you. It is not just the carpet, the books, or the music. It is the fact that there is all this energy there. People come in and they are like-minded, because they are open, they are seeking, they are curious. Even if they have different views than yours.

PSD: *Did you start out with this kind of an atmosphere in mind?*
TK: No, it was never that thought out, which was appealing in a sense. I remember when we talked about what magazines we would carry, it was appealing to me to have *Christian Living* next to *The Buddhist Times,* so that everybody would know it was their store.

PSD: *The store is a tool or forum for social expression.*
TK: We have a legitimacy because we are just a retail store and have no political position outside of supporting the First Amendment and free speech. We have no agenda, so we can have varied speakers come like Newt Gingrich or Gloria Steinem, though not on the same night. (She laughs.) Being able to do these kinds of things is the part that is exciting to me.

PSD: *With all due respect to other large bookstores in the area, your store has a magical feel. What do you think is responsible for that?*
TK: That's a great question, because we are exploring this with our new store in Jackson, Tennessee. So I don't really know. All you can do is create a space and allow stuff to

happen, rather than force things. It feels very much like a balance between the masculine and the feminine. You give it enough direction and clear orientation and keep it on track. These are sort of the stereotypical, masculine, goal-directed things. The other side is much more allowing and invites people in without knowing what is going to happen.

PSD: *Has it been fun to go from a little bookstore to running a big business?*
TK: Yes, it has been fun. There are parts I like as much as being in the store and selling. I like the organizational part. I honestly think that I am one of those people who is a real entrepreneur. Not every entrepreneur is a good business person, and it is not always so great to be an entrepreneur, but that profile really fits me. Which for me is coming up with new ideas and being creative in how to do them. I really grow much less interested on day eight hundred of the whole process when you really have to plan everything, when other people get involved and you really have to make it work. Then it becomes a different skill.

PSD: *You like the part of creation and birth.*
TK: That is absolutely right. I have a pretty high tolerance for risk.

PSD: *That is key, because this whole thing could not have happened without risk.*
TK: It is. It really did not matter to me if we made money. That is the truth. I was never doing this to make money. We spent two years looking for a location and I got really discouraged, thinking this will never, ever happen. I just needed enough money to support myself. We opened and were actually close to breaking even in the first year. I always paid attention to sales and expenses, but I was never that concerned with the bottom line. I was never focused on whether my investment was paying off. In the last few years, as I have become more focused on the

bottom line and my return on investment, it is frankly less fun. There is much less of that sense of magic.

PSD: *Are you distressed by how few people are reading these days?*
TK: What I worry about is related to that but is a little different. Not reading is just sort of a symptom that has more to do with the fast pace, the quick gratification, and the unwillingness to wait. Like investing in the stock market. We have such a short view of what matters and what we will wait for. We also have an uncomfortableness and an unwillingness about not being or doing anything. To not be producing, to not be active, to not have noise coming in. I think this is a big part of why people don't read. You have to be content with some stillness and silence to sit down and read a book. All of this concerns me along with the fact that there is so much less contemplation.

PSD: *Do you think you might ever say, "I have done the bookstore phase of my life and I am now going to move in another direction?"*
TK: You bet! Absolutely. This summer, I am sponsoring a workshop on Esalen. I have also been thinking of opening a little stationery store.

PSD: *Who influenced you and fostered that entrepreneurial spirit?*
TK: I would have never thought about my father being like this. He was a carpenter and a building contractor who had a fourth grade education. But he was in business for himself and he was successful doing that. Looking back now, I see that he was really artistic doing house plans and landscaping.

PSD: *Were there a lot of books in your house growing up?*
TK: We didn't have a lot of books. When I was 14, my mother died of cancer. She was 42 years old. She was young and I was

young. There is no doubt that played a huge part in who I became and the way I turned out — probably a lot of the independence, the sensitivity, and taking care of myself. I am stronger in many ways because of that.

PSD: *Spiritually, where do you find yourself today?*
TK: "Open" would be a word that feels really nice. Being in touch with my own spiritual being and feeling more comfortable with the universe at large. This has made me feel much more like a whole person.

PSD: *What matters most to you?*
TK: What matters most to me is my children. I have two great children. It is really fulfilling for me to have nice, good kids. Also, enjoying what I do and doing what I like. Doing as little as possible of the things I don't like, which are draining. Those things that take away from me and don't enrich me. Part of me struggles between self-exploration and being self-indulgent. I don't want to be self-indulgent, but I do want to be self-respecting. To allow whatever is happening to happen, and to nurture whoever I am on the core level. I don't want to be completely self-absorbed.

PSD: *Was it hard to raise a daughter not having your own maternal role model?*
TK: I was actually thrilled when I found out that I was having a girl, and looked forward to the chance of being mother and daughter again. Having a lot of personal therapy helped me deal with my own stuff without putting it on her. We have a beautiful relationship

PSD: *How would you define success?*
TK: When all is said and done, I would like to know that my life had been of value, that I had made some positive difference in the world. That somehow the lives around me had been made better because of something I had done and who I am. In addition, I would like to enjoy the process of providing that for people. Then I would feel like my life had been a success.

PSD: *That is beautiful. It is about giving and enjoying the process of giving.*
TK: I like hearing that we are doing a good business or we are doing a good job at different things. But what is really wonderful is when people talk about how they feel when they go into the store or what the store means to them. People have been very magnanimous and eloquent about what it is like for them being in our store. People feel they have been nurtured there, and that is what we need to keep on doing. It is about being respectful of people.

PSD: *The store is there to enhance the community.*
TK: Absolutely. The reason we do this is we want the store to be a resource for the community.

PSD: *That is the social worker in you.*
TK: That is the social worker. The bankers were always concerned that we would just give the books away. They really were.

PSD: *What do you think makes you want to give?*
TK: It makes you feel good. My mother was a very giving person, so I picked up some of it from her. And my daughter is very giving. Maybe we are just born with it. I'm sure I was loved and taken care of as a child and that is probably why. When somebody is loved, it nurtures that part of them that will want to give something back. That is my job.

PSD: *Is that why Thelma Kidd is here?*
TK: Right. To somehow facilitate this.

PSD: *What brings you the most pleasure?*
TK: A couple of years ago, I remodeled my

house. I really love having created a space that is comfortable, that is mine, and that is home. Because of my mother getting sick and dying, my childhood home didn't have the greatest connotations. I missed out on some of what creating a home is all about. I love just being in my home.

PSD: *What advice would you pass on to your children as they go out into the world?*

TK: I did this last year when my daughter went away to college. Some of the things I said were, 'Go to sleep. You will feel better in the morning, and everything will look better when you wake up.' I think that is great advice that took me years to learn. 'Listen to your heart and trust your heart to guide you.' My mother had a wonderful saying on our wall when I was growing up. It said, "Never take life so seriously, you'll never get out of it alive." There is something to that, to embrace the absurdity and to laugh. 'Never lose your sense of humor.'

One thing that is truly important is to take care of yourself. To know what you need and take responsibility for getting it. Whatever it is you need, do not depend on other people to take care of it for you.

PSD: *Is there a void in not having a companion to share the experience of your life?*

TK: It is a sadness as much as anything. I feel a sadness for that loss. I do incredibly well alone, and don't get lonely a lot, which sometimes makes me wonder. But I do feel sadness in wishing for that intimacy and partnership.

PSD: *How would you like to be remembered?*

TK: As a caring and creative person. I would want my children to remember me as thinking they were the greatest things that walked on earth. I really love my kids.

230

Duncan Callicott

Landscape Architect and Horticulturist

"For what I do, you have to have a mix of creativity and love of nature. An appreciation of nature and a desire to enhance."

PSD: *Do you feel successful?*
DC: What I am curious about was whether you perceived me to be successful or perceived me as believing that I was successful?

PSD: *Both. How would you define success?*
DC: I don't think I want to. I don't think I am successful.

PSD: *If you don't believe you are successful, then you must have some definition for success. Otherwise, how could you make such a judgment?*
DC: Many, many years ago a woman came to Montgomery Bell Academy when I was a freshman and each of us mocked her, to each other, afterwards. She had this expression, "I want to belong." What this woman speaker said was there was a someone in each of us who wanted to belong. She really hit a special nerve with us. You have this balance whether you feel like you are successful or feel like you have an inferiority complex that you override when you are in public.

PSD: *For instance...*
DC: I consider the last speaking tour I had in Tallahassee a success because I cut up and carried on and it all went over all right. I enjoyed taking an audience for a ride, which gets back to the 'I want to belong' thing. I always liked public speaking. We even did a thing called The Freedom Forum that grew into a program that John Seigenthaler is the head of now. Public speaking was actually forced upon me by my father, who wanted me to be an attorney. The fun of communicating is when you get some response. There is a clown in everybody.

I have been extremely fortunate in that I grew up in a time when life was simple, though complex in many ways, but all prescribed. There was no latitude, you did what was done, you did the program. My wife and I didn't do that with our children, we let them create their own program. As a child I was always concerned with birds. I loved birds. They were your companions. I had every kind of animal as a pet growing up. The best pet I ever had was a crow.

PSD: *How did you slip through the cracks and escape a career in law?*
DC: By the grace of God. (He laughs.) Also some very good friends of my parents who realized how unhappy I was at the prospect. I went to Vanderbilt because I had to, and got in by the skin of my teeth.

PSD: *Did you feel called to work with the land?*
DC: It was more of an opportunity. During my junior year, I quit playing football and I swapped fathers with a friend whose father was in the landscape business. It was called Jones Nursery, so in a sense, I was trying to keep up with the Joneses. We had moved to Golf Club Lane at the time and were living on three acres. So I spent a lot of time improving the property around our home. I ended up leaving Vanderbilt and going down to Athens, Georgia to the University of Georgia. That is also where I met my wife.

PSD: *Did you always love working with land and having your hands in the soil?*
DC: Oh yeah, it started out very early. I was born in 1936 on thirty acres of land in Brentwood on Hardscuffle Road. There were no other children around, nothing but animals. I didn't learn to ride a bicycle until I was forty because I grew up on a hill with a horse. My ancestors had conservatories and greenhouses, so we had this horticulture thing in our blood. My father had a love of the land.

PSD: *Do you ever feel a personal connection to plants and trees as one would to a pet?*
DC: Yes. For instance, I am looking at a Dwarf Iris out there that has come into

bloom. It has been all over this yard and some years it hasn't been happy. I can't wait to get out there.

PSD: *So they have personalities?*
DC: Oh yeah, they are very temperamental. If they don't like where you put them, they will say, "so long." If they do like where you put them, then they will multiply and thrive, just like people. My compost pile is about an acre in size with some wonderful things growing out of it.

PSD: *Has all this work with nature made you more philosophical about life?*
DC: That is more of a conscious thing. I'm not one to expound on those sorts of topics.

PSD: *So there is more going on than what will surface in this interview?*
DC: Yes.

PSD: *What advice would you give a young person about finding their calling?*
DC: In the landscape design business, they have been coming to me for years but I tell them I am not a very good example. I am just one of the oldest. For what I do, you have to have a mix of creativity and love of nature. An appreciation of nature and a desire to enhance. Sometimes the chemistry is not right.

The plant growing cycle includes everything in life you are trying to do. You do something that creates beauty. You want to create beauty. By doing so, you generate praise from your fellow man, which we all love. You also get to see if, indeed, you can do it. There are things that I can't grow on this spot or on any spot, for whatever reason. And that goes for 'life', too. So success, to get back to your original question, is really about whether you can grow it or not.

PSD: *What a great metaphor.*
DC: And it is not just a matter of the relationship between the plant and you, it's

whether or not you can create an environment for it.

PSD: *So one does not create success, one creates the environment for success — whether for yourself, other people, or plant life.*
DC: And if they thrive, they grow. The definition of a perennial is, 'If it does not die, it will continue to grow from year to year.'

PSD: *So in a sense we can all be perennials if we continue to grow and learn?*
DC: You can look at it that way.

PSD: *What is it about nature that you love so much?*
DC: Going out in the morning to see what is in bloom, what has emerged, what has turned a different color. In other words, seeing what has happened out there. It is different every minute of every day. It never reaches a peak, it is either in ascension or decline. Always changing. This business of change, when it works, that is success. When you deal with a painting, the only thing that changes is where you put it on the wall or how you light it. But nature is ever-changing.

PSD: *Someone with absolutely no expertise in horticulture can still look at nature and experience its holistic beauty.*
DC: That's right.

PSD: *Is nature perfect?*
DC: Well of course it is. You may not consider it perfect, but it is. "Ours is not to reason why."

PSD: *Are you concerned about what we are doing to the environment and the world's ecology?*
DC: Yes, I am concerned. I am not as active as I once was and I regret this. I used to be in the Sierra Club and the Tennessee Scenic River Club. One way I am active is that I almost never, ever use any sort of herbicide.

PSD: *How about environmental issues on a national level?*

DC: The attitude of the Republican majority in trying to undo everything conservationists worked so hard for over the years is alarming. It indicates to me these elected people were always more of the unwashed, now they are the recently washed. You have this huge group of people who are completely ignorant of or unconcerned with the environment. Maybe they don't even have any appreciation, either. In the past, they didn't know any better. Now, everyone has had the opportunity to learn what is good and bad. The recycling movement is good. It has made a difference, I suppose.

PSD: *Let's go back to your own paradigm of success in terms of growth. If we don't take care of our environment, how will we as a species grow and flourish?*

DC: Well, I don't know if the great, recently washed really care that much, if Governor Sundquist could pull this pollution thing in the Smokies and grant a permit to whoever it was — and then turn right around after getting rid of a conservation-minded commissioner and name the grandson of one of the most notorious coal miners in his place. This is business-oriented. You don't see a professional forester being named as a commissioner. There are people out there who are doing as much as I used to. I guess I am cynical because the people who really care about the environment are such a minority.

PSD: *You do what you love and get paid to do it. Is that success?*

DC: That is success. Also, not striving for monetary things that do not matter to me. I was also very lucky in terms of all this.

PSD: *Was there an element of fate involved?*

DC: Being an Episcopalian, I would call it predestination rather than fate. I followed the flow of things. You have your choice. When I left Cheekwood, it opened up a new day for me and it has been extremely rewarding on many levels. I used to do this sort of thing just for scotch and water, so to speak.

PSD: *How would you like to be remembered?*

DC: I think it was Rhett Butler who said, "Frankly, my dear, I don't give a damn." I have seen so many things that so many people have done. And what they did has either been entirely obliterated or forgotten. The only solace you might have is that what these people did at the time might have helped someone or something. You have to believe in the afterlife because nothing lasts here.

Wynonna Judd

Recording Artist

"Music has always been the outlet for my sensitive and tender heart."

PSD: *Your singing has a very spiritual quali-*
ty. When did you first realize, "I can really
sing. This is my gift."?

WJ: I knew you were going to ask me that
question. This is sort of a two-part answer. I
have always known that I was weird, that I
wasn't like all the other kids. The second part
of the answer would be that it wasn't until the
last few years that I really knew, flying on my
own, that my gift was such that it now
astounds even me.

I feel very separate, almost like I am two people. Because when I step into the light to
sing, I am merely the vehicle of the anointing.
Yet when I am outside of that light, I am sort
of like everybody else. I have told people
before that I feel ordinary when I am not
singing, and that something extraordinary
happens to me when I am. So it is an odd
existence, because when I leave the studio, I
am just another goof waiting to make my next
error, kind of like we all do throughout our
day.

If I go through my day and start to feel arrogant, that doesn't work. I think that is why
God put Mom with me for ten years. (She
laughs.) Because God knew that I would
have probably thought I was Elvis, and that I
would be too busy with my head up my
behind to pay attention to what the lesson
here really is. And the lesson I have learned,
in the last few years really, is just how truly
ordinary I am, but how extraordinary it is
when I open my mouth and God comes
through me.

PSD: *When did you first become aware of*
your purpose?
WJ: I am thirty-two. So it is a very interesting
phenomenon that I have only recently discovered. When I was younger, I took it all for
granted. I thought I was bulletproof. I was too
busy following after my mother, too busy
reacting. Now I am pro-active, I know the dif-

ference. So I spent the first several years of
my success very scattered. To be honest with
you, success is as equally devastating as failure, because it is not normal to win the lottery and the next day quit your job and
change your lifestyle. That's a shock!

And that is what happened to me when I was
eighteen. I was cast into a role of being trau-
matized by success and reacting to that role
while just trying to keep up. Now I am able
to sit back and push the buttons, saying "yes,
no, I'll get to that later." Balance has finally
come into my life. So it is a very interesting
journey.

PSD: *Thank God you have discovered this at*
age thirty-two. Sadly, some people never get it.
WJ: Well, it has taken six years of Christian
counseling to figure it out at $80 an hour!
(She laughs.)

PSD: *You talked about feeling different, or in*
a sense, alienated. I know there are people
who will read this and relate. That is a part of
the burden of any gift.
WJ: It is a burden. It is a blessing and a
curse. When I say these things, I don't want
to sound arrogant. But when someone has a
gift, when God chooses someone, I think it is
because they have the heart for it. Even so, I
have walked around most of my life with a
"Why me, Lord?" syndrome. It's both unfortunate and fortunate that the reason I sing the
way I do is because I feel things so deeply,
maybe too deeply. For most of my life I have
been "turned down." Yet when I sing, I am
"turned up." It's a funny thing.

People would say "Don't feel that way,
Wynonna. You are too sensitive." But when I
sing, people turn me up to eleven because
they dig me. Yet when I am not singing, they
turn me down, saying that I am too dramatic.
I have always been this way, and it is really
hard for me to be in a world that is so cruel
and harsh at times. Music has always been the

outlet for my sensitive and tender heart. I think that is why God knew I couldn't handle having a corporate job or being a mother with eight kids at once. This is what I am supposed to do because I have the heart for it and I am ready to accept the responsibility and the burden of it.

PSD: *What would you tell someone who is feeling a bit different and estranged?*

WJ: The simplest and best advice I ever got came through a man named Don Potter. Don is both a spiritual mentor who helped lead my heart to the Lord at eighteen, and has made every record with me up until this one. Don said something to me that really put it into perspective, "You have to have the gift in order to do something." For instance, if you are blind, you are never going to be a race car driver. I meet people every day who ask for advice and I tell them, "If you don't have the heart for hearing and feeling the gift you have, then don't do it."

PSD: *Whatever that gift may be?*

WJ: Whatever it is. If you want to be rich and famous, be very careful. Much is given and much is expected. You must be really willing, and this is so important, because I hear many people say they want the authority but not the responsibility, and that is the ego. That is the part of us that says "I want to be the big IT!!"

I am responsible for fifty people, and while that doesn't compare to a big corporation, it is still enough for me to go to bed some nights and feel a bit overwhelmed. So I ask people what their reasons are for wanting to be in the music business. If it is about going backstage to meet Reba or hang out with Garth, they might want to consider something else. Because it isn't about that. It is about an awful lot of really hard work.

PSD: *What are your feelings about the times in which we now live?*

WJ: Unfortunately, I see a lot of people around me losing faith, and that is why I think your book is very timely. People are losing their way and are unable to hang on and have faith. They are missing the point that happiness can be found all along the way, not just at the end of the road. You must go with the process. For me, my music comes out of the need to celebrate and to praise. That's not where I was at eighteen, though. Back then, I wanted to be somebody and to be America's sweetheart. In the last five years, I have been slammed with a lot of scandal in the tabloids, things that have caused some really dark times. What I have learned is that it is a test.

PSD: *Fame always struck me as a prison. It seems that a lot is projected onto people and what they may represent, rather than be about anything close to who they are.*

WJ: This is true in some ways. I am definitely the target of a lot weirdness and I accept that responsibility. I sometimes look at Elvis and wonder what it was like for him to be so incredibly successful. Then I realize he is just like us! So, to me, we idolize and set people up on pedestals like they are such magical beings. I feel I am being used through my music to open their hearts to God.

PSD: *You seem to have a pretty good outlook on life.*

WJ: Something I have learned is that 90% of life is really attitude. That is why you see a lot of people who may not seem very talented make it big and win the prize. That is why I try to wake up everyday with an attitude of, "What do I get to do?" rather than "What do I have to do?" There is a big difference. This is important because I am of the belief that every thought you have manifests itself in your body. My mom does a whole thing on how important your thoughts are and how your body responds to those thoughts. She is living proof! It is a matter of your faith and your ability to believe. I keep one foot on the ground, one foot going forward, and my eyes to the heavens.

PSD: *I have a feeling that you have become much more centered in the past couple of years. What effect has being a mother had?*

WJ: God gave me a break. I have not had a great life when it comes to people being honest with me, even members of my own family. This is a very tricky subject, but it is important for me to talk about it for my own growth.

My whole life, I was always doing shows and leading what people thought was this incredible life. I had two families that never really got along, since my parents were divorced, and I was always in the middle of the chaos. I would watch people jockey for position with me because of my fame. And I don't blame my family any more for that, because fame is very alluring. It's just natural for people to be curious about people in the spotlight.

So I had to deal with a lot of people who have not been very honest with me. Now it has taken me thirty-two years to understand what unconditional love is, and that is when God sent my children, Elijah and Grace, to me. I think that Elijah and Grace chose me and this is the first time I have felt unconditional love. They are the closest thing to the angels. There is no purer love than what they give back to me.

PSD: *What was it like to carry life inside you?*

WJ: I sang the best I have ever sung when I was pregnant. When you are that full of life, you are obviously tapped into the heavens. Your feet are on the ground and you are getting fatter by the day, yet your mind is somewhere else. I daydreamed all the time. You are constantly aware of this being inside of you. You are absolutely caught up in this miracle.

PSD: *How is the relationship with your mother these days?*

WJ: We are closer than we have ever been. We finish each other's sentences. It is a very complicated dynamic. We are WAY close. It is almost like, "OK, Mom, cut the cord." (She laughs.) When I was in the delivery room giving birth, she was patting me on the head telling me I was still her baby. She is still my Mama. I heard once that you are truly not an adult until your parents move on from this world.

PSD: *Are you a "gut instinct" type of person? Do you follow your heart?*

WJ: In my music I do, because I trust myself there. I lack belief in myself though, but I have an incredible faith in God. I also know that, when it comes to my music, I don't have to worry. For some reason, I don't have as much faith in myself in my personal life. I have such doubt in my abilities. I am just as desperate in my feelings at times as everybody else, and that happens just about every day. Once I tap into the outside world, I am just a walking goober waiting to meet someone who is going to hurt my feelings. The only thing that keeps me going is my faith.

PSD: *What brings you the most pleasure these days?*

WJ: There is a feeling I have had — and I know every mother can relate to this — when I have just got Elijah to sleep. He is resting, it is peaceful, and all is right with the world. There is such contentment in the feeling that "my kids are OK." There was also a feeling the day after I had married Arch, a peace that surpasses all understanding. I had heard people talk about getting married, but there really is something different after you have married someone. There is this covenant. The third feeling would be right after I have come off stage and I go to my dressing room and take off my sweaty jacket. There is this feeling of satisfaction, "a job well done."

PSD: *Do you do anything to stay grounded?*
WJ: I am a seeker, and am definitely on the path. I just don't have great discipline when it comes to me. I am struggling to put myself on the list somewhere, but there are so many things going on, I sacrifice myself, which I know is wrong. I am learning how to say "No," and take a few minutes for myself. I'm learning to replenish and rejuvenate. It is hard because I am such a doer. Five weeks after I had Grace, I was back on the road.

PSD: *What do you do to relax?*
WJ: I procrastinate! (She laughs.) I procrastinate very well.

PSD: *I need to get you some of Anthony Robbins' tapes.*
WJ: I met Anthony Robbins and he gave me all of his stuff, but I haven't got to it yet. (She laughs.) Mom laughs at me because she will call to ask if I'm wasting time, and I will say, "Yes." Usually, it is really late at night. I was up until 4:00 a.m. last night. My favorite thing to do is be at my house, put on my pajamas, put my hair in a ponytail, stay up late, and do whatever I want to do. It's the greatest! It is really quiet, no one is bugging me about anything, and I can drink straight from the milk carton if I want to. I'll do a lot of dreaming, and feel more like a human "being" rather than a human "doing."

PSD: *Those can be sweet moments.*
WJ: I love it. There are also times out on the road in the bus that I can feel the same way. Like when the sun is just about to go down and it is really quiet. There is this feeling that this is how heaven will be.

PSD: *How would you personally define success?*
WJ: It sounds really corny, but our greatest journey is that to inner peace. I have been close to death a couple of times, once when I was delivering my daughter Grace. Inner peace comes from knowing that when I die, I am going to heaven, that I am eternal. That is a promise I don't have to question. Success is knowing that when I die I am going to heaven, and if I never sing another note, I am worthy. It took me twelve years to feel that way. If I never make another record, I am OK.

PSD: *That is beautiful. You are worthy by just being you.*
WJ: We set conditional goals like, "If I lose ten pounds, then I am fine." There is not enough celebration in life. I remember meeting Donald Trump and thinking "You are really not satisfied with a billion dollars. Maybe if you get five or six billion, then what will it take?" For me, it is not about money. Now, it is strictly "I am worthy, I am a child of God." Period. That's what it is for me.

PSD: *What would you tell your daughter if she was eighteen and asking for advice before she went out into the world to find herself?*
WJ: You know what my first thought was? "Go ask your father!" (She laughs.) That is such a tough question. I think it would have to come down to Scripture. There will come a point when Grace is going to know that I don't have it all figured out. I would tell her to trust God even if she didn't trust me. Take it to Him. I would tell her to follow her gut instinct even if I told her something different.

Follow your gut. "People yell, God whispers." So I would give Grace this advice someday, "I don't care if it is a boy pressuring you, a teacher telling you something, I don't care what it is, follow your heart."

Your gut, gut, gut instinct. The instinct that is way beneath pride and ego, and the need to please others. This is the only thing that has served me through every situation. "People yell and God whispers." If I get still and quiet, I will hear my inner voice. So this would be my advice to her; get still and know

God, and know that inner voice. It will serve you the rest of your life, even after I am not here.

PSD: *Speaking of that, how would you like to be remembered?*

WJ: I would just like to be remembered. "Oh, that Wynonna, she was a great singer. She sang from her heart." Just for someone to remember, to bring up the idea of me. To be remembered for kindness to strangers, for the acts of random kindness.

Nashville Area Community Foundation, Inc.
210 23rd Avenue North
Nashville, Tennessee 37203-1502

Enclosed please find a check payable to the Nashville Area Community Foundation, Inc. (the "Foundation"), a Tennessee not-for-profit corporation, exempt under IRC { } 501(c)(3) for its charitable, educational public purposes.

This gift, which is based on proceeds from the sale of the book *What Matters Most*, hereby creates a Designated Fund as provided for in the Charter and Bylaws establishing the Foundation, subject to all the terms and conditions contained therein, and any amendments or additions thereto at any time made, except as hereinafter set forth.

By this gift it is the intention of Paul Dolman ("Donor") to create the WHAT MATTERS MOST FUND to benefit young people involved in the YMCA's Y-CAP program by providing them scholarship funds to help with the expense of post-secondary school education within the Foundation (the "Fund"). Donor hereby retains the right to add to this fund from time to time, and it is the hope of the Donor that other individuals, organizations, and corporations will also add to the Fund.

It is understood that the Foundation shall have the ultimate authority and control over all property of the Fund, and the income derived therefrom, for the charitable purposes of the Foundation. The Fund will be charged by the Foundation 1.25% of principal of the Fund annually, payable quarterly in arrears on an accrued basis, valued as of the last business day of each quarter.

Donor asks that the Y-CAP program select the most deserving scholarship recipients and work to ensure that they pick the optimal post-secondary experience. Donor also asks that Y-CAP structure the use of these scholarship funds to ensure that grants from this Fund augment rather than displace other sources of scholarship dollars. Donor further asks that, in years where there are no suitable candidates for these scholarships or when the Funds available exceed the need of Y-CAP clients, the Foundation help in the search for opportunities to support students fitting the Y-CAP profile but not necessarily in the Y-CAP program. Donor suggests that all the proceeds of the Fund as determined under the Foundation's Total Return Concept be paid to Y-CAP no less often than annually.

Please indicate below your acceptance of this gift and of the terms and conditions noted above.

Very truly yours,

Paul Samuel Dolman